SPURGEON
ON THE PSALMS

BOOK ONE

Psalm 1 through Psalm 25

SPURGEON
ON THE PSALMS

BOOK ONE

Psalm 1 through Psalm 25

CHARLES H. SPURGEON

Compiled and Edited by Beverlee J. Chadwick

BRIDGE LOGOS

Newberry, FL 32669

Bridge-Logos

Newberry, FL 32669 USA

Spurgeon on the Psalms
Charles H. Spurgeon
Compiled and Edited by Beverlee J. Chadwick

Printed in the United States of America.

Library of Congress Catalog Card Number: 2014953407
International Standard Book Number 978-1-61036-137-8

Scripture quotations are from the *King James Version* of the Bible.

VP 08-19-16

TABLE OF CONTENTS

FOREWORD
WHAT ARE THE PSALMS?

THE BASIC AND SIMPLEST ANSWER to that question is that the Psalms were the Holy Spirit inspired prayer-and-praise book of Israel in the Old Covenant. Their timeless guidance, comfort, and wording of musical beauty continue to bless and inspire the praise and prayers of all generations. In terms of human experience, they are revelations of truth as they are worked out in the emotions, sufferings and desires of the people of God by the circumstances through which they pass.

We see ourselves in the lives of those noble souls mentioned in the Psalms as they struggled with their problems and themselves. They bared their hearts, analyzed their problems, chided and encouraged themselves and each other. Sometimes they were happy and sometimes depressed but always honest with themselves. That's one of the reasons why the Psalms are so valuable to us in our daily walk and spiritual growth. The Psalms have always proven to be a great source of solace and encouragement—both to the children of Israel and the Christian Church throughout the centuries.

Spurgeon's comments are understood by people from a wide range of backgrounds and levels of knowledge because they touch on the basic experiences of love, hate, guilt, repentance, forgiveness, death, life, etc., and God's Word for all of them.

Charles Spurgeon's commentaries on the Psalms have a universal appeal that is unequaled in inspiration, clarity of speech, and timeless encouragement. As we apply them to our lives they will not only inspire, comfort and guide us, they will become the motivating factor that will increase our desire to know God's Word and His will for our lives to His glory and praise.

— Beverlee J. Chadwick, Senior Editor
Bridge-Logos, Inc.

PREFACE

BY CHARLES H. SPURGEON

MY PREFACE shall at least possess the virtue of brevity, as I find it difficult to impart to it any other. The delightful study of the Psalms has yielded me boundless profit and ever growing pleasure; common gratitude constrains me to communicate to others a portion of the benefit, with the prayer that it may induce them to search further for themselves. That I have nothing better of my own to offer upon this peerless book is to me matter of deepest regret; that I have anything whatever to present is subject for devout gratitude to the Lord of grace. I have done my best, but, conscious of many defects, I heartily wish I could have done far better.

The here given is my own. I consulted a few authors before penning it, to aid me in interpretation and arouse my thoughts; but, still I can claim originality for my comments, at least so I honestly think. Whether they are better or worse for that, I know not; at least I know I have sought heavenly guidance while writing them, and therefore I look for a blessing on the printing of them.

The research expended on this volume would have occupied far too much of my time, had not my friend and amanuensis[1] Mr. John L. Keys, most diligently aided me in investigations at the British Museum, Dr. William's Library, and other treasuries of theological lore. With his help I have ransacked books by the hundred, often without finding a memorable line as a reward, but at other times with the most satisfactory result. Readers little know how great labor the finding of but one pertinent extract may involve;

---

1. A literary or artistic assistant.

labor certainly I have not spared: my earnest prayer is that some measure of good may come of it to my brethren in the ministry and to the Church at large.

Should this first volume meet with the approbation of the judicious, I shall hope by God's grace to continue the work as rapidly as I can consistently with the research demanded and my incessant pastoral duties. Another volume will follow in all probability in twelve months' time, if life be spared and strength be given.

It may be added, that although the comments were the work of my health, the rest of the volume is the product of my sickness. When protracted illness and weakness laid me aside from daily preaching, I resorted to my pen as an available means of doing good. I would have preached had I been able, but as my Master denied me the privilege of thus serving Him, I gladly availed myself of the other method of bearing testimony for His name. O that He may give me fruit in this field also, and His shall be all the praise.

— C. H. Spurgeon
Clapham, December, 1869

"God's thoughts of you are many; let not yours be few in return."

— Charles H. Spurgeon

A Brief Biography
of
Charles Haddon Spurgeon

CHARLES HADDON SPURGEON was born on June 19, 1834, in Kelvedon, Essex, England, forty miles northeast of London. Early in his life it was obvious he was destined to be a preacher, like his father and grandfather, who were both independent ministers. Charles Spurgeon's conversion took place on January 6, 1850. He was fifteen years old at the time and here in his own words is how it happened.

"I sometimes think I might have been in darkness and despair now, had it not been for the goodness of God in sending a snowstorm one Sunday morning, when I was going to a place of worship. When I could go no further, I turned down a court and came to a little Primitive Methodist Chapel. There might be a dozen or fifteen people in that chapel. The minister did not come that morning: snowed in, I suppose. A poor man, a shoemaker, a tailor, or something of that sort, went up into the pulpit to preach. He was obliged to stick to his text, for the simple reason he had nothing else to say. The text was, 'Look unto me, and be ye saved, all the ends of the earth' [Isaiah 45:22]. He did not even pronounce the words rightly, but that did not matter.

"There was, I thought, a glimpse of hope for me in the text. He began thus: 'My dear friends, this is a very simple text indeed. It says, "Look." Now that does not take a deal of effort. It ain't lifting your foot or your finger; it is just "look." Well, a man need not go to college to learn to look. You may be the biggest fool, and yet you can look. A man need not be worth a thousand a year to look. Anyone can look; a child can look. But this is what the text says. Then it says, "Look unto Me."'

"'Ay,' said he, in broad Essex, 'many of ye are looking to yourselves. No use looking there. You'll never find comfort in yourselves.' Then the good man followed up his text in this way: 'Look unto Me: I am sweating great drops of blood. Look unto Me; I am hanging on the Cross. Look: I am dead and buried. Look unto Me; I rise again. Look unto Me; I ascend; I am sitting at the Father's right hand. O, look to Me! Look to Me!' When he had got about that length, and managed to spin out ten minutes, he was at the length of his tether.

"Then he looked at me under the gallery, and I daresay, with so few present, he knew me to be a stranger. He then said, 'Young man, you look very miserable.' Well, I did; but I had not been accustomed to having remarks made on my personal appearance from the pulpit before. However, it was a good blow struck. He continued: 'And you will always be miserable—miserable in life and miserable in death—if you do not obey my text. But if you obey now, this moment, you will be saved.'

"Then he shouted, as only a Primitive Methodist can, 'Young man, look to Jesus Christ.' Then and there the cloud was gone, the darkness had rolled away, and in that moment I saw the sun. I had been waiting to do fifty things, but when I heard the word look, I could have almost looked my eyes away. I could have risen that instant and sung with the most enthusiastic of them of the precious blood of Christ, and the simple faith that looks alone to Him.

"I thought I could dance all the way home and I now understand what John Bunyan meant when he declared he wanted to tell the crows on the plowed land all about his conversion. He was too full to hold it in. He must tell somebody. There was no doubt about his conversion; it went through every part of his being.

"As Richard Knill [a missionary] said, 'At such a time of the day, clang went every harp in Heaven, for Richard Knill was born again'; it was even so with me." Spurgeon later said if there had been a pile of blazing faggots [bundles of sticks] next to the church door, he could have stood in the midst of them without chains, happy to give his flesh and blood and bones to be burned, if only such action might have testified of the love he felt for Jesus. "Between half past ten, when I entered that chapel, and half past twelve, when I returned home, what a change had taken place in me!"

Spurgeon, who was soon to become known as "the boy preacher," was admitted to the church at Newmarket on April 4, 1850. At that time, he had not yet received the Lord's Supper, because though he had never heard of Baptists until he was fourteen, he had become convinced, by the Church of England catechism and by study of the New Testament, that believers in Christ should be baptized in His name after they received Him, and so he naturally desired baptism before his first communion.

He could not find a Baptist minister anywhere nearer than Isleham, where a Reverend W. W. Cantlow, who was a former missionary in Jamaica, ministered. Having decided to go there to be baptized, Charles first wrote to his parents to ask permission. They readily consented, although his father warned him that he must not trust in his baptism, and his mother reminded him that though she often prayed that her son would be a Christian, she had never asked that he would be a Baptist. Spurgeon playfully responded that the Lord had dealt with her in His usual bounty, and had given her exceedingly, abundantly, above all that she had asked.

It was on his mother's birthday, May 3, 1850, that Spurgeon "put on Christ," just short of his sixteenth birthday.

He rose early in the morning, spent two hours in prayer and dedication, and walked eight miles to Isleham Ferry, on the river Lark, which is a beautiful stream that divides Suffolk from Cambridgeshire. Though there were not as many people at the baptism as there normally were on a Sunday baptism, there were a sufficient number watching to make Spurgeon, who had never seen a baptism before, a bit nervous. Here is his description of the scene.

"The wind blew down the river with a cutting blast as my turn came to wade into the flood; but after I had walked a few steps, and noted the people on the ferryboat, and in boats, and on either shore, I felt as if Heaven and Earth and hell might all gaze upon me, for I was not ashamed, then and there, to declare myself a follower of the Lamb. My timidity was washed away; it floated down the river into the sea, and must have been devoured by the fishes, for I have never felt anything of the kind since. Baptism also loosed my tongue, and from that day it has never been quiet."

The evening a prayer meeting was held in the Isleham vestry, at which time the newly baptized Spurgeon prayed openly—"And people wondered and wept for joy as they listened to the lad." In the morning he went back to Newmarket, and the next Sunday he had communion for the first time, and was appointed a Sunday school teacher.

Some years later he wrote, "I did not fulfill the outward ordinance to join a party and to become a Baptist, but to be a Christian after the apostolic fashion; for they, when they believed, were baptized. It is now questioned whether John Bunyan was baptized, but the same question can never be raised concerning me. I, who scarcely belong to any sect, am nevertheless by no means willing to have it doubted in time to come whether or not I followed the conviction of my heart."

Later that year he moved to Cambridge. In the winter of

1850–1851, when he was just sixteen, he preached his first sermon in a cottage at Teversham, Cambridge. He hadn't planned on preaching there; in fact, he hadn't known he was going to, but he was tricked into it by a Mr. James Vinter in Cambridge, who was president of the Preachers' Association. Bishop Vinter, as he was generally known, called on Spurgeon one morning just as school was dismissed, and told him "to go over to Teversham the next evening, for a young man was to preach there who was not much used to services, and very likely would be glad of company."

Bishop Vinter apparently knew Spurgeon well, for a direct request for him to preach probably would have been refused. But Vinter knew that the young man had in him those qualities that make great preachers, and he only had to get started. Considering Vinter's reason for the ruse, it was excusable—it was also successful. Spurgeon and the other young man Vinter had mentioned, started off in the early evening along the Newmarket Road to Teversham. After walking some distance in silence, Spurgeon expressed the hope that his companion, who was a bit older, would sense the presence of God when he preached. Horrified, the older man said he had never preached, could not preach, and would not preach. The older man said there would be no sermon at all unless Spurgeon preached. Spurgeon hesitated at first, saying he did not know what he could preach. The older man replied that if Spurgeon would just give one of his Sunday school teachings it should do quite well. Spurgeon then agreed to preach, and reproached himself for his hesitation: "Surely I can tell a few poor cottagers of the sweetness and love of Jesus, since I feel them in my own soul." Now having settled the matter, it was as if the Lord himself walked with them as He did with the two men on the road to Emmaus.

Spurgeon's text that memorable evening was "Unto you therefore which believe he is precious" [1 Peter 2:7]. Then he expounded the praises of his Lord for nearly an hour, while those gathered in that thatched cottage listened attentively, enthralled with the eloquence of the young lad. When he finished, he was happy with the fact that he had been able to complete his sermon, which showed how little he thought of his preaching ability. Spurgeon then picked up a hymnbook to close out the service with praise and worship songs. Before he could start singing, however, an aged woman called out, "Bless your dear heart, how old are you?" Perhaps a bit prideful, or embarrassed to tell how young he was, Spurgeon replied, "You must wait until the service is over before making any such inquiries. Let us now sing."

During the friendly conversation that followed the singing, the elderly woman asked Spurgeon again, "How old are you?"

To this Spurgeon replied, "I am under sixty."

"Yes," said the elderly woman, "and under sixteen."

"Never mind," Spurgeon said, "think of the Lord Jesus Christ and His preciousness." Then upon the urging of several of the church members, he promised he would come back—if Bishop Vinter thought he was fit to preach again.

From that small but notable beginning, Charles Spurgeon's fame as a preacher spread around the countryside, and he was invited to preach in Teversham both on Sundays and weekdays. Over the years in his writings and sermons, Spurgeon described his daily routine in those days. He would rise early in the morning for prayer and reading the Bible, and then he would attend to school duties until about five in the evening. Almost every evening he would visit the villages near Cambridge to tell the people what he had learned during the day. He found that those things took solid hold of him when he proclaimed them to others. He also said he made many blunders in those days, but he usually had a friendly audience and there were no reporters at that time writing down his every word.

Spurgeon promised to preach at the small Baptist church in October of 1851 in Waterbeach, six miles from Cambridge. The chapel at Waterbeach was a primitive building with a thatched roof, which was common in those days. Spurgeon promised to preach for a few Sundays, but continued for more than two years. It was here that he published his first literary work: a gospel tract written in 1853. When Spurgeon took up the pulpit at Waterbeach, the village was notorious for its godlessness, public drunkenness and profanity, like many of the towns where Charles Finney preached during the Great American Awakening. And like those towns, Waterbeach was soon to come under the power of the gospel, for God had sent His chosen messenger there. Here is Spurgeon's account of the changes that took place.

"In a short time the little thatched chapel was crammed, the biggest vagabonds of the village were weeping floods of tears, and those who had been the curse of the parish became its blessing. I can say with joy and happiness that almost from one end of the village to the other, at the hour of eventide, one might have heard the voice of song coming from every rooftree, and echoing from almost every heart."

Spurgeon's first convert in Waterbeach was a laborer's wife, and he said he prized that soul more than the thousands that came afterward. She received Christ at the Sunday service, and early the next morning the seventeen-year-old Spurgeon hurried down to see his first spiritual child. "If anybody had said to me, 'Somebody has left you twenty thousand pounds,' I would not have given a snap of my fingers for it compared with the joy I felt when I was told that God had saved a soul through my ministry. I felt like a boy who had earned his first guinea, or like a diver who had been down to the depth of the sea, and brought up a rare pearl."

Spurgeon's style and ability were considered to be far above the average from the beginning of his ministry. Of these early days, his brother James wrote, "When I drove my brother about the country to preach, I thought then, as I have thought ever since, what an extraordinary preacher he was. What wonderful unction and power I remember in some of those early speeches! The effect upon the people listening to him I have never known exceeded in after years. He seemed to have leaped full-grown into the pulpit. The breadth and brilliance of those early sermons, and the power that God's Holy Spirit evidently gave to him, made them perfectly marvelous. When he went to Waterbeach his letters came home, and were read as family documents, discussed, prayed over and wondered at. We were not surprised, however, for we all believed that it was in him."

It's a measure of how much Spurgeon ministered in the country where God had placed him that by the time he was called to London he had preached six hundred and seventy sermons.

While the young Spurgeon was busy in Waterbeach and content to stay there, the New Park Street Baptist Church in London was looking for a pastor who could revive its fallen condition. It was an influential church because of having probably the largest chapel of any Baptist church building—it could seat nearly 1200 people, and was one of only six churches that had a listed membership of over three hundred. For a number of years, however, the church had been unable to find pastors of any distinction and the active membership had dwindled to less than two hundred. At this time the pastorate had been vacant for three months, and then they discovered nineteen-year-old Charles Spurgeon.

It happened unexpectedly. George Gould, a deacon of the church at Loughton, Essex, was in Cambridge and attended the anniversary meeting of the Cambridge Sunday School Union. Charles Spurgeon was one of the speakers. During their speeches, the two older speakers scorned Spurgeon's youth. Spurgeon asked if he could reply. Both his speech and his reply so impressed Gould that when he returned to London one of the New Park Street deacons, Thomas Olney, complained to him that they had been unable to find a suitable pastor, Gould suggested young Spurgeon. The suggestion was ignored the first time it was made, but when it was made again at a later date, Olney spoke to another New Park Street deacon and they agreed "to try the experiment" and wrote to Waterbeach, which was the only address they had, and invited Spurgeon to preach one Sunday.

When the invitation reached Spurgeon on the last Sunday of 1853, he was certain it was a mistake and passed the letter to Robert Coe, one of his church deacons. Coe said he was certain it *wasn't* a mistake, and that what he had long dreaded had happened. But he was surprised at the invitation coming so soon and coming from London, which was "a great step from this little place." Spurgeon still wasn't convinced, but on November 28, he wrote a cautious answer to the invitation, and said that he was willing to go to London for a Sunday, but suggested that the invitation was probably a mistake since he was only nineteen, and was quite unknown outside of the Waterbeach area. A second letter from London, however, eased his mind and he arranged to preach at New Park Street on December 18, 1853.

When the reluctant Spurgeon reached London he was greeted with a total lack of hospitality. Rather than house him in the home of one of the affluent members, as was often the custom with visiting clergy, they sent him to a boarding house in Queen's Square, Bloomsbury, where he was given a bedroom barely large enough to hold a bed. The clothing he wore clearly showed his country breeding and upon hearing he was going to preach at New Park Street, the other boarders told him tall tales of London's wonderful preachers. By the time Spurgeon went to his small bedroom to sleep, he was thoroughly discouraged, which, added to the unaccustomed street noise, kept him awake most of the night.

When he went to New Park Street the next morning and saw the imposing building, he was amazed at his own recklessness at thinking he could preach there. If he hadn't been certain of his calling, he probably would have returned immediately to Waterbeach.

But once in front of the sparse congregation that attended that morning—only about eighty people, he regained his normal confidence and delivered his sermon from James 1:17: "Every good gift and every perfect gift is from above, and cometh down from the Father of lights, with whom is no variableness, neither shadow of turning." His message so affected the congregation that after the meeting one of the deacons said that if Spurgeon was only with them for three months the church would be filled. News of the splendid young preacher from Waterbeach spread by word-of-mouth all Sunday afternoon, and that evening the congregation had more than tripled what it was in the morning. Among them was the young lady who was later to become Spurgeon's wife. His text that evening was from Revelation 14:5b: "they are without fault before the throne of God."

The people were so excited at the end of the service that they would not leave until the deacons had convinced Spurgeon to come again, and before he left the building he agreed to return. Here is his account of that service. "The Lord helped me very graciously. I had a happy Sabbath in the pulpit, and spent the interval with warm-hearted friends; and when at night I trudged back to the Queen's Square narrow lodging, I was not alone, and I no longer looked on Londoners as flinty-hearted barbarians. My tone was altered, I wanted no pity of anyone; I did not care a penny for the young gentlemen lodgers and their miraculous ministers, nor for the grind of the cabs, nor for anything else under the sun. The lion had been looked at all around, and his majesty did not appear to be a tenth as majestic as when I had heard his roar miles away."

No other preacher who had spoken at New Park Street during the three months when the pastorate was vacant had been invited a second time, but Spurgeon was invited back on the first, third, and fifth Sundays of January, 1854. His ministry was so successful that on January 25, the Wednesday before the last Sunday, he was invited to occupy the pulpit for six months, with a view to becoming their new pastor.

Spurgeon was in Cambridge when the invitation from the church reached him, and he immediately wrote back stating that he dared not accept an unqualified invitation for such a long time. "My objection is not to the length of the time of probation, but it ill becomes a youth to promise to preach to a London congregation so long until he knows them and they know him. I would engage to supply for three months of that time, and then, should the congregation fail or the church disagree, I would reserve to myself the liberty, without breach of engagement, to retire, and you on your part would have the right to dismiss me without seeming to treat me ill. Enthusiasm and popularity are often like the crackling of thorns, and soon expire. I do not wish to be a hindrance if I cannot be a help."

The suggested probation was cut short, however, when fifty of the men members signed a request to the deacons that a special meeting be called. The meeting was held on April 19, and a resolution was passed in which they expressed with thankfulness the esteem in which their new preacher was held and the extraordinary increase in attendance at all the church meetings. Thus they "consider it prudent to secure as early as possible his permanent settlement among us."

On April 28, just over four months after he arrived in London, the nineteen-year-old Spurgeon replied, "There is but one answer to so loving and candid an invitation. I accept it." Then he asked for their prayers, "Remember my youth and inexperience, and I pray that these may not hinder my usefulness. I trust also the remembrance of these will lead you to forgive mistakes I may make, or unguarded words that I may utter."

Spurgeon was a man of great courage, especially when it came to spiritual matters and defense of the Bible. He once said, "I have hardly ever known what the fear of man means." Along with this, God increasingly added courage to his faith, until there was literally nothing that could stop him from doing the work to which God had called him.

In his exposition of the ninety-first Psalm in *The Treasury of David*, perhaps one of his greatest works, he wrote this: "In the year 1854, when I had scarcely been in London twelve months, the neighborhood in which I lived was visited by Asiatic cholera, and my congregation suffered from its inroads. Family after family summoned me to the bedside of the smitten, and almost every day I was called to visit the grave. I gave myself up with youthful ardor to the visitation of the sick, and was sent for from all quarters of the district by persons of all ranks and religions. I became weary in body and sick at heart. My friends seemed falling one by one, and I felt or fancied that I was sickening like those around me. A little more work and weeping would have laid me low among the rest; I felt that my burden was heavier than I could bear, and I was ready to sink under it. As God would have it, I was returning mournfully from a funeral, when my curiosity led me to read a paper that was wafered [taped] up in a shoemaker's shop in the Dover Road. It did not look like a trade announcement, nor was it, for it bore in a good bold handwriting these words: "Because thou hast made the Lord, which is my refuge, even the most High, thy habitation; there shall no evil befall thee, neither shall any plague come nigh thy dwelling" [Psalm 91:9–10]. The effect on my heart was immediate. Faith appropriated the passage as her own. I felt secure, refreshed, girded with immortality. I went on with my visitation of the dying in a calm and peaceful spirit; I felt no fear of evil and I suffered no harm. The providence which moved the tradesman to place those verses on the window I gratefully acknowledge, and in the remembrance of its marvelous power I adore the Lord my God."

Though only about eighty people attended Spurgeon's first service at New Park Street, it soon became impossible to crowd into the building all the people who wanted to hear and see "the boy preacher," and the services moved to increasingly larger buildings. Soon the decision was made to enlarge the New Park Street chapel, and the services were moved to a public building, Exeter Hall. Although using a public place for church services is common practice today, it was virtually unheard of in Spurgeon's day. However, even though Exeter Hall held several thousand more than the Park Street Chapel, it also wasn't large enough to contain the increasing crowds flocking to his meetings.

The work on the chapel took place from February 11 to May 27, 1855, and during this time Spurgeon became increasingly busy. Besides all his other ministerial duties and his writing, he was preaching as much as thirteen times a week. Soon his voice was overtaxed and the services in Exeter Hall were too much for him (keep in mind that there were no sound systems in those days and the preacher had to speak loudly enough for all in even the largest hall to hear him). About his voice, his wife later wrote: "Sometimes his voice would almost break and fail as he pleaded with sinners to come to Christ, or magnified the Lord in His sovereignty and righteousness. A glass of chili vinegar always stood on a shelf under the desk before him, and I knew what to expect when he had recourse to that remedy.

"I remember with strange vividness the Sunday evening when he preached from the text, 'His name shall endure for ever' [Psalm 72:17]. It was a subject in which he reveled, it was his chief delight to exalt his glorious Savior, and he seemed in that discourse to be pouring out his very soul and life in homage and adoration before his gracious King. However, I really thought he was going to die there, in the face of all those people. At the end he made a mighty effort to recover his voice; but utterance well nigh failed, and only in broken accents could the pathetic peroration [conclusion of the sermon] be heard—'Let my name perish, but let Christ's name last forever! Jesus! Jesus! *Jesus!* Crown Him Lord of all! You will not hear me say anything else. These are my last words in Exeter Hall for this time. Jesus! Jesus! *Jesus!* Crown Him Lord of all!' and then he fell back almost fainting in the chair behind him."

Their return to the enlarged New Park Street Chapel on May 31 was disappointing for it was discovered that the money spent on it was almost wasted. Several hundred more could get into the chapel, however, the crowds were larger than before and thousands were disappointed. They remained there for about a year before it became necessary to rent Exeter Hall again.

In the meantime, like George Whitefield, Spurgeon preached in the open air whenever the opportunity was offered, once in a field to a crowd of almost twenty thousand. Writing on June 3 of the same year to the soon-to-be Mrs. Spurgeon, Spurgeon said: "Yesterday I climbed to the summit of a minister's glory. My congregation was enormous; I think ten thousand, but certainly twice as many as at Exeter Hall. The Lord was with me, and the profoundest silence was observed; but oh, the close—never did mortal man receive a more enthusiastic oration! I wonder I am alive! After the service five or six gentlemen endeavored to clear a passage, but I was borne along, amid cheers, and prayers, and shouts, for about a quarter of an hour—it really seemed more like a week! I was hurried round and round the field without hope of escape until, suddenly seeing a nice open carriage, with two occupants, standing near; I sprang in, and begged them to drive away. This they most kindly did, and I stood up, waving my hat, and crying, 'The blessing of God be with you!' while from thousands of heads the hats were lifted and cheer after cheer was given. Surely amid these plaudits I can hear the low rumbling of an advancing storm of reproaches; but even this I can bear for the Master's sake."

As if on cue, the storms rumbled and rolled in. Spurgeon soon had almost as many detractors as he did admirers. On one occasion when his carriage was driven through a crowd in London, he was heartily hooted and booed. All throughout his ministry a portion of the press was scornfully critical of him. Spurgeon once said, "A true Christian is one who fears God, and is hated by the *Saturday Review.*" But no matter how highly and often he was criticized, he never changed one dot of what he believed to be the truth of God. His Pauline Calvinism, his sturdy Puritanism, his old-fashioned apostolic gospel, remained unchanged to the end.

A criticism that followed him all his life was that he was conceited. His biographer, W. Y Fullerton, wrote about this: As to the question of conceit, in later years he gave a sufficient answer. "A friend of mine was calling upon him some time ago," wrote one after his death, "and happened to say, 'Do you know, Mr. Spurgeon, some people think you are conceited?' The great preacher smiled indulgently, and after a pause said, 'Do you see those bookshelves? They contain hundreds, nay, thousands of my sermons translated into every language under heaven. Well, now, add to this that ever since I was twenty years old there never has been built a place large enough to hold the numbers of people who wished to hear me preach, and, upon my honor, when I think of it, I wonder I am not more conceited than I am.'" Upon which the writer remarks, "That is the kind of bonhomie [geniality] that disarms criticism."

Spurgeon became known through much of London, but not all its inhabitants had heard of him. Strangely, what quickly made him known in every part of the city was an accident. The owners of Exeter Hall said they could no longer rent the hall to one congregation, so plans were immediately formulated to build a structure larger than the Hall that would hold the thousands the Hall could not accommodate. In the meantime, some temporary building was needed. Fortunately, the Surrey Music Hall, which could hold ten to twelve thousand people, became available. The news that Spurgeon was to preach in the Music Hall spread like wildfire, and on Sunday evening, October 19, 1856, the hall was jammed with ten thousand people and another ten thousand in the gardens surrounding the hall. The building was so crowded that the service began before its appointed time. A prayer was offered, then a hymn with the customary running commentary, then another hymn. Prayer before the sermon was being offered when suddenly a loud cry of "Fire!" rang throughout the hall. There was instant panic and bedlam. In the ensuing rush for the door, a stairway gave way and toppled people to the floor; others were knocked down and trampled underfoot. Seven were killed and twenty-eight were taken to the hospital seriously injured. There was, however, no fire; it was a false alarm, given perhaps out of malice against Spurgeon.

In the midst of it all, Spurgeon was unaware of the extent of the disaster, and did not know there had been any fatal injuries. He attempted to quiet the people, and at the urging of repeated cries endeavored to preach. He told the crowd the text he had intended to use was the thirty-third verse of the third chapter of Proverbs, "The curse of the Lord is in the house of the wicked: but he blesseth the habitation of the just," and asked the people to remain quiet or retire gradually if they felt they must leave. But there was more disturbance, and the service had to be discontinued. Spurgeon was so distressed by it all; he had to be carried from the pulpit.

The next day every newspaper in London carried vivid descriptions of the disaster and the deaths and injuries and vilified Spurgeon for holding services in a public Music Hall. One leading newspaper said, "This hiring of places of amusement for Sunday preaching is a novelty, and a powerful one. It looks as if religion were at its last shift [a qualitative change]. It is a confession of weakness, rather than a sign of strength. It is not wrestling with Satan in his strongholds—to use the old earnest Puritan language—but entering into a very cowardly truce and alliance with the world." Within days every part of London was talking about the young preacher, and when he resumed preaching, after spending several days deeply depressed and discouraged, the crowds were larger than ever. Hoping to turn people against Spurgeon, the newspapers had done just the opposite, and made him the best known preacher in all of London. What the enemy had intended for evil, God had turned to good.

Through all the years of his ministry, Spurgeon's popularity increased until he was known all over the civilized world. His sermons were reproduced by the millions in virtually every language. Even today they are read more than any other sermons ever printed.

On March 25, 1861, Spurgeon preached his first sermon in his newest and largest building, the Metropolitan Tabernacle at Elephant and Castle, Southwark. The building would seat four thousand six hundred people, but often another thousand, and often more, found some place to sit or stand. One of the deacons once claimed that on a special occasion they had crammed eight thousand people into it. "We counted eight thousand out of her" he said. "I don't know where she put 'em, but we did."

D. L. Moody had not yet arrived on the London scene, but Spurgeon invited him to preach at the tabernacle, to which Moody replied, "In regard to coming to your tabernacle, I consider it a great honor to be invited; and, in fact, I should consider it an honor to black your boots, but to preach to your people would be out of the question. If they will not turn to God under your preaching, neither will they be persuaded though one rose from the dead." Moody did later preach for Spurgeon, and in writing to thank him, Spurgeon said, "I wish you could give us every night you can for the next sixty days. There are so few men who can draw on a weeknight."

That was the wonder of it, Spurgeon built a tabernacle seating between five and six thousand persons, able to contain over seven thousand, and for thirty-eight years he maintained that congregation there and elsewhere in London. Other great preachers, like Wesley and Whitefield, gathered as great crowds, but they traveled to various places to do so. Spurgeon remained rooted in London.

At a prayer meeting on May 26, 1890, Spurgeon looked around the Metropolitan Tabernacle and exclaimed, "How many thousands have been converted here! There has not been a single day but what I have heard of two, three or four having been converted; and that not for one, two, or three years, but for the last ten years!" It is an interesting note that additions to the church year by year were double the additions to New Park Street in the same periods of time, which shows that the number of new converts bears a relationship to the size of the congregation. With few exceptions, that great building was crowded every Sunday morning and evening for thirty years, and the attendance at the Thursday night meeting was usually even larger.

Spurgeon once said, "Somebody asked me how I got my congregation. I never got it at all. I did not think it was my duty to do so. I only had to preach the gospel. Why, my congregation got my congregation. I had eighty, or scarcely a hundred, when I preached first. The next time I had two hundred. Everyone who heard me was saying to his neighbor, 'You must go and hear this young man!' Next meeting we had four hundred, and in six weeks, eight hundred. That was the way in which my people got my congregation. Now the people are admitted by tickets. That does very well; a member can give his ticket to another person and say, 'I will stand in the aisle'; or 'I will get in with the crowd.' Some persons, you know, will not go if they can get in easily, but they will go if you tell them they cannot get in without a ticket. That is the way congregations ought to bring a congregation about a minister. A minister preaches all the better if he has a large congregation."

On October 26, 1891, Spurgeon, though he was feeling increasingly ill and weak from a combination of rheumatism, gout, and Bright's disease [chronic inflammation in the kidneys], which he had suffered from for many years, started out on a journey to Menton, France, where he often went to rest and recuperate. When he and Mrs. Spurgeon reached the Hotel Beau-Rivage, where they were staying, he enjoyed three months of "earthy paradise" without difficulty, and despite his weakness. By the middle of January, however, he began to weaken rapidly, though he conducted brief services in his room on January 10 and 17. These services were the last of his earthly work for his Lord. He died at the age of 58 on January 31, 1892. His wife and two sons outlived him, as did his father, who died at the age of almost ninety-two.

The news of his home-going flashed around the world. One London newspaper had the terse headline, "Death of

Spurgeon." That day it was difficult to obtain a newspaper anywhere in England, the demand was so great. Spurgeon's coffin was brought back from Menton, France, and arrived at Victoria Station, London, on Monday, February 9, 1892. It was met by a small group of friends and taken to the Pastor's College, where it remained for the rest of the day. That night it was carried into the Metropolitan Tabernacle, and over sixty thousand people passed by it to pay their homage. Four funeral services were held on Wednesday to accommodate the crowds. Ira D. Sankey, Moody's associate, was there and sang twice. Evan Herber Evans, a Welsh Nonconformist minister, spoke briefly and concluding said, "But there is one Charles Haddon Spurgeon whom we cannot bury; there is not earth enough in Norwood to bury him—the Spurgeon of history. The good works that he has done will live. You cannot bury them."

The funeral was on Thursday, and one newspaper said you could search all of London and not find three women who were not wearing black. At the graveside, Archibald G. Brown, a close friend and one of Spurgeon's most distinguished associates, gave a eulogy that some have said will be remembered forever.

"Beloved President, faithful Pastor, Prince of Preachers, brother beloved, dear Spurgeon—we bid thee not 'Farewell,' but only for a little while 'Goodnight.' Thou shalt rise soon at the first dawn of the Resurrection day of the redeemed. Yet is the 'goodnight' not ours to bid, but thine; it is we who linger in the darkness; thou art in God's holy light. Our night shall soon be passed, and with it all our weeping. Then, with thine, our songs shall greet the morning of a day that knows no cloud nor close; for there is no night there.

"Hard worker in the field, thy toil is ended. Straight has been the furrow thou hast ploughed. No looking back has marred thy course. Harvests have followed thy patient sowing, and heaven is already rich with thine ingathered sheaves, and shall still be enriched through the years yet lying in eternity.

"Champion of God, thy battle, long and nobly fought, is over; thy sword, which clave to thy hand, has dropped at last: a palm branch takes it place. No longer does the helmet press thy brow, oft weary with its surging thoughts of battle; a victor's wreath from the great Commander's hand has already proved thy full reward.

"Here, for a little while, shall rest thy precious dust. Then shall thy Well-beloved come; and at His voice thou shalt spring from thy couch of earth, fashioned like unto His body, into glory. Then spirit, soul, and body shall magnify the Lord's redemption. Until then, beloved, sleep. We praise God for thee, and by the blood of the everlasting covenant, hope and expect to praise God with thee. Amen."

Spurgeon's coffin was then lowered into the ground. On it was a Bible open to the text that led Spurgeon to the Lord and Savior he had served faithfully for more than forty years, "Look unto me, and be ye saved, all the ends of the earth: for I am God, and there is none else" [Isaiah 45:22].

PSALM 1

PSALM 1:1–PSALM 1:6

Psalm 1:1 *Blessed is the man that walketh not in the counsel of the ungodly, nor standeth in the way of sinners, nor sitteth in the seat of the scornful.*

EXPOSITION: **Verse 1.** "Blessed"—see how this Book of Psalms opens with a benediction, even as did the famous Sermon of our Lord upon the Mount! The word translated "blessed" is a very expressive one. The original word is plural, and it is a controversial matter whether it is an adjective or a substantive. Hence we may learn the multiplicity of the blessings which shall rest upon the man whom God has justified, and the perfection and greatness of the blessedness he shall enjoy. We might read it, Oh, the blessednesses! and

we may well regard it (as Ainsworth[2] does) as a joyful acclamation of the gracious man's felicity. May the same

---

2. Henry Ainsworth, English clergyman, scholar, and author (1571–1622)

27

benediction rest on us!

Here the gracious man is described both negatively (Psalm 1:1) and positively (Psalm 1:2). He is a man who does not walk in the counsel of the ungodly. He takes wiser counsel, and walks in the commandments of the Lord his God. To him the ways of piety are paths of peace and pleasantness. His footsteps are ordered by the Word of God, and not by the cunning and wicked devices of carnal men. It is a rich sign of inward grace when the outward walk is changed, and when ungodliness is put far from our actions. Note next *"he standeth not in the way of sinners."* His company is of a choicer sort than it was. Although a sinner himself, he is now a blood-washed sinner, quickened by the Holy Spirit, and renewed in heart. Standing by the rich grace of God in the congregation of the righteous, he dares not mingle with the multitude that do evil. Again it is said, *"nor sitteth in the seat of the scornful."* He finds no rest in the atheist's jeers. Let others make a mockery of sin, of eternity, of hell and Heaven, and of the Eternal God; this man has learned better philosophy than that of the infidel, and has too much sense of God's presence to endure to hear His name blasphemed. The seat of the scorner may be very lofty, but it is very near to the gate of hell; let us flee from it, for it shall soon be empty, and destruction shall swallow up the man who sits therein. Mark the gradation in the first verse:

> He walketh not in the counsel of the ungodly,
> Nor standeth in the way of sinners,
> Nor sitteth in the seat of the scornful.

When men are living in sin they go from bad to worse. At first they merely walk in the counsel of the careless and ungodly, who forget God. The evil is rather practical than habitual—but after that, they become accustomed to evil. They stand in the way of open sinners who willfully violate God's commandments; and if let alone, they go one step further, and they themselves become pestilent teachers and tempters of others, and thus they sit in the seat of the scornful. They have taken their degree in vice, and as true Doctors of Damnation they are installed, and are looked up to by others as Masters in Belial. But the blessed man, the man to whom all the blessings of God belong, can hold no communion with such characters as these. He keeps himself pure from these lepers; he puts away evil things from him as garments spotted by the flesh; he comes out from among the wicked, and goes outside the camp, bearing the reproach of Christ. O for grace to be thus separate from sinners.

Psalm 1:2 *But his delight is in the law of the Lord; and in his law doth he meditate day and night.*

EXPOSITION: Verse 2. And now mark his positive character. His delight is in the law of the Lord. He is not under the law as a curse and condemnation, but he is in it, and he delights to be in it as his rule of life; he delights, moreover, to meditate in it, to read it by day, and think upon it by night. He takes a text and carries it with him all day long; and in the night watches, when sleep forsakes his eyelids, he muses upon the Word of God. In the day of his prosperity he sings psalms out of the Word of God, and in the night of his affliction he comforts himself with promises out of the same book.

The Law of God is the daily bread of the true believer. And yet, in David's day, how small was the volume of inspiration, for they had scarcely anything save the first five Books of Moses! How much more, then, should we prize the whole written Word which it is our privilege to have in all our houses! But, alas, what ill treatment is given to this angel from Heaven! We are not all Berean searchers of the Scriptures. How few among us can lay claim to the benediction of the text! Perhaps some of you can claim a sort of negative purity, because you do not walk in the way of the ungodly; but let me ask you—is your delight in The Law of God? Do you study God's Word? Do you make it the man of your right hand—your best companion and hourly guide? If not, this blessing belongs not to you.

Psalm 1:3 *And he shall be like a tree planted by the rivers of water, that bringeth forth his fruit in his season; his leaf also shall not wither; and whatsoever he doeth shall prosper.*

EXPOSITION: **Verse 3.** And he shall be like a tree planted—not a wild tree, but "a tree planted," chosen, considered as property, cultivated and secured from the last terrible uprooting, for *"every plant which my heavenly Father hath not planted, shall be rooted up:"* Matthew 15:13. By the rivers of water; so that even if one river should fail, He has another. The rivers of pardon and the rivers of grace, the rivers of the promise and the rivers of communion with Christ, are never failing sources of supply. He *is "like a tree planted by the rivers of water, that bringeth forth his fruit in his season;"* not unseasonable graces, like untimely figs, which are never full flavored. But the man who delights in God's Word, being taught by it, brings forth patience in the time of suffering, faith in the day of trial, and holy joy in the hour of prosperity. Fruitfulness is an essential quality of a gracious man, and that fruitfulness should be seasonable. *"His leaf also shall not wither;"* his faintest word shall be everlasting; his little deeds of love shall be had in remembrance. Not simply shall his fruit be preserved, but his leaf also. He shall neither lose his beauty nor his fruitfulness.

"And whatsoever he doeth shall prosper." Blessed is the

man who has such a promise as this. But we must not always estimate the fulfillment of a promise by our own eye sight. How often, my brethren, if we judge by feeble sense, may we come to the mournful conclusion of Jacob, "All these things are against me!" [See Genesis 42:36.]. For though we know our interest in the promise, yet we are so tried and troubled, that sight sees the very reverse of what that promise foretells. But to the eye of faith this word is sure, and by it we perceive that our works are prospered, even when everything seems to go against us.

It is not outward prosperity which the Christian most desires and values; it is soul prosperity which he longs for. We often, like Jehoshaphat, make ships to go to Tarshish for gold, but they are broken at Eziongeber. But even here there is a true prospering, for it is often for the soul's health that we would be poor, bereaved, and persecuted. Our worst things are often our best things. As there is a curse wrapped up in the wicked man's mercies, so there is a blessing concealed in the righteous man's crosses, losses, and sorrows. The trials of the saint are a divine husbandry, by which he grows and brings forth abundant fruit.

Psalm 1:4 *The ungodly are not so: but are like the chaff which the wind driveth away.*

EXPOSITION: **Verse 4.** We have now come to the second head of the Psalm. In this verse the contrast of the ill estate of the wicked is employed to heighten the coloring of that fair and pleasant picture which precedes it. The more forcible translation of the Vulgate and of the Septuagint version is: Not so the ungodly, not so. And we are hereby to understand that whatever good thing is said of the righteous is not true in the case of the ungodly. Oh! How terrible is it to have a double negative put upon the promises! And yet this is just the condition of the ungodly.

Mark the use of the term ungodly, for, as we have seen in the opening of the Psalm, these are the beginners in evil, and are the least offensive of sinners. Oh! If such is the sad state of those who quietly continue in their morality, and neglect their God, what must be the condition of open sinners and shameless infidels? The first sentence is a negative description of the ungodly, and the second is the positive picture. Here is their character: They are like chaff, intrinsically worthless, dead, unserviceable, without substance, and easily carried away. Here, also, mark their doom: The wind drives away; death shall hurry them with its terrible blast into the fire in which they shall be utterly consumed.

Psalm 1:5 *Therefore the ungodly shall not stand in the judgment, nor sinners in the congregation of the righteous.*

EXPOSITION: **Verse 5.** They shall stand there to be judged, but not to be acquitted. Fear shall lay hold upon them there; they shall not stand their ground; they shall flee away; they shall not stand in their own defense; for they shall blush and be covered with eternal contempt. Well may the saints long for Heaven, for no evil men shall dwell there, nor sinners in the congregation of the righteous. All our congregations upon Earth are mixed. Every church has one devil in it. The tares grow in the same furrows as the wheat. There is no floor which is as yet thoroughly purged from chaff. Sinners mix with saints, as dross mingles with gold. God's precious diamonds still lie in the same field with pebbles.

Righteous Lots are this side of Heaven continually vexed by the men of Sodom. Let us rejoice then, that in *the general assembly and church of the firstborn* above, there shall by no means be admitted a single unrenewed soul. [See Hebrews

12:23.]. Sinners cannot live in Heaven. They would be out of their element. Sooner could a fish live upon a tree than the wicked in Paradise. Heaven would be an intolerable hell to an impenitent man, even if he could be allowed to enter; but such a privilege shall never be granted to the man who perseveres in his iniquities. May God grant that we may have a name and a place in His courts above!

Psalm 1:6 *For the Lord knoweth the way of the righteous: but the way of the ungodly shall perish.*

EXPOSITION: Verse 6. Or, as the Hebrew has it yet more fully, The Lord is knowing the way of the righteous. He is constantly looking on their way, and though it may be often in mist and darkness, yet the Lord knows it. If it is in the clouds and tempest of affliction, He understands it. He numbers the hairs of our head; He will not suffer any evil to befall us. *He knoweth the way that I take: when He hath tried me, I shall come forth as gold.* [See Job 23:10.]

"But the way of the ungodly shall perish." Not only shall they perish themselves, but their way shall perish too. The righteous carves his name upon the rock, but the wicked writes his remembrance in the sand. The righteous man plows the furrows of earth, and sows a harvest here, which shall never be fully reaped until he enters the enjoyments of eternity.

But as for the wicked, he plows the sea, and though there may seem to be a shining trail behind his keel, yet the waves shall pass over it, and the place that knew him shall know him no more forever. The very "way" of the ungodly shall perish. If it exists in remembrance, it shall be in the remembrance of the bad; for the Lord will cause the name of the wicked to rot, to become a stench in the nostrils of the good, and to be only known to the wicked themselves by its putridity.

May the Lord cleanse our hearts and our ways, that we may escape the doom of the ungodly, and enjoy the blessedness of the righteous!

PSALM 2
PSALM 2:1–PSALM 2:10

Psalm 2:1 *Why do the heathen rage, and the people imagine a vain thing?*

EXPOSITION: **Verse 1.** We have, in these first three verses, a description of the hatred of human nature against the Christ of God. No better comment is needed upon it than the apostolic song in Acts 4:27–28, *For of a truth against thy holy child Jesus, whom thou hast anointed, both Herod, and Pontius Pilate, with the Gentiles, and the people of Israel, were gathered together, for to do whatsoever thy hand and thy counsel determined before to be done.* The psalm begins abruptly with an angry interrogation; and well it may: it is surely but little to be wondered at, that the sight of creatures in arms against their God should amaze the psalmist's mind. We see the heathen raging, roaring like the sea, tossed to and fro with restless waves, as the ocean in a storm; and then we mark the people in their hearts imagining a vain thing against God. Where there is much rage there is generally some folly, and in this case there is an excess of it.

Psalm 2:2 *The kings of the earth set themselves, and the rulers take counsel together, against the Lord, and against his anointed, saying . . .*

EXPOSITION: **Verse 2.** Note that the commotion is not caused by the people only, but their leaders foment the rebellion. The kings of the Earth set themselves. In determined malice they arrayed themselves in opposition against God. It was not temporary rage, but deep-seated hate, for they set themselves resolutely to withstand the Prince of Peace. And the rulers take counsel together. They go about their warfare craftily, not with foolish haste, but deliberately. They use all the skill which art can give. Like Pharaoh, they cry, *Let us deal wisely with them* [See Exodus 1:10.]. O that men were half as careful in God's service to serve Him wisely, as His enemies are to attack His kingdom craftily. Sinners have their wits about them, and yet saints are dull. But what say they? What is the meaning of this commotion?

Psalm 2:3 *Let us break their bands asunder, and cast away their cords from us.*

EXPOSITION: **Verse 3.** *Let us break their bands asunder*—let us be free to commit all manner of abominations. Let us be our own gods. Let us rid ourselves of all restraint. Gathering impudence by the traitorous proposition of rebellion, they add—let us cast away; as if it were an easy matter. What! O ye kings, do you think yourselves to be as Samson, and are the bands of omnipotence but as green wreaths before you? Do you dream that you shall snap to pieces and destroy the mandates of God—the decrees of the Most High—as if they were but tow?[3]

And do you say, "And cast away their cords from us?" Yes! There are monarchs who have spoken thus, and there are still rebels upon thrones. However mad the resolution to revolt from God, it is one in which man has persevered ever since his creation, and he continues in it to this very day. The glorious reign of Jesus in the latter day will not be consummated, until a terrible struggle has convulsed the nations. His coming will be as a refiner's fire, and like fuller's

---

3. A bundle of flax, hemp or jute.

soap, and the day thereof shall burn as an oven. Earth loves not her rightful monarch, but clings to the usurper's sway: the terrible conflicts of the last days will illustrate both the world's love of sin and Jehovah's power to give the Kingdom to His only Begotten. To a graceless neck the yoke of Christ is intolerable, but to the saved sinner it is easy and light. We may judge ourselves by this, do we love that yoke, or do we wish to cast it from us?

Psalm 2:4 *He that sitteth in the heavens shall laugh: the Lord shall have them in derision.*

EXPOSITION: Verse 4. Let us now turn our eyes from the wicked council chamber and raging tumult of man, to the secret place of the majesty of the Most High. What does God say? What will the King do unto the men who reject His only begotten Son, the Heir of all things?

Mark the quiet dignity of the Omnipotent One, and the contempt which He pours upon the princes and their raging people. He has not taken the trouble to rise up and do battle with them—He despises them, He knows how absurd, how irrational, how futile are their attempts against Him—He therefore laughs at them.

Psalm 2:5 *Then shall he speak unto them in his wrath, and vex them in his sore displeasure.*

EXPOSITION: Verse 5. After He has laughed He shall speak; He needs not smite; the breath of His lips is enough. At the moment when their power is at its height and their fury most violent, then shall His Word go forth against them. And what is it that He says? It is a very galling sentence. "Yet," says He, "despite your malice, despite your tumultuous gatherings, despite the wisdom of your counsels, despite the craft of your lawgivers, yet have I set my King upon my holy hill of Zion." Is not that a grand exclamation! He has already done that which the enemy seeks to prevent. While they are proposing, He has disposed the matter.

Jehovah's will is done, and man's will frets and raves in vain. God's Anointed is appointed, and shall not be disappointed. Look back through all the ages of infidelity, hearken to the high and hard things which men have spoken against the Most High, listen to the rolling thunder of Earth's volleys against the Majesty of Heaven, and then think that God is saying all the while, *Yet have I set my king upon my holy hill of Zion.*

Psalm 2:6 *Yet have I set my king upon my holy hill of Zion.*

EXPOSITION: Verse 6. Yet Jesus reigns, yet He sees the travail of His soul, and His unsuffering kingdom yet shall come when He shall take unto himself His great power, and reign from the river unto the ends of the Earth. Even now He reigns in Zion, and our glad lips sound forth the praises of the Prince of Peace. Greater conflicts may here be foretold, but we may be confident that victory will be given to our Lord and King. Glorious triumphs are yet to come; hasten them, we pray you, O Lord! It is Zion's glory and joy that her King is in her, guarding her from foes, and filling her with good things. Jesus sits upon the throne of grace, and the throne of power in the midst of His Church. In Him is Zion's best safeguard; let her citizens be glad in Him.

> Thy walls are strength, and at thy gates
> a guard of heavenly warriors waits;
> Nor shall thy deep foundations move,
> Fixed on His counsels and His love.

Thy foes in vain designs engage;
Against His throne in vain they rage,
Like rising waves, with angry roar,
That dash and die upon the shore.[4]

Psalm 2:7 *I will declare the decree: the Lord hath said unto me, Thou art my Son; this day have I begotten thee.*

EXPOSITION: Verse 7. This psalm wears something of a dramatic form, for now another person is introduced as speaking. We have looked into the council chamber of the wicked, and to the throne of God, and now we behold the Anointed declaring His rights of sovereignty, and warning the traitors of their doom. God has laughed at the counsel and ravings of the wicked, and now Christ the Anointed himself comes forward, as the Risen Redeemer, *declared to be the Son of God with power, according to the spirit of holiness, by the resurrection from the dead* (Romans 1:14). Looking into the angry faces of the rebellious kings, the Anointed One seems to say, "If this suffices not to make you silent, *'I will declare the decree.'*"

Now this decree is directly in conflict with the device of man, for its tenor is the establishment of the very dominion against which the nations are raving. *You are my Son.* Here is a noble proof of the glorious Divinity of our Immanuel. *For unto which of the angels said he at any time, Thou art my Son, this day have I begotten thee?* [Hebrews 1:5–6.]. What a mercy to have a Divine Redeemer in whom to rest our confidence!

This day have I begotten thee. If this refers to the Godhead

---

4. Hymn # 558, "God the Glory and Defense of the Church" in the *Church Hymnbook*, by William Salter (1821–1910).

of our Lord, let us not attempt to fathom it, for it is a great truth, a truth reverently to be received, but not irreverently to be scanned. It may be added, that if this relates to the Begotten One in His human nature, we must here also rejoice in the mystery, but not attempt to violate its sanctity by intrusive prying into the secrets of the Eternal God. The things which are revealed are enough, without venturing into vain speculations. In attempting to define the Trinity, or unveil the essence of Divinity, many men have lost themselves: here great ships have foundered. What have we to do in such a sea with our frail skiffs[5]?

Psalm 2:8 *Ask of me, and I shall give thee the heathen for thine inheritance, and the uttermost parts of the earth for thy possession.*

EXPOSITION: **Verse 8.** *Ask of me.* It was a custom among great kings to give to favored ones whatever they might ask. [See Esther 5:6 and Matthew 14:7.]. Jesus has but to ask and have. Here He declares that His very enemies are His inheritance. To their face He declares this decree, and "Lo! here", cries the Anointed One, as He holds aloft in that once-pierced hand the scepter of His power, "He hath given me this, not only the right to be a king, but the power to conquer."

Psalm 2:9 *Thou shalt break them with a rod of iron; thou shalt dash them in pieces like a potter's vessel.*

EXPOSITION: **Verse 9.** Yes! Jehovah has given to His Anointed a rod of iron with which He shall break rebellious nations in pieces, and, despite their imperial strength, they shall be but as potters' vessels, easily dashed into shivers,

5. A small boat propelled by oars or sails.

when the rod of iron is in the hand of the omnipotent Son of God. Those who will not bend must break. Potters' vessels are not to be restored if dashed in pieces, and the ruin of sinners will be hopeless if Jesus shall smite them.

> Ye sinners seek His grace,
> Whose wrath ye cannot bear;
> Fly to the shelter of his cross,
> And find salvation there.[6]

Psalm 2:10 *Be wise now therefore, O ye kings: be instructed, ye judges of the earth.*

EXPOSITION: Verse 10. The scene again changes, and counsel is given to those who have taken counsel to rebel. They are exhorted to obey, and give the kiss of homage and affection to Him whom they have hated. Be wise. It is always wise to be willing to be instructed, especially when such instruction tends to the salvation of the soul. *Be wise now, therefore;* delay no longer, but let good reason weigh with you. Your warfare cannot succeed, therefore desist and yield cheerfully to Him who will make you bow if you refuse His yoke. O how wise, how infinitely wise is obedience to Jesus, and how dreadful is the folly of those who continue to be His enemies!

Psalm 2:11 *Serve the Lord with fear and trembling.*

EXPOSITION: Verse 11. *Serve the Lord with fear;* let reverence and humility be mingled with your service. He is a great God, and you are but puny creatures; bend therefore, in lowly worship, and let a filial fear mingle with all your

---

6. Hymn # 610 in the Lutheran Hymnal, "And Will the Judge Descend" by Philip Doddridge 1702–1751.

obedience to the great Father of the Ages. Rejoice with trembling—there must ever be a holy fear mixed with the Christian's joy. This is a sacred compound, yielding a sweet aroma, and we must see to it that we burn no other upon the altar. Fear, without joy is torment; and joy without holy fear, would be presumption.

Psalm 2:12 *Kiss the Son, lest he be angry, and ye perish from the way, when his wrath is kindled but a little. Blessed are all they that put their trust in him.*

EXPOSITION: **Verse 12.** Mark the solemn argument for reconciliation and obedience. It is an awful thing to perish in the midst of sin, in the very way of rebellion; and yet how easily could His wrath destroy us suddenly. It needs not that His anger should be heated seven times hotter; let the fuel kindle but a little, and we are consumed. O sinner! Take heed of the terrors of the Lord; for *our God is a consuming fire* [Hebrews 12:29]. Note the benediction with which the psalm closes: *Blessed are all they that put their trust in Him.* Have we a share in this blessedness? Do we trust in Him? Our faith may be slender as a spider's thread; but if it be real, we are in our measure blessed. The more we trust, the more fully shall we know this blessedness. We may therefore close the psalm with the prayer of the apostles: *Lord, increase our faith* [Luke 17:5].

The first psalm was a contrast between the righteous man and the sinner; the second psalm is a contrast between the tumultuous disobedience of the ungodly world and the sure exaltation of the righteous Son of God. In the first psalm, we saw the wicked driven away like chaff; in the second psalm we see them broken in pieces like a potter's vessel. In the first psalm, we beheld the righteous like a tree planted by the rivers of water; and here, we contemplate Christ the

Covenant Head of the righteous, made better than a tree planted by the rivers of water, for He is made king of all the islands, and all the heathen bow before Him and kiss the dust; while He himself gives a blessing to all those who put their trust in Him.

The two psalms are worthy of the very deepest attention; they are, in fact, the preface to the entire Book of Psalms, and were by some of the ancients, joined into one. They are, however, two psalms; for Paul speaks of this as the second psalm. [See Acts 13:33.]. The first shows us the character and lot of the righteous; and the next teaches us that the psalms are Messianic, and speak of Christ the Messiah—the Prince who shall reign from the river even unto the ends of the Earth. That they have both a far reaching prophetic outlook we are well assured, but we do not feel competent to open up that matter, and must leave it to abler hands.

PSALM 3
PSALM 3:1–PSALM 3:8

Psalm 3:1 *Lord, how are they increased that trouble me! many are they that rise up against me.*

EXPOSITION: **Verse 1.** The poor brokenhearted father complains of the multitude of his enemies, and if you turn to 2 Samuel 15:2, you will find it written that *the conspiracy was strong; for the people increased continually with Absalom,* while the troops of David constantly diminished! *Lord, how are they increased that trouble me!* Here is a note of exclamation to express the wonder of woe which amazed and perplexed the fugitive father. Alas! I see no limit to my misery, for my troubles are enlarged! There was enough at first to sink me very low; but lo my enemies multiply! When Absalom, my darling, is in rebellion against me, it is enough to break my heart; but lo! Ahithophel has forsaken me, my faithful counselors have turned their backs on me; lo, my generals and soldiers have deserted my standard! "How are they increased that trouble me!" Troubles always come in flocks. Sorrow has a numerous family.

Many are they that rise up against me. Their hosts are far superior to mine! Their numbers are too great for my reckoning! Let us here recall to our memory the innumerable host which beset our Divine Redeemer. The legions of our sins, the armies of fiends, the crowd of bodily pains, the host of spiritual sorrows, and all the allies of death and hell, set themselves in battle against the Son of Man. O how precious to know and believe that He has routed their hosts, and trodden them down in His anger! They who would have troubled us He has removed into captivity, and those who would have risen up against us He has laid low. The dragon lost his sting when he dashed it into the soul of Jesus.

Psalm 3:2 *Many there be which say of my soul, There is no help for him in God. Selah.*

EXPOSITION: **Verse 2.** David complains before his loving God of the worst weapon of his enemies' attacks, and the bitterest drop of his distresses. "Oh!" saith David, many there be that say of my soul, *There is no help for him in God.* Some of his distrustful friends said this sorrowfully, but his enemies exultingly boasted of it, and longed to see their words proved by his total destruction. This was the most unkind cut of all, when they declared that his God had forsaken him. Yet David knew in his own conscience that he had given them some ground for this exclamation, for he had committed sin against God in the very light of day. Then they flung his crime with Bathsheba into his face, and they said, "Go up, thou bloody man; God hath forsaken thee and left thee."

Shimei cursed him, and swore at him to his very face, for he was bold because of his backers, since multitudes of the men of Belial thought of David in like fashion. Doubtless, David felt this infernal suggestion to be staggering to his faith. If all the trials which come from Heaven, all the temptations which ascend from hell, and all the crosses which arise from Earth, could be mixed and pressed together, they would not make a trial so terrible as that which is contained in this verse. It is the most bitter of all afflictions to be led to fear that there is no help for us in God.

And yet remember our most blessed Savior had to endure

this in the deepest degree when He cried, *My God, my God, why hast thou forsaken me?* [Psalm 22:1]. He knew full well what it was to walk in darkness and to see no light. This was the curse of the curse. This was the wormwood mingled with the gall. To be deserted of His Father was worse than to be the despised of men. Surely we should love Him who suffered this bitterest of temptations and trials for our sake. It will be a delightful and instructive exercise for the loving heart.

Psalm 3:3 *Thou, O Lord, art a shield for me.*

EXPOSITION: **Verse 3.** *Thou, O Lord, art a shield for me.* The word in the original signifies more than a shield; it means a buckler round about, a protection which shall surround a man entirely, a shield above, beneath, around, without and within. Oh! What a shield is God for His people! He wards off the fiery darts of Satan from beneath, and the storms of trials from above, while, at the same instant, He speaks peace to the tempest within the breast. You are my glory Lord—David knew that though he was driven from his capital in contempt and scorn, he could yet return in triumph, and by faith he looks upon God as honoring and glorifying him.

O for grace to see our future glory amid present shame! Indeed, there is a present glory in our afflictions, if we could but discern it; for it is no mean thing to have fellowship with Christ in His sufferings. David was honored when he made the ascent of Olivet, weeping, with his head covered; for he was in all this made like unto his Lord. May we learn, in this respect, to glory in tribulations also! And the lifter up of mine head—you shall yet exalt me. Though I hang my head in sorrow, I shall very soon lift it up in joy and thanksgiving. What a divine trio of mercies is contained in this verse!—

Defense for the defenseless, glory for the despised, and joy for the comfortless. Verily we may well say, "there is none like the God of Jeshurun" [See Deuteronomy 33:26.].

Psalm 3:4 *I cried unto the Lord with my voice, and he heard me out of his holy hill. Selah.*

EXPOSITION: **Verse 4.** *I cried unto the Lord with my voice.* Why does he say, "with my voice?" Surely, silent prayers are heard. Yes, but good men often find that, even in secret, they pray better aloud than they do when they utter no vocal sound. Perhaps, moreover, David would think thus—"My cruel enemies clamor against me; they lift up their voices, and, behold, I lift up mine and my cry out soars them all." They clamor, but the cry of my voice in great distress pierces the very skies, and is louder and stronger than all their tumult; for there is One in the sanctuary who harkens to me from the seventh heaven, and He has heard me out of his holy hill. Answers to prayers are sweet cordials for the soul. We need not fear a frowning world while we rejoice in a prayer-hearing God.

Psalm 3:5 *I laid me down and slept; I awaked; for the Lord sustained me.*

EXPOSITION: **Verse 5.** David's faith enabled him to lie down; anxiety would certainly have kept him on tiptoe, watching for an enemy. Yet, he was able to sleep, to sleep in the midst of trouble, surrounded by foes. *So he giveth his beloved sleep* [See Psalm 127:2.]. There is a sleep of presumption; God deliver us from it! There is a sleep of holy confidence; God help us so to close our eyes! But David says he awaked also. Some sleep the sleep of death; but he, though exposed to many enemies, reclined his head on the bosom of his God, slept happily beneath the wing of Providence in sweet security, and then awoke in safety.

For the Lord sustained me. The sweet influence of the Pleiades[7] of promise shone upon the sleeper, and he awoke conscious that the Lord had preserved him. An excellent divine has well remarked—"This quietude of a man's heart by faith in God, is a higher sort of work than the natural resolution of manly courage, for it is the gracious operation of God's Holy Spirit upholding a man above nature, and therefore the Lord must have all the glory of it."

Psalm 3:6 *I will not be afraid of ten thousands of people, that have set themselves against me round about.*

EXPOSITION: **Verse 6.** Buckling on his harness for the day's battle, our hero sings, *I will not be afraid of ten thousands of people, that have set themselves against me round about.* Observe that he does not attempt to underestimate the number or wisdom of his enemies. He reckons them at tens of thousands, and he views them as cunning huntsmen chasing him with cruel skill. Yet he trembles not, but looking his enemy in the face he is ready for the battle. There may be no way of escape; they may hem me in as the deer are surrounded by a circle of hunters; they may surround me on every side, but in the name of God I will dash through them; or, if I remain in the midst of them, yet shall they not hurt me; I shall be free in my very prison. But David is too wise to venture to the battle without prayer; he therefore takes himself to his knees, and cries aloud to Jehovah.

---

7. The Pleiades or the Seven Star Sisters is a star cluster located in the constellation of Taurus. It appears in spring and early summer, and therefore connotes mild weather and consolation.

Psalm 3:7 *Arise, O Lord; save me, O my God: for thou hast smitten all mine enemies upon the cheek bone; thou hast broken the teeth of the ungodly.*

EXPOSITION: Verse 7. His only hope is in his God, but that is so strong a confidence, that he feels the Lord has but to arise and he is saved. It is enough for the Lord to stand up, and all is well. He compares his enemies to wild beasts, and he declares that God has broken their jaws, so that they could not injure him; "You have broken the teeth of the ungodly." Or else he alludes to the peculiar temptations to which he was then exposed. They had spoken against him; God, therefore, has "smitten them upon the cheek bone." They seemed as if they would devour him with their mouths; God has broken their teeth, and let them say what they will, their toothless jaws shall not be able to devour him. Rejoice, O believer, you have to do with a dragon whose head is broken, and with enemies whose teeth are dashed from their jaws!

Psalm 3:8 *Salvation belongeth unto the Lord: thy blessing is upon thy people. Selah.*

EXPOSITION: Verse 8. This verse contains the sum and substance of Calvinistic doctrine. Search Scripture through, and you must, if you read it with a candid mind, be persuaded that the doctrine of salvation by grace alone is the great doctrine of the Word of God: *Salvation belongeth unto the Lord.* This is a point concerning which we are daily fighting. Our opponents say, "Salvation belongs to the free will of man; if not to man's merit, yet at least to man's will;" but we hold and teach that salvation from first to last, in every iota of it, belongs to the Most High God. It is God that chooses His people. He calls them by His grace; He quickens them by His Spirit, and keeps them by His power. It is not of man, neither by man; *not of him that willeth, nor of him that runneth, but of God that sheweth mercy* [Romans 9:16].

May we all learn this truth experimentally, for our proud flesh and blood will never permit us to learn it in any other way. In the last sentence the peculiarity and specialty of salvation are plainly stated: Your blessing is upon your people. Neither upon Egypt, nor upon Tyre, nor upon Nineveh; your blessing is upon your chosen, your blood-bought, your everlastingly beloved people.

Selah: lift up your hearts, and pause, and meditate upon this doctrine. *Thy blessing is upon thy people.* Divine, discriminating, distinguishing, eternal, infinite, immutable love, is a subject for constant adoration. Pause, my soul, at this Selah, and consider your own interest in the salvation of God; and if by humble faith you are enabled to see Jesus as yours by His own free gift of himself to you, if this greatest of all blessings is upon you, rise up and sing:

> "Rise, my soul! adore and wonder!
> Ask, 'O why such love to me?'
> Grace hath put me in the number
> Of the Saviour's family: Hallelujah!
> Thanks, eternal thanks, to thee!"[8]

---

8. Hymn #452 in the Protestant Episcopal Church Hymnbook. "On Sovereign Grace," written in 1845.

PSALM 4
PSALM 4:1–PSALM 4:8

Psalm 4:1 *Hear me when I call, O God of my righteousness: thou hast enlarged me when I was in distress; have mercy upon me, and hear my prayer.*

EXPOSITION: Verse 1. This is another instance of David's common habit of pleading past mercies as a ground for present favor. Here he reviews his Ebenezers[9] and takes comfort from them. It is not to be imagined that he who has helped us in six troubles will leave us in the seventh. God does nothing by halves, and He will never cease to help us until we cease to need. The manna shall fall every morning until we cross the Jordan.

Observe, that David speaks first to God and then to men. Surely we should all speak the more boldly to men if we had more constant converse with God. He who dares to face his Maker will not tremble before the sons of men.

The name by which the Lord is here addressed, God of my righteousness, deserves notice, since it is not used in any other part of Scripture. It means, Lord, you are the author, the witness, the maintainer, the judge, and the rewarder of my righteousness; to you I appeal from the calumnies and harsh judgments of men. Herein is wisdom, let us imitate it and always take our suit, not to the petty courts of human opinion, but into the superior court, the King's Bench of Heaven.

---

9. "Ebenezer" was the name of a stone commemorating the Lord's help, placed by Samuel. (See 1 Samuel 7:12.)

Thou has enlarged me when I was in distress—a figure taken from an army enclosed in a defile, and hard pressed by the surrounding enemy. God has dashed down the rocks and given me room; He has broken the barriers and set me in a large place. Or, we may understand it thus: "God has enlarged my heart with joy and comfort, when I was like a man imprisoned by grief and sorrow." God is a never failing comforter. Have mercy upon me. Though you may justly permit my enemies to destroy me, on account of my many and great sins, yet I flee to your mercy, and I beseech you to hear my prayer, and bring your servant out of his troubles. The best of men need mercy as truly as the worst of men. All the deliverances of saints, as well as the pardons of sinners, are the free gifts of heavenly grace.

Psalm 4:2 *O ye sons of men, how long will ye turn my glory into shame? how long will ye love vanity, and seek after leasing? Selah.*

EXPOSITION: **Verse 2.** In this second division of the psalm, we are led from the closet of prayer into the field of conflict. Note the undaunted courage of the man of God. He recognizes that his enemies are great men for such is the meaning of the Hebrew words translated—sons of men, but still he believes them to be foolish men, and therefore chides them, as though they were but children. He tells them that they love vanity, and seek after leasing, that is, lying, empty fancies, vain conceits, wicked fabrications. He asks them how long they mean to make his honor a jest, and his fame a mockery? A little of such mirth is too much, why need they continue to indulge in it? Had they not been long enough upon the watch for his stopping? Had not repeated disappointments convinced them that the Lord's anointed was not to be overcome by all their calumnies? Did they mean to jest their souls into hell, and go on with their laughter until swift vengeance would turn their merriment into howling? In the contemplation of their perverse continuance in their vain and lying pursuits, the psalmist solemnly pauses and inserts a Selah.

Surely we too may stop awhile, and meditate upon the deep seated folly of the wicked, their continuance in evil, and their sure destruction; and we may learn to admire that grace which has made us to differ, and taught us to love truth, and seek after righteousness.

Psalm 4:3 *But know that the Lord hath set apart him that is godly for himself: the Lord will hear when I call unto him.*

EXPOSITION: Verse 3. But know. Fools will not learn, and therefore they must again and again be told the same thing, especially when it is such a bitter truth which is to be taught them, viz.—the fact that the godly are the chosen of God, and are, by distinguishing grace, set apart and separated from among men. Election is a doctrine which unrenewed men cannot endure, but nevertheless, it is a glorious and well-attested truth, and one which should comfort the tempted believer. Election is the guarantee of complete salvation, and an argument for success at the throne of grace. He who chose us for himself will surely hear our prayer. The Lord's elect shall not be condemned, nor shall their cry be unheard. David was king by divine decree, and we are the Lord's people in the same manner: let us tell our enemies to their faces, that they fight against God and destiny, when they strive to overthrow our souls. O beloved, when you are on your knees, the fact of your being set apart as God's own peculiar treasure, should give you courage and inspire you with fervency and faith. *Shall not God avenge his own* *elect, which cry day and night unto him?* [Luke 18:7]. Since He chose to love us He cannot but choose to hear us.

Psalm 4:4 *Stand in awe, and sin not: commune with your own heart upon your bed, and be still. Selah.*

EXPOSITION: **Verse 4.** Tremble and sin not. How many reverse this counsel and sin but tremble not. O that men would take the advice of this verse and commune with their own hearts. Surely a want of thought must be one reason why men are so mad as to despise Christ and hate their own mercies. O that for once their passions would be quiet and let them be still, that so in solemn silence they might review the past, and meditate upon their inevitable doom. Surely a thinking man might have enough sense to discover the vanity of sin and the worthlessness of the world. Stay, rash sinner, stay, before you take the last leap. Go to your bed and think upon your ways. Ask counsel of your pillow, and let the quietude of night instruct you! Throw not away your soul for nothing! Let reason speak! Let the clamorous world be still awhile, and let your poor soul plead with you to think before you seal its fate, and ruin it forever! Selah. O sinner! Pause while I question you awhile in the words of a sacred poet:

> "Sinner, is thy heart at rest?
> Is thy bosom void of fear?
> Art thou not by guilt oppressed?
> Speaks not conscience in thine ear?
> Can this world afford thee bliss?
> Can it chase away thy gloom?
> Flattering, false, and vain it is;
> Tremble at the worldling's doom!

Think, O sinner, on thy end,
See the judgment day appear,
Thither must thy spirit wend,
There thy righteous sentence hear.
Wretched, ruined, helpless soul,
To a Saviour's blood apply;
He alone can make thee whole,
Fly to Jesus, sinner, fly!"[10]

Psalm 4:5 *Offer the sacrifices of righteousness, and put your trust in the Lord.*

EXPOSITION: Verse 5. Provided that the rebels had obeyed the voice of the last verse, they would now be crying—"What shall we do to be saved?" And in the present verse, they are pointed to the sacrifice, and exhorted to trust in the Lord. When the Jew offered sacrifice righteously, that is, in a spiritual manner, he thereby set forth the Redeemer, the great sin atoning Lamb; there is, therefore, the full gospel in this exhortation of the psalmist. O sinners, flee ye to the sacrifice of Calvary, and there put your whole confidence and trust, for He who died for men is the Lord Jehovah.

Psalm 4:6 *There be many that say, Who will shew us any good? Lord, lift thou up the light of thy countenance upon us.*

EXPOSITION: Verse 6. We have now entered upon the third division of the psalm, in which the faith of the afflicted one finds utterance in sweet expressions of contentment and peace.

There were many, even among David's own followers, who wanted to see rather than to believe. Alas! This is the

---

10. Hymn, "Sinner, Is Thy Soul at Rest?" by Jared Bell
Waterbury, 1779–1876.

tendency of us all! Even the regenerate sometimes groan after the sense and sight of prosperity, and are sad when darkness covers all good from view. As for worldlings, this is their unceasing cry.

Who will show us any good? Never satisfied, their gaping mouths are turned in every direction, their empty hearts are ready to drink in any fine delusion which impostors may invent; and when these fail, they soon yield to despair, and declare that there is no good thing in either Heaven or Earth. The true believer is a man of a very different mold. His face is not downward like the beasts', but upward like the angels'. He drinks not from the muddy pools of Mammon, but from the fountain of life above. The light of God's countenance is enough for him. This is his riches, his honor, his health, his ambition, his ease. Give him this, and he will ask no more. This is joy unspeakable, and full of glory. Oh, for more of the indwelling of the Holy Spirit, that our fellowship with the Father and with His Son Jesus Christ may be constant and abiding!

Psalm 4:7 *Thou hast put gladness in my heart, more than in the time that their corn and their wine increased.*

EXPOSITION: **Verse 7.** "It is better," said one, "to feel God's favor one hour in our repenting souls, than to sit whole ages under the warmest sunshine that this world affords." Christ in the heart is better than corn in the barn or wine in the vat. Corn and wine are but fruits of the world, but the light of God's countenance is the ripe fruit of Heaven. "Thou art with me," is a far more blessed cry than "Harvest home." Let my granary be empty, I am yet full of blessings if Jesus Christ smiles upon me; but if I have all the world, I am poor without Him.

We should not fail to remark that this verse is the saying of the righteous man, in opposition to the saying of the many. How quickly does the tongue betray the character! "Speak, that I may see you!" said Socrates to a fair boy. The metal of a bell is best known by its sound. Birds reveal their nature by their song. Owls cannot sing the carol of the lark, nor can the nightingale hoot like the owl. Let us, then, weigh and watch our words, lest our speech should prove us to be foreigners, and aliens from the commonwealth of Israel.

Psalm 4:8 *I will both lay me down in peace, and sleep: for thou, Lord, only makest me dwell in safety.*

EXPOSITION: Verse 8. Sweet Evening Hymn! I shall not sit up to watch through fear, but I will lie down; and then I will not lie awake listening to every rustling sound, but I will lie down in peace and sleep, for I have nothing to fear. He that has the wings of God above him needs no other curtain. Better than bolts or bars is the protection of the Lord. Armed men kept the bed of Solomon, but we do not believe that he slept more soundly than his father, whose bed was the hard ground, and who was haunted by bloodthirsty foes. Note the word only, which means that God alone was his keeper and that though alone, without man's help, he was even then in good keeping, for he was "alone with God." A quiet conscience is a good bedfellow. How many of our sleepless hours might be traced to our untrusting and disordered minds. They slumber sweetly whom faith rocks to sleep. No pillow so soft as a promise; no coverlet so warm as an assured interest in Christ.

O Lord, give us this calm repose on you, that like David we may lie down in peace, and sleep each night while we live; and joyfully may we lie down in the appointed season, to sleep in death, to rest in God! Dr. Hawker's[11] reflection upon this psalm is worthy to be prayed over and fed upon with sacred delight. We cannot help transcribing it:

O dear reader let us never lose sight of the Lord Jesus while reading this Psalm. He is the Lord our righteousness; and therefore, in all our approaches to the mercy seat, let us go there in a language corresponding to this which calls Jesus the Lord our righteousness. While men of the world, from the world are seeking their chief good, let us desire his favor which infinitely transcends corn and wine, and all the good things which perish in the using. Yes, Lord, your favor is better than life itself. You cause them that love you to inherit substance, and fill all their treasure.

Oh gracious God and Father, have you in such a wonderful manner set apart one in our nature for yourself? Have you indeed chosen one out of the people? Have you seen Him in the purity of His nature—a one in every point Godly? Have you given Him as the covenant of the people? And have you declared yourself well pleased in Him? Oh! Then, well may my soul be well pleased in Him also. Now do I know that my God and Father will hear me when I call upon him in Jesus' name, and when I look up to him for acceptance for Jesus' sake! Yes, my heart is fixed, O Lord, my heart is fixed; Jesus is my hope and righteousness; the Lord will hear me when I call. And henceforth will I both lay me down in peace and sleep securely in Jesus, accepted in the Beloved; for this is the rest wherewith the Lord causes the weary to rest, and this is the refreshing.

---

11. Robert Stephen Hawker, English Clergyman, 1753–1827.

Psalm 5
Psalm 5:1–Psalm 5:12

Psalm 5:1 *Give ear to my words, O Lord, consider my meditation.*

EXPOSITION: Verse 1. There are two sorts of prayers—those expressed in words, and the unuttered longings which abide as silent meditations. Words are not the essence but the garments of prayer. Moses at the Red Sea cried to God, though he said nothing. Yet the use of language may prevent distraction of mind, may assist the powers of the soul, and may excite devotion. David, we observe, uses both modes of prayer, and craves for the one a hearing, and for the other a consideration. What an expressive word!

Consider my meditation. If I have asked that which is right, give it to me; if I have omitted to ask that which I most needed, fill up the vacancy in my prayer. *Consider my meditation.* Let your holy soul consider it as presented through my all glorious Mediator: then regard it in your wisdom, weigh it in the scales, judge my sincerity, and of the true state of my necessities, and answer me in due time for your mercy's sake! There may be prevailing intercession where there are no words; and alas, there may be words where there is no true supplication. Let us cultivate the spirit of prayer which is even better than the habit of prayer. There may be seeming prayer where there is little devotion. We should begin to pray before we kneel down, and we should not cease when we rise up.

Psalm 5:2 *Hearken unto the voice of my cry, my King, and my God: for unto thee will I pray.*

EXPOSITION: **Verse 2.** *The voice of my cry.* In another psalm we find the expression, *The voice of my weeping.* Weeping has a voice—a melting, plaintive tone, an ear-piercing shrillness, which reaches the very heart of God; and crying has a voice—a soul-moving eloquence; coming from our heart it reaches God's heart. Ah! My brothers and sisters, sometimes we cannot put our prayers into words: they are nothing but a cry: but the Lord can comprehend the meaning, for He hears a voice in our cry. To a loving father his children's cries are music, and they have a magic influence which his heart cannot resist.

My King, and my God. Observe carefully these little pronouns, *my* King, and *my* God. They are the pith and marrow of the plea. Here is a grand argument why God should answer prayer—because He is our King and our God. We are not aliens to Him: He is the King of our country. Kings are expected to hear the appeals of their own people. We are not strangers to Him; we are His worshippers, and He is our God: ours by covenant, by promise, by oath, by blood. *For unto thee will I pray.* Here David expresses his declaration that he will seek to God, and to God alone. God is to be the only object of worship: the only resource of our soul in times of need. Leave broken cisterns to the godless, and let the godly drink from the Divine fountain alone. *Unto thee will I pray.* He makes a resolution, that as long as he lived he would pray. He would never cease to supplicate, even though the answer may not come.

Psalm 5:3 *My voice shalt thou hear in the morning, O Lord; in the morning will I direct my prayer unto thee, and will look up.*

EXPOSITION: **Verse 3.** Observe, this is not so much
a prayer as a resolution, *"My voice shall you hear;* I will
not be dumb, I will not be silent, I will not withhold my
speech, I will cry to you for the fire that dwells within compels
me to pray."* We can sooner die than live without prayer.
None of God's children are possessed with a dumb devil. *In
the morning.* This is the fittest time for prayer with God.
An hour in the morning is worth two in the evening. While
the dew is on the grass, let grace drop upon the soul. Let us
give to God the mornings of our days and the morning of
our lives. Prayer should be the key of the day and the lock
of the night. Devotion should be both the morning star and
the evening star.

If we merely read our English version, and want an
explanation of these two sentences, we find it in the figure
of an archer, I will direct my prayer unto you, I will put my
prayer upon the bow, I will direct it towards Heaven, and
then when I have shot up my arrow, I will look up to see
where it has gone. But the Hebrew has a still fuller meaning
than this—"I will direct my prayer." It is the word that is
used for the laying in order of the wood and the pieces of
the victim upon the altar, and it is used also for the putting
of the shewbread upon the table. It means just this: "I will
arrange my prayer before you;" I will lay it out upon the
altar in the morning, just as the priest lays out the morning
sacrifice. I will arrange my prayer; or, as old Master Trapp
has it, "I will marshal up my prayers," I will put them in
order, call up all my powers, and bid them stand in their
proper places, that I may pray with all my might, and pray
acceptably. And will look up, or, as the Hebrew might better
be translated, "'I will look out,' I will look out for the answer;
after I have prayed; I will expect that the blessing shall come."
It is a word that is used in another place where we read of
those who watched for the morning. So will I watch for your

answer, O my Lord! I will spread out my prayer like the victim on the altar, and I will look up, and expect to receive the answer by fire from Heaven to consume the sacrifice.

Two questions are suggested by the last part of this verse. Do we not miss very much of the sweetness and efficacy of prayer by a want of careful meditation before it, and of hopeful expectation after it? We too often rush into the presence of God without forethought or humility. We are like men who present themselves before a king without a petition, and what wonder is it that we often miss the end of prayer?

We should be careful to keep the stream of meditation always running; for this is the water to drive the mill of prayer. It is idle to pull up the flood gates of a dry brook, and then hope to see the wheel revolve. Prayer without fervency is like hunting with a dead dog, and prayer without preparation is hawking with a blind falcon. Prayer is the work of the Holy Spirit, but He works by means. God made man, but He used the dust of the Earth as a material: the Holy Ghost is the author of prayer, but He employs the thoughts of a fervent soul as the gold with which to fashion the vessel. Let not our prayers and praises be the flashes of a hot and hasty brain, but the steady burning of a well-kindled fire.

But, furthermore, do we not forget to watch the result of our supplications? We are like the ostrich, which lays her eggs and looks not for her young. We sow the seed, and are too idle to seek a harvest. How can we expect the Lord to open the windows of His grace, and pour us out a blessing, if we will not open the windows of expectation and look up for the promised favor? Let holy preparation link hands with patient expectation, and we shall have far larger answers to our prayers.

Psalm 5:4 *For thou art not a God that hath pleasure in wickedness: neither shall evil dwell with thee.*

EXPOSITION: **Verse 4.** And now the psalmist having thus expressed his resolution to pray, you hear him putting up his prayer. He is pleading against his cruel and wicked enemies. He uses a most mighty argument. He begs of God to put them away from him, because they were displeasing to God himself. For you are not a God that has pleasure in wickedness: neither shall evil dwell with thee. "When I pray against my tempters," says David, "I pray against the very things which you yourself abhor." You hate evil: Lord, I beseech you, deliver me from it! Let us learn here the solemn truth of the hatred which a righteous God must bear toward sin. He has no pleasure in wickedness, however wittily, grandly, and proudly it may array itself. Its glitter has no charm for Him. Men may bow before successful villainy, and forget the wickedness of the battle in the gaudiness of the triumph, but the Lord of Holiness is not such a one as we are. Neither shall evil dwell with you. You will not afford it the meanest shelter. Neither on Earth nor in Heaven shall evil share the mansion of God. Oh, how foolish are we if we attempt to entertain two guests so hostile to one another as Christ Jesus and the devil! Rest assured Christ will not live in the parlor of our hearts if we entertain the devil in the cellar of our thoughts.

Psalm 5:5 *The foolish shall not stand in thy sight: thou hatest all workers of iniquity.*

EXPOSITION: **Verse 5.** The foolish shall not stand in your sight. Sinners are fools written large. A little sin is a great folly, and the greatest of all folly is great sin. Such sinful fools as these must be banished from the court of Heaven. Earthly kings wanted to have fools in their trains, but the only wise God will have no fools in His palace above.

You hate all workers of iniquity. It is not a little dislike, but a thorough hatred which God bears to workers of iniquity. To be hated of God is an awful thing. O let us be very faithful in warning the wicked around us, for it will be a terrible thing for them to fall into the hands of an angry God!

Psalm 5:6 *Thou shalt destroy them that speak leasing: the Lord will abhor the bloody and deceitful man.*

EXPOSITION: Verse 6. Observe that evil speakers must be punished as well as evil workers, for thou shalt destroy them that speak leasing. All liars shall have their portion in the lake which burns with fire and brimstone. A man may lie without danger of the law of man, but he will not escape the law of God. Liars have short wings, their flight shall soon be over, and they shall fall into the fiery floods of destruction.

The Lord will abhor the bloody and deceitful man. Bloody men shall be made drunk with their own blood, and they who began by deceiving others shall end with being deceived themselves. Our old proverb says, "Bloody and deceitful men dig their own graves." The voice of the people is in this instance the voice of God. How forcible is the word abhor! Does it not show us how powerful and deep seated is the hatred of the Lord against the workers of iniquity?

Psalm 5:7 *But as for me, I will come into thy house in the multitude of thy mercy: and in thy fear will I worship toward thy holy temple.*

EXPOSITION: Verse 7. With this verse the first part of the psalm ends. The psalmist has bent his knee in prayer; he has described before God, as an argument for his deliverance, the character and the fate of the wicked; and now he contrasts this with the condition of the righteous.

But as for me, I will come into your house. I will not

stand at a distance; I will come into your sanctuary, just as a child comes into his father's house. But I will not come there by my own merits; no, I have a multitude of sins, and therefore I will come in the multitude of your mercy. I will approach you with confidence because of your immeasurable grace. God's judgments are all numbered, but His mercies are innumerable; He gives His wrath by weight, but without weight His mercy.

And in thy fear will I worship toward thy holy temple— toward the temple of your holiness. The temple was not built on Earth at that time; it was but a tabernacle; but David was wanting to turn his eyes spiritually to that temple of God's holiness where between the wings of the Cherubim Jehovah dwells in light ineffable. Daniel opened his window toward Jerusalem, but we open our hearts toward Heaven.

Psalm 5:8 *Lead me, O Lord, in thy righteousness because of mine enemies; make thy way straight before my face.*

EXPOSITION: Verse 8. Now we come to the second part, in which the psalmist repeats his arguments, and goes over the same ground again. *Lead me, O Lord,* as a little child is led by its father, as a blind man is guided by his friend. It is safe and pleasant walking when God leads the way. In your righteousness, not in my righteousness, for that is imperfect, but in yours, for you are righteousness itself. Make your way, not my way, straight before my face. Brethren, when we have learned to give up our own way, and long to walk in God's way, it is a happy sign of grace; and it is no small mercy to see the way of God with clear vision straight before our face. Errors about duty may lead us into a sea of sins, before we know where we are.

Psalm 5:9 *For there is no faithfulness in their mouth; their inward part is very wickedness; their throat is an open sepulchre; they flatter with their tongue.*

EXPOSITION: Verse 9. This description of depraved man has been copied by the Apostle Paul, and, together with some other quotations, he has placed it in the second chapter of Romans, as being an accurate description of the whole human race, not of David's enemies only, but of all men by nature. Note that remarkable figure: Their throat is an open sepulcher, a sepulcher full of loathsomeness, of miasma, of pestilence and death. But, worse than that, it is an open sepulcher, with all its evil gases issuing forth, to spread death and destruction all around. So, with the throat of the wicked, it would be a great mercy if it could always be closed. If we could seal in continual silence the mouth of the wicked it would be like a sepulcher shut up, and would not produce much mischief.

But, "their throat is an open sepulchre," consequently all the wickedness of their heart exhales, and comes forth. How dangerous is an open sepulcher; men in their journeys might easily stumble therein, and find themselves among the dead. Ah! Take heed of the wicked man, for there is nothing that he will not say to ruin you; he will long to destroy your character, and bury you in the hideous sepulcher of his own wicked throat.

One sweet thought here, however. At the resurrection there will be a resurrection not only of bodies, but characters. This should be a great comfort to a man who has been abused and slandered. *Then shall the righteous shine forth as the sun.* [See Matthew 13:43.] The world may think you vile, and bury your character; but if you have been upright, in the day when the graves shall give up their dead, this open sepulcher of the sinner's throat shall be compelled to give up your heavenly character and you shall come forth and be honored in the sight of men.

They flatter with their tongue. Or, as we might read it, "They have an oily tongue, a smooth tongue." A smooth tongue is a great evil; many have been bewitched by it. There are many human anteaters that with their long tongues covered with oily words entice and entrap the unwary and make their gain thereby. When the wolf licks the lamb, he is preparing to wet his teeth in its blood.

Psalm 5:10 *Destroy thou them, O God; let them fall by their own counsels; cast them out in the multitude of their transgressions; for they have rebelled against thee.*

EXPOSITION: **Verse 10.** Against you: not against me. If they were my enemies I would forgive them, but I cannot forgive yours. We are to forgive our enemies, but God's enemies it is not in our power to forgive. These expressions have often been noticed by men of over refinement as being harsh, and grating on the ear. "Oh!" say they, "they are vindictive and revengeful." Let us remember that they might be translated as prophecies, not as wishes; but we do not care to avail ourselves of this method of escape. We have never heard of a reader of the Bible who, after perusing these passages, was made revengeful by reading them, and it is but fair to test the nature of a writing by its effects. When we hear a judge condemning a murderer, however severe his sentence, we do not feel that we should be justified in condemning others for any private injury done to us. The psalmist here speaks as a judge, *ex officio*[12]; he speaks as God's mouth, and in condemning the wicked he gives us no excuse whatever for uttering anything in the way of malediction upon those who have caused us personal offence.

---

12. By right of office.

The most shameful way of cursing another is by pretending to bless him. Now, in direct contrast we put this healthy petition of David, which is intended to be a blessing by warning the sinner of the impending curse. O impenitent man, be it known unto you that all your godly friends will give their solemn assent to the awful sentence of the Lord, which He shall pronounce upon you in the day of doom! Our verdict shall applaud the condemning curse which the Judge of all the Earth shall thunder against the godless.

In the following verse we once more find the contrast which has marked the preceding Psalms.

Psalm 5:11 *But let all those that put their trust in thee rejoice: let them ever shout for joy, because thou defendest them: let them also that love thy name be joyful in thee.*

EXPOSITION: Verse 11. Joy is the privilege of the believer. When sinners are destroyed our rejoicing shall be full. They laugh first and weep ever after; we weep now, but shall rejoice eternally. When they howl we shall shout, and as they must groan forever, so shall we ever shout for joy. This holy bliss of ours has a firm foundation, for, O Lord, we are joyful in you. The eternal God is the wellspring of our bliss. We love God, and therefore we delight in Him. Our heart is at ease in our God. We fare sumptuously every day because we feed on Him. We have music in the house, music in the heart, and music in Heaven, for the Lord Jehovah is our strength and our song; He also is become our salvation.

Psalm 5:12 *For thou, Lord, wilt bless the righteous; with favour wilt thou compass him as with a shield.*

EXPOSITION: **Verse 12.** Jehovah has ordained His people the heirs of blessedness, and nothing shall rob them of their inheritance. With all the fullness of His power He will bless them, and all His attributes shall unite to satiate them with divine contentment. Nor is this merely for the present, but the blessing reaches into the long and unknown future. *Thou, Lord, wilt bless the righteous.* This is a promise of infinite length, of unbounded breadth, and of unutterable preciousness.

As for the defense which the believer needs in this land of battles, it is here promised to him in the fullest measure. There were vast shields used by the ancients as extensive as a man's whole person, which would surround him entirely. So says David, *With favour wilt thou compass him as with a shield.* According to Ainsworth there is here also the idea of being crowned, so that we wear a royal helmet, which is at once our glory and defense. O Lord, ever give to us this gracious coronation!

PSALM 6
PSALM 6:1–PSALM 6:10

Psalm 6:1 *O Lord, rebuke me not in thine anger, neither chasten me in thy hot displeasure.*

EXPOSITION: **Verse 1.** Having read through the first division, in order to see it as a whole, we will now look at it verse by verse. *O Lord, rebuke me not in thine anger.* The psalmist is very conscious that he deserves to be rebuked, and he feels, moreover, that the rebuke in some form or other must come upon him, if not for condemnation, yet for conviction and sanctification.

"Corn is cleaned with wind, and the soul with chastening."[13]

It would be folly to pray against the golden hand which enriches us by its blows. He does not ask that the rebuke may be totally withheld, for he might thus lose a blessing in disguise; but, *Lord, rebuke me not in thine anger.* If you remind me of my sin, it is good; but, oh, remind me not of it as one incensed against me, lest your servant's heart should sink in despair. Thus says Jeremiah, *O Lord, correct me, but with judgment; not in thine anger, lest thou bring me to nothing* [Jeremiah 10:24]. I know that I must be chastened, and though I shrink from the rod yet do I feel that it will be for my benefit; but, oh, my God, chasten me not in thy hot displeasure, lest the rod become a sword, and lest in smiting, you would also kill. So may we pray that the chastisements of our gracious God, if they may not be entirely removed, may at least be sweetened by the consciousness that they are

---

13. George Herbert, Welsh poet, 1593–1633.

73

not in anger, but in His dear covenant love.

Psalm 6:2 *Have mercy upon me, O Lord; for I am weak: O Lord, heal me; for my bones are vexed.*

EXPOSITION: **Verse 2.** *Have mercy upon me, O Lord; for I am weak.* Though I deserve destruction, yet let your mercy pity my frailty. This is the right way to plead with God if we would prevail. Urge not your goodness or your greatness, but plead your sin and your littleness. Cry, "I am weak," therefore, O Lord, give me strength and crush me not. Send not forth the fury of your tempest against so weak a vessel. Temper the wind to the shorn lamb. Be tender and pitiful to a poor withering flower, and break it not from its stem. Surely this is the plea that a sick man would urge to move the pity of his fellow if he were striving with him, "Deal gently with me, 'for I am weak.'" A sense of sin had so spoiled the psalmist's pride, so taken away his vaunted strength that he found himself weak to obey the law, weak through the sorrow that was in him, too weak, perhaps, to lay hold on the promise. "I am weak." The original may be read, "I am one who droops," or withered like a blighted plant. Ah! Beloved, we know what this means, for we, too, have seen our glory stained, and our beauty like a faded flower.

Psalm 6:3 *My soul is also sore vexed: but thou, O Lord, how long?*

EXPOSITION: **Verse 3.** O Lord, heal me; for my bones are vexed. Here he prays for healing, not merely the mitigation of the ills he endured, but their entire removal, and the curing of the wounds which had arisen from them. His bones were "shaken," as the Hebrew has it. His terror had become so great that his very bones shook; not only did his flesh quiver, but the bones, the solid pillars of the house of manhood, were made to tremble. "My bones are shaken." Ah, when the soul has a sense of sin, it is enough to make the bones shake; it is enough to make a man's hair stand up on end to see the flames of hell beneath him, an angry God above him, and danger and doubt surrounding him.

Well might he say, "My bones are shaken." Lest, however, we should imagine that it was merely bodily sickness— although bodily sickness might be the outward sign—the psalmist goes on to say, *My soul is also sore vexed.* Soul-trouble is the very soul of trouble. It matters not that the bones shake if the soul be firm, but when the soul itself is also sore vexed this is agony indeed.

But thou, O Lord, how long? This sentence ends abruptly, for words failed, and grief drowned the little comfort which dawned upon him. The psalmist had still, however, some hope; but that hope was only in his God. He therefore cries, "O Lord, how long?" The coming of Christ into the soul in His priestly robes of grace is the grand hope of the penitent soul; and, indeed, in some form or other, Christ's appearance is, and ever has been, the hope of the saints.

Calvin's favorite exclamation was, *"Domine usquequo"*—O Lord, how long? Nor could his sharpest pains, during a life of anguish, force from him any other word. Surely this is the cry of the saints under the altar, "O Lord, how long?" And this should be the cry of the saints waiting for the millennial glories, "Why are His chariots so long in coming; Lord, how long?" Those of us who have passed through conviction of sin knew what it was to count our minutes as hours, and our hours as years, while mercy delayed its coming. We watched for the dawn of grace, as they that watch for the morning. Earnestly did our anxious spirits ask, "O Lord, how long?"

Psalm 6:4 *Return, O Lord, deliver my soul: oh save me for thy mercies' sake.*

EXPOSITION: **Verse 4.** *Return, O Lord; deliver my soul.* As God's absence was the main cause of his misery, so His return would be enough to deliver him from his trouble. *Oh save me for thy mercies' sake.* He knows where to look, and what arm to lay hold upon. He does not lay hold on God's left hand of justice, but on His right hand of mercy. He knew his iniquity too well to think of merit, or appeal to anything but the grace of God. *For your mercies' sake.* What a plea that is! How prevalent it is with God! If we turn to justice, what plea can we urge? But if we turn to mercy we may still cry, notwithstanding the greatness of our guilt, *Save me for thy mercies' sake.* Observe how frequently David here pleads the name of Jehovah, which is always intended where the word Lord is given in capitals. Five times in four verses we here meet with it. Is not this a proof that the glorious name is full of consolation to the tempted saint? Eternity, Infinity, Immutability, Self-existence, are all in the name Jehovah, and all are full of comfort.

Psalm 6:5 *For in death there is no remembrance of thee: in the grave who shall give thee thanks?*

EXPOSITION: **Verse 5.** And now David was in great fear of death—death temporal, and perhaps death eternal. Read the passage as you will, the following verse is full of power.

> *"For in death there is no remembrance of thee; in the grave who shall give thee thanks?"*

Churchyards are silent places; the vaults of the sepulcher echo not with songs. Damp earth covers dumb mouths.

"O Lord!" said he, "if you will spare me I will praise you. If I die, then must my mortal praise at least be suspended; and if I perish in hell, then you will never have any thanksgiving from me. Songs of gratitude cannot rise from the flaming pit of hell. True, you will doubtless be glorified, even in my eternal condemnation, but then O Lord, I cannot glorify you voluntarily; and among the sons of men, there will be one heart the less to bless you." Ah! Poor trembling sinners, may the Lord help you to use this forcible argument! It is for God's glory that a sinner should be saved. When we seek pardon, we are not asking God to do that which will stain His banner, or put a blot on His escutcheon [shield]. He delights in mercy. It is His peculiar, darling attribute. Mercy honors God. Do not we ourselves say, "Mercy blesses him that gives, and him that takes?" And surely, in some diviner sense, this is true of God, who, when He gives mercy, glorifies himself.

Psalm 6:6 *I am weary with my groaning; all the night make I my bed to swim; I water my couch with my tears.*

EXPOSITION: Verse 6. The psalmist gives a fearful description of his long agony: *I am weary with my groaning.* He has groaned until his throat was hoarse; he had cried for mercy until prayer became a labor. God's people may groan, but they may not grumble. Yes, they must groan, being burdened, or they will never shout in the day of deliverance. The next sentence, we think, is not accurately translated. It should be, I shall make my bed to swim every night (when nature needs rest, and when I am most alone with my God). That is to say, my grief is fearful even now, but if God does not soon save me, it will not stay of itself, but will increase, until my tears will be so many, that my bed itself shall swim. A description rather of what he feared would be, than of what had actually taken place. May not our forebodings of future woe become arguments which faith may urge when seeking present mercy?

Psalm 6:7 *Mine eye is consumed because of grief; it waxeth old because of all mine enemies.*

EXPOSITION: **Verse 7.** I water my couch with my tears. Mine eye is consumed because of grief; it waxes old because of all my enemies. As an old man's eye grows dim with years, so, says David, my eye is grown red and feeble through weeping. Conviction sometimes has such an effect upon the body that even the outward organs are made to suffer. May not this explain some of the convulsions and hysterical attacks which have been experienced under convictions in the revivals in Ireland? Is it surprising that some souls are smitten to the earth, and begin to cry aloud; when we find that David himself made his bed to swim, and grew old while he was under the heavy hand of God? Ah! Brethren, it is no light matter to feel one's self a sinner, condemned at the bar of God. The language of this psalm is not strained and forced, but perfectly natural to one in so sad a plight.

Psalm 6:8 *Depart from me, all ye workers of iniquity; for the Lord hath heard the voice of my weeping.*

EXPOSITION: **Verse 8.** Hitherto, all has been mournful and disconsolate, but now—

> Your harps, ye trembling saints,
> Down from the willows take.[14]

---

14. "Your Harps, Ye Trembling Saints," hymn written by Augustus Toplady in 1772.

78

You must have your times of weeping, but let them be short. Get yourself up; get up, from your dunghills! Cast aside your sackcloth and ashes! *Weeping may endure for a night, but joy cometh in the morning* [Psalm 30:5].David has found peace, and rising from his knees he begins to sweep his house of the wicked. *Depart from me, all ye workers of iniquity.* The best remedy for us against an evil man is a long space between us both. "Get yourself gone; I can have no fellowship with you." Repentance is a practical thing. It is not enough to bemoan the desecration of the temple of the heart; we must scourge out the buyers and sellers, and overturn the tables of the money changers. A pardoned sinner will hate the sins which cost the Savior His blood. Grace and sin are quarrelsome neighbors, and one or the other must go to the wall.

For the Lord has heard the voice of my weeping. What a fine Hebraism, and what grand poetry it is in English! *He hath heard the voice of my weeping.* Is there a voice in weeping? Does weeping speak? In what language does it utter its meaning? Why, in that universal tongue which is known and understood in all the Earth, and even in Heaven above. When a man weeps, whether he is a Jew or Gentile, Barbarian, Scythian, bond or free, it has the same meaning in it. Weeping is the eloquence of sorrow. It is an orator who does not stammer, needing no interpreter, but understood of all. Is it not sweet to believe that our tears are understood even when words fail? Let us learn to think of tears as liquid prayers, and of weeping as a constant dropping of importunate intercession which will wear its way right surely into the very heart of mercy, despite the stony difficulties which obstruct the way. My God, I will "weep" when I cannot plead, for you hear the voice of my weeping.

Psalm 6:9 *The Lord hath heard my supplication; the Lord will receive my prayer.*

EXPOSITION: Verse 9. The Lord has heard my supplication. The Holy Spirit had wrought into the psalmist's mind the confidence that his prayer was heard. This is frequently the privilege of the saints. Praying the prayer of faith, they are often infallibly assured that they have prevailed with God. We read of Luther that, having on one occasion wrestled hard with God in prayer, he came leaping out of his closet crying, *"Vicimus, vicimus;"* that is, "We have conquered, we have prevailed with God." Assured confidence is no idle dream, for when the Holy Ghost bestows it upon us, we know its reality, and could not doubt it, even though all men should deride our boldness.

The Lord will receive my prayer. Here is past experience used for future encouragement. He has, He will. Note this, O believer, and imitate its reasoning.

Psalm 6:10 *Let all mine enemies be ashamed and sore vexed: let them return and be ashamed suddenly.*

EXPOSITION: Verse 10. *Let all mine enemies be ashamed and sore vexed.* This is rather a prophecy than an imprecation, it may be read in the future, "All my enemies shall be ashamed and sore vexed." They shall return and be ashamed instantaneously—in a moment—their doom shall come upon them suddenly. Death's day is doom's day, and both are sure and may be sudden. The Romans often said, "The feet of the avenging Deity are shod with wool." With noiseless footsteps vengeance nears its victim, and sudden and overwhelming shall be its destroying stroke. If this were an imprecation, we must remember that the language of the old dispensation is not that of the new. We pray for our enemies, not against them. God have mercy on them, and bring them into the right way.

Thus the psalm, like those which precede it, shows the different estates of the godly and the wicked. O Lord, let us be numbered with your people, both now and forever!

PSALM 7

PSALM 7:1–PSALM 7:17

Psalm 7:1 *O Lord my God, in thee do I put my trust: save me from all them that persecute me, and deliver me.*

EXPOSITION: Verse 1. David appears before God to plead with Him against the Accuser, who had charged him with treason and treachery. The case is here opened with an avowal of confidence in God. Whatever may be the emergency of our condition we shall never find it amiss to retain our reliance upon our God. O Lord my God, mine by a special covenant, sealed by Jesus' blood, and ratified in my own soul by a sense of union to you; in you, and in you only, do I put my trust, even now in my sore distress. I shake, but my rock moves not. It is never right to distrust God, and never vain to trust Him. And now, with both divine relationship and holy trust to strengthen him, David utters the burden of his desire—save me from all them that persecute me.

His pursuers were very many, and any one of them cruel enough to devour him; he cries, therefore, for salvation from them all. We should never think our prayers complete until we ask for preservation from all sin, and all enemies. And deliver me, extricate me from their snares, acquit me of their accusations, give a true and just deliverance in this trial of my injured character. See how clearly his case is stated; let us see to it, that we know what we would have when we are come to the throne of mercy. Pause a little while before you pray, that you may not offer the sacrifice of fools. Get a distinct idea of your need, and then you can pray with the more fluency of fervency.

Psalm 7:2 *Lest he tear my soul like a lion, rending it in pieces, while there is none to deliver.*

EXPOSITION: Verse 2. *Lest he tear my soul.* Here is the plea of fear co-working with the plea of faith. There was one among David's foes mightier that the rest, who had dignity, strength, and ferocity, and was, therefore, like a lion. From this foe he urgently seeks deliverance. Perhaps this was Saul, his royal enemy; but in our own case there is one who goes about like a lion, seeking whom he may devour, concerning whom we should ever cry, "Deliver us from the Evil One." Notice the vigor of the description—*rending it in pieces, while there is none to deliver.*

It is a picture from the shepherd life of David. When the fierce lion had pounced upon the defenseless lamb, and had made it his prey, he would rend the victim in pieces, break all the bones, and devour all, because no shepherd was near to protect the lamb or rescue it from the ravenous beast. This is a soul-moving portrait of a saint delivered over to the will of Satan. This will make the bowels of Jehovah yearn.

A father cannot be silent when a child is in such peril. No, he will not endure the thought of his darling in the jaws of a lion; he will arise and deliver his persecuted one. Our God is very pitiful, and He will surely rescue His people from so desperate a destruction. It will be well for us here to remember that this is a description of the danger to which the psalmist was exposed from slanderous tongues. Verily this is not an overdrawn picture, for the wounds of a sword will heal, but the wounds of the tongue cut deeper than the flesh, and are not soon cured. Slander leaves a slur, even if it is wholly disproved. Common fame, although notoriously a common liar, has very many believers. Once let an ill word get into men's mouths, and it is not easy to get it fully out again.

The Italians say that good repute is like the cypress, once cut it never puts forth leaf again; this is not true if our character is cut by a stranger's hand, but even then it will not soon regain its former verdure. Oh, it is a meanness most detestable to stab a good man in his reputation, but diabolical hatred observes no nobility in its mode of warfare. We must be ready for this trial, for it will surely come upon us. If God was slandered in Eden, we shall surely be maligned in this land of sinners. Gird up your loins, you children of the resurrection, for this fiery trial awaits you all.

Psalm 7:3–5 O *Lord my God, if I have done this; if there be iniquity in my hands; If I have rewarded evil unto him that was at peace with me; (yea, I have delivered him that without cause is mine enemy): Let the enemy persecute my soul, and take it; yea, let him tread down my life upon the earth, and lay mine honour in the dust. Selah.*

EXPOSITION: Verses 3–5. The second part of this wandering hymn contains a protestation of innocence, and an invocation of wrath upon his own head, if he were not clear from the evil imputed to him. So far from hiding treasonable intentions in his hands, or ungratefully requiting the peaceful deeds of a friend, he had even suffered his enemy to escape when he had him completely in his power. Twice had he spared Saul's life; once in the Cave of Adullam,[15] and again when he found him sleeping in the midst of his slumbering camp: he could, therefore, with a clear conscience, make his appeal to Heaven.

---

15. Cave of Adullam: the cave that both Saul and King David took refuge in near the city of Adullam.

He needs not fear the curse whose soul is clear of guilt. Yet is the imprecation a most solemn one, and only justifiable through the extremity of the occasion, and the nature of the dispensation under which the psalmist lived. We are commanded by our Lord Jesus to let our yes be yes, and our no, no: *for whatsoever is more than these cometh of evil.* [See Matthew 5:37.] If we cannot be believed on our word, we are surely not to be trusted on our oath; for to a true Christian his simple word is as binding as another man's oath. Especially beware, O unconverted men! of trifling with solemn imprecations! Remember the woman at Devizes, who wished she might die if she had not paid her share in a joint purchase, and who fell dead there and then with the money in her hand.

Selah. David enhances the solemnity of this appeal to the dread tribunal of God by the use of the usual pause. From these verses we may learn that no innocence can shield a man from the calumnies of the wicked. David had been scrupulously careful to avoid any appearance of rebellion against Saul, whom he constantly styled "the Lord's anointed;" but all this could not protect him from lying tongues. As the shadow follows the substance, so envy pursues goodness. It is only at the tree laden with fruit that men throw stones. If we would live without being slandered we must wait till we get to Heaven. Let us be very heedful not to believe the flying rumors which are always harassing gracious men. If there are no believers in lies there will be but a dull market in falsehood, and good men's characters will be safe. Ill will never spoke well. Sinners have an ill will to saints, and therefore, be sure they will not speak well of them.

Psalm 7:6 *Arise, O Lord, in thine anger, lift up thyself because of the rage of mine enemies: and awake for me to the judgment that thou hast commanded.*

EXPOSITION: **Verse 6.** We now listen to a fresh prayer, based upon the avowal which he has just made. We cannot pray too often, and when our heart is true, we shall turn to God in prayer as naturally as the needle to its pole. Arise, O Lord, in your anger. His sorrow makes him view the Lord as a judge who had left the judgment seat and retired into His rest. Faith would move the Lord to avenge the quarrel of His saints. Lift up yourself because of the rage of mine enemies—a still stronger figure to express his anxiety that the Lord would assume His authority and mount the throne. Stand up, O God, rise above them all, and let your justice tower above their villainies.

Awake for me to the judgment that you have commanded. This is a bolder utterance still, for it implies sleep as well as inactivity, and can only be applied to God in a very limited sense. He never slumbers, yet He often seems to do so; for the wicked prevail, and the saints are trodden in the dust. God's silence is the patience of longsuffering, and if wearisome to the saints, they should bear it cheerfully in the hope that sinners may thereby be led to repentance.

Psalm 7:7 *So shall the congregation of the people compass thee about: for their sakes therefore return thou on high.*

EXPOSITION: **Verse 7.** *So shall the congregation of the people compass thee about.* Your saints shall crowd to your tribunal with their complaints, or shall surround it with their solemn homage: for their sakes therefore return on high. As when a judge travels at the assizes,[16] all men take their cases to his court that they may be heard, so will the righteous gather to their Lord.

Here he fortifies himself in prayer by pleading that if

---

16. English county courts.

the Lord will mount the throne of judgment, multitudes of the saints would be blessed as well as himself. If I be too base to be remembered, yet, for their sakes, for the love you bear to your chosen people, come forth from your secret pavilion, and sit in the gate dispensing justice among the people. When my suit includes the desires of all the righteous it shall surely speed, for, *shall not God avenge his own elect?* [See Luke 18:7.]

Psalm 7:8 *The LORD shall judge the people: judge me, O LORD, according to my righteousness, and according to mine integrity that is in me.*

EXPOSITION: **Verse 8.** If I am not mistaken, David has now seen in the eye of his mind the Lord ascending to His judgment seat, and beholding Him seated there in royal state, he draws near to Him to urge his suit anew. In the last two verses he besought Jehovah to arise, and now that He is arisen, he prepares to mingle with "the congregation of the people" who compass the Lord about. The royal heralds proclaim the opening of the court with the solemn words, *The Lord shall judge the people.* Our petitioner rises at once, and cries with earnestness and humility, *Judge me, O Lord, according to my righteousness, and according to mine integrity that is in me.* His hand is on an honest heart, and his cry is to a righteous Judge.

Psalm 7:9 *Oh let the wickedness of the wicked come to an end; but establish the just: for the righteous God trieth the hearts and reins.*

EXPOSITION: **Verse 9.** He sees a smile of complacency upon the face of the King, and in the name of all the assembled congregation he cries aloud, *Oh let the wickedness of the* *wicked come to an end; but establish the just.* Is not this the universal longing of the whole company of the elect? When shall we be delivered from the filthy conversation of these men of Sodom? When shall we escape from the filthiness of Mesech and the blackness of the tents of Kedar? What a solemn and weighty truth is contained in the last sentence of the ninth verse! How deep is the divine knowledge!—He tries. How strict, how accurate, how intimate His search!—He tries the hearts, the secret thoughts, and reins, the inward affections. *All things are naked and opened to the eyes of him with whom we have to do.* [See Hebrews 4:13.]

Psalm 7:10 *My defence is of God, which saveth the upright in heart.*

EXPOSITION: Verse 10. The judge has heard the cause, has cleared the guiltless, and uttered his voice against the persecutors. Let us draw near, and learn the results of the great assize. Yonder is the slandered one with his harp in hand, hymning the justice of his Lord, and rejoicing aloud in his own deliverance.

My defense is of God, which saveth the upright in heart. Oh, how good to have a true and upright heart. Crooked sinners, with all their craftiness, are foiled by the upright in heart. God defends the right. Filth will not long abide on the pure white garments of the saints, but shall be brushed off by divine providence, to the vexation of the men by whose base hands it was thrown upon the godly. When God shall try our cause, our sun has risen, and the sun of the wicked is set forever. Truth, like oil, is ever above, no power of our enemies can drown it; we shall refute their slanders in the day when the trumpet wakes the dead, and we shall shine in honor when lying lips are put to silence. O believer, fear not all that your foes can do or say against you, for the tree which God plants no winds can hurt.

Psalm 7:11 *God judgeth the righteous, and God is angry with the wicked every day.*

EXPOSITION: Verse 11. *God judgeth the righteous;* He has not given you up to be condemned by the lips of persecutors. Your enemies cannot sit on God's throne, nor blot your name out of His book. Let them alone, then, for God will find time for His revenge.

God is angry with the wicked every day. He not only detests sin, but is angry with those who continue to indulge in it. We have no insensible and stolid God to deal with; He can be angry, no, He is angry today and every day with you, you ungodly and impenitent sinners. The best day that ever dawns on a sinner brings a curse with it. Sinners may have many feast days, but no safe days. From the beginning of the year even to its ending, there is not an hour in which God's oven is not hot, and burning in readiness for the wicked, who shall be as stubble.

Psalm 7:12 *If he turn not, he will whet his sword; he hath bent his bow, and made it ready.*

EXPOSITION: Verse 12. *If he turn not, He will whet His sword.* What blows are those which will be dealt by that long uplifted arm! God's sword has been sharpening upon the revolving stone of our daily wickedness, and if we will not repent, it will speedily cut us in pieces. Turn or burn is the sinner's only alternative. He has bent His bow and made it ready.

Psalm 7:13 *He hath also prepared for him the instruments of death; he ordaineth his arrows against the persecutors.*

EXPOSITION: Verse 13. Even now the thirsty arrow longs to wet itself with the blood of the persecutor. The bow is bent, the aim is taken, the arrow is fitted to the string, and what, O sinner, if the arrow should be let fly at you even now! Remember, God's arrows never miss the mark, and are, every one of them, "instruments of death." Judgment may tarry, but it will not come too late. The Greek proverb says, "The mill of God grinds late, but grinds to powder."

Psalm 7:14 *Behold, he travaileth with iniquity, and hath conceived mischief, and brought forth falsehood.*

EXPOSITION: Verse 14. In three graphic pictures we see the slanderer's history. A woman in travail furnishes the first metaphor. He travails with iniquity. He is full of it, pained until he can carry it out, he longs to work his will, and he is full of pangs until his evil intent is executed. He has conceived mischief. This is the original of his base design. The devil has had doings with him, and the virus of evil is in him. And now behold the progeny of this unhallowed conception. The child is worthy of its father, his name of old was, "the father of lies," and the birth does not belie the parent, for he brought forth falsehood. Thus, one figure is carried out to perfection; the psalmist now illustrates his meaning by another, taken from the stratagems of the hunter.

Psalm 7:15 *He made a pit, and digged it, and is fallen into the ditch which he made.*

EXPOSITION: **Verse 15.** *He made a pit, and digged it.*
He was cunning in his plans, and industrious in his labors.
He stooped to the dirty work of digging. He did not fear
to soil his own hands; he was willing to work in a ditch if
others might fall therein. What mean things men will do to
wreak revenge on the godly. They hunt for good men, as
if they were brute beasts; no, they will not give them the
fair chase afforded to the hare or the fox, but must secretly
entrap them, because they can neither run them down nor
shoot them down.

Our enemies will not meet us to the face, for they fear
us as much as they pretend to despise us. But let us look on
to the end of the scene. The verse says he is fallen into the
ditch which he made. Ah! There he is, let us laugh at his
disappointment. Lo! He is himself the beast, he has hunted
his own soul, and the chase has brought him a goodly victim.
Aha, aha, so should it ever be. Come hither and make merry
with this entrapped hunter, this biter who has bitten himself.
Give him no pity, for it will be wasted on such a wretch. He
is but rightly and richly rewarded by being paid in his own
coin. He cast forth evil from his mouth, and it has fallen
into his bosom. He has set his own house on fire with the
torch which he lit to burn a neighbor. He sent forth a foul
bird, and it has come back to its nest.

Psalm 7:16 *His mischief shall return upon his own
head, and his violent dealing shall come down upon
his own pate.*

EXPOSITION: **Verse 16.** The rod which he lifted on
high has smitten his own back. He shot an arrow upward,
and it has returned upon his own head. He hurled a stone
at another and it has come down upon his own pate. Curses
are like young chickens, they always come home to roost.

Ashes always fly back in the face of him that throws them. *As he loved cursing, so let it come unto him* [Psalm 109:17].

How often has this been the case in the histories of both ancient and modern times. Men have burned their own fingers when they were hoping to brand their neighbor. And if this does not happen now, it will hereafter. The Lord has caused dogs to lick the blood of Ahab in the midst of the vineyard of Naboth. Sooner or later the evil deeds of persecutors have always leaped back into their arms. So it will be in the last great day, when Satan's fiery darts shall all be quivered in his own heart, and all his followers shall reap the harvest which they themselves have sown.

Psalm 7:17 *I will praise the LORD according to his righteousness: and will sing praise to the name of the LORD most high.*

EXPOSITION: Verse 17. We conclude with the joyful contrast. In this all these psalms are agreed; they all exhibit the blessedness of the righteous, and make its colors the more glowing by contrast with the miseries of the wicked. The bright jewel sparkles in a black foil. Praise is the occupation of the godly, their eternal work, and their present pleasure. Singing is the fitting embodiment for praise, and therefore do the saints make melody before the Lord Most High. The slandered one is now a singer: his harp was unstrung for a very little season, and now we leave him sweeping its harmonious chords, and flying on their music to the third heaven of adoring praise.

PSALM 8

PSALM 8:1–PSALM 8:9

Psalm 8:1 O Lord, our Lord, how excellent is thy name in all the earth! who hast set thy glory above the heavens.

EXPOSITION: **Verse 1.** Unable to express the glory of God, the psalmist utters a note of exclamation. O Jehovah our Lord! We need not wonder at this, for no heart can measure, no tongue can utter, the half of the greatness of Jehovah. The whole creation is full of His glory and radiant with the excellency of His power; His goodness and His wisdom are manifested on every hand. The countless myriads of terrestrial beings, from man the head, to the creeping worm at the foot, are all supported and nourished by the Divine bounty. The solid fabric of the universe leans upon His eternal arm. Universally He is present, and everywhere is His name excellent. God works ever and everywhere. There is no place where God is not. The miracles of His power await us on all sides. Traverse the silent valleys where the rocks enclose you on either side, rising like the battlements of Heaven until you can see but a strip of the blue sky far overhead.

You may be the only traveler who has passed through that glen; the bird may start up frightened, and the moss may tremble beneath the first tread of human foot; but God is there in a thousand wonders, upholding yon rocky barriers, filling the flower cups with their perfume, and refreshing the lonely pines with the breath of His mouth. Descend, if you will, into the lowest depths of the ocean, where undisturbed the water sleeps, and the very sand is motionless in unbroken quiet, but the glory of the Lord is there, revealing its excellence in the silent palace of the sea.

Borrow the wings of the morning and fly to the uttermost parts of the sea, but God is there. Mount to the highest Heaven, or dive into the deepest hell, and God is in both hymned in everlasting song, or justified in terrible vengeance. Everywhere, and in every place, God dwells and is manifestly at work. Nor on Earth alone is Jehovah extolled, for His brightness shines forth in the firmament above the Earth. His glory exceeds the glory of the starry heavens; above the region of the stars He has set fast His everlasting throne, and there He dwells in light ineffable.

> Let us adore Him [*who*] *alone spreadeth out the heavens, and treadeth upon the waves of the sea;*[*who*] *maketh Arcturus, Orion, and Pleiades, and the chambers of the south* (Job 9:8–9). We can scarcely find more fitting words than those of Nehemiah 9:6, *Thou, even thou, art Lord alone; thou hast made heaven, the heaven of heavens, with all their host, the earth, and all things that are therein, the seas, and all that is therein, and thou preservest them all; and the host of heaven worshippeth thee.*

Returning to the text we are led to observe that this psalm is addressed to God, because none but the Lord himself can fully know His own glory. The believing heart is ravished with what it sees, but God only knows the glory of God. What a sweetness lies in the little word "our," how much is God's glory endeared to us when we consider our interest in Him as our Lord.

How excellent is your name! No words can express that excellency; and therefore it is left as a note of exclamation. The very name of Jehovah is excellent, what must His person be. Note the fact that even the heavens cannot contain His glory; it is set above the heavens, since it is and ever must be too great for the creature to express. When wandering among the Alps, we felt that the Lord was infinitely greater than all His grandest works, and under that feeling we roughly wrote these few lines:

Yet in all these how great seer they be, we see not Him.

The glass is all too dense and dark, or else our earthborn eyes too dim.

Yon Alps, that lift their heads above the clouds,

And hold familiar converse with the stars,

Are dust, at which the balance trembles not,

Compared with His divine immensity.

The snow crowned summits fail to set Him forth,

Who dwells in eternity, and bears

Alone, the name of High and Lofty One.

Depths unfathomed are too shallow to express

The wisdom and the knowledge of the Lord.

The mirror of the creatures has no space

To bear the image of the Infinite.

It is true the Lord has fairly writ His name,

And set His seal upon creation's brow.

But as the skilful potter much excels,

The vessel which He fashions on the wheel,

Even so, but in proportion greater far,

Jehovah's self transcends His noblest works.

Earth's ponderous wheels would break,
her axles snap,

If freighted with the load of Deity.

Space is too narrow for the Eternal's rest,

And time too short a footstool for His throne.

Even avalanche and thunder lack a voice,

To utter the full volume of His praise.

How then can I declare Him? Where are words

With which my glowing tongue may speak
His name?

Silent I bow, and humbly I adore.[17]

Psalm 8:2 *Out of the mouth of babes and sucklings hast thou ordained strength because of thine enemies, that thou mightest still the enemy and the avenger.*

EXPOSITION: **Verse 2.** Nor only in the heavens above is the Lord seen, but the Earth beneath is telling forth His majesty. In the sky, the massive orbs, rolling in their stupendous grandeur, are witnesses of His power in great things, while here below, the lisping utterances of babes are the manifestations of His strength in little ones. How often will children tell us of a God whom we have forgotten! How does their simple prattle refute those learned fools who deny the being of God! Many men have been made to hold their tongues, while sucklings have borne witness to the glory of the God of Heaven.

---

17. Poem by Charles H. Spurgeon

It is singular how clearly the history of the Church expounds this verse. Did not the children cry "Hosanna!" in the temple, when proud Pharisees were silent and contemptuous? And did not the Savior quote these very words as a justification of their infantile cries? Early Church history records many amazing instances of the testimony of children for the truth of God, but perhaps more modern instances will be the most interesting.

John Fox tells us, in the *Foxe's Book of Martyrs,* that when Mr. Lawrence was burnt in Colchester, he was carried to the fire in a chair, because through the cruelty of the Papists, he could not stand upright, several young children came to the fire, and cried as well as they could speak, "Lord, strengthen thy servant, and keep thy promise." God answered their prayer, for Mr. Lawrence died as firmly and calmly as anyone could wish to breathe his last.

When one of the Popish chaplains told Mr. Wishart, the great Scotch martyr, that he had a devil in him, a child that stood by cried out, "A devil cannot speak such words as that man speaks."

One more instance is still nearer to our time. In a postscript to one of his letters, in which he details his persecution when first preaching in Moorfields, London, George Whitefield says, "I cannot help adding that several little boys and girls, who were fond of sitting around me on the pulpit while I preached, and handed to me people's notes—though they were often pelted with eggs, dirt, &etc., thrown at me—never once gave way; but on the contrary, every time I was struck, they turned up their little weeping eyes, and seemed to wish they could receive the blows for me. God make them, in their growing years, great and living martyrs for Him who, *out of the mouths of babes and sucklings, perfects praise!*" [See Matthew 21:16.] He who delights in the songs of angels is pleased to honor himself in the eyes of His enemies by the praises of little children. What a contrast between the glory above the heavens, and the mouths of babes and sucklings! Yet by both the name of God is made excellent.

Psalm 8:3–4 *When I consider thy heavens, the work of thy fingers, the moon and the stars, which thou hast ordained; What is man, that thou art mindful of him? and the son of man, that thou visitest him?*

EXPOSITION: **Verses 3–4.** At the close of that excellent little manual entitled "The Solar System," written by Dr. Thomas Dick, we find an eloquent passage which beautifully expounds the text:

A survey of the solar system has a tendency to moderate the pride of man and to promote humility. Pride is one of the distinguishing characteristics of puny man, and has been one of the chief causes of all the contentions, wars, devastations, systems of slavery, and ambitious projects which have desolated and demoralized our sinful world. Yet there is no disposition more incongruous to the character and circumstances of man.

Perhaps there are no rational beings throughout the universe among whom pride would appear more unseemly or incompatible than in man, considering the situation in which he is placed. He is exposed to numerous degradations and calamities, to the rage of storms and tempests, the devastations of earthquakes and volcanoes, the fury of whirlwinds, and the tempestuous billows of the ocean, to the ravages of the sword, famine, pestilence, and numerous diseases; and at length he must sink into the grave, and his body must become the companion of worms!

The most dignified and haughty of the sons of men are liable to these and similar degradations as well as the meanest of the human family. Yet, in such circumstances, man—that puny worm of the dust, whose knowledge is so limited, and whose follies are so numerous and glaring—has the effrontery to strut in all the haughtiness of pride, and to glory in his shame. When other arguments and motives produce little effect on certain minds, no considerations seem likely to have a more powerful tendency to counteract this deplorable propensity in human beings, than those which are borrowed from the objects connected with astronomy.

They show us what an insignificant being—what a mere atom, indeed, man appears amidst the immensity of creation! Though he is an object of the paternal care and mercy of the Most High, yet he is but as a grain of sand to the whole Earth, when compared to the countless myriads of beings that people the amplitudes of creation. What is the whole of this globe on which we dwell compared with the solar system, which contains a mass of matter ten thousand times greater?

What is it in comparison of the hundred millions of suns and worlds which by the telescope have been descried throughout the starry regions? What, then, is a kingdom, a province, or a baronial territory, of which we are as proud as if we were the lords of the universe and for which we engage in so much devastation and carnage? What are they, when set in competition with the glories of the sky? Could we take our station on the lofty pinnacles of Heaven, and look down on this scarcely distinguishable speck of Earth, we should be ready to exclaim with Seneca, "Is it to this little spot that the great designs and vast desires of men are confined?

Is it for this there is so much disturbance of nations, so much carnage, and so many ruinous wars?

"Oh, the folly of deceived men, to imagine great kingdoms in the compass of an atom, to raise armies to decide a point of earth with the sword!"

Dr. Chalmers,[18] in his Astronomical Discourses, very truthfully says: "We gave you but a feeble image of our comparative insignificance, when we said that the glories of an extended forest would suffer no more from the fall of a single leaf, than the glories of this extended universe would suffer though the globe we tread upon, 'and all that it inherits, should dissolve.'"

Psalm 8:5 – 8 *For thou hast made him a little lower than the angels, and hast crowned him with glory and honour. Thou madest him to have dominion over the works of thy hands; thou hast put all things under his feet: All sheep and oxen, yea, and the beasts of the field; The fowl of the air, and the fish of the sea, and whatsoever passeth through the paths of the seas.*

EXPOSITION: Verses 5 – 8. These verses may set forth man's position among the creatures before he fell; but as they are, by the Apostle Paul, appropriated to man as represented by the Lord Jesus, it is best to give most weight to that meaning. In order of dignity, man stood next to the angels, and a little lower than they; in the Lord Jesus this was accomplished, for He was made a little lower than the angels by the suffering of death. Man in the Garden of Eden had the full command of all creatures, and they came before him to receive their names as an act of homage to him as

---

18. Thomas Chalmers, a Scottish minister and leader of the Church of Scotland.

the vice-regent of God to them.

Jesus in His glory is now Lord, not only of all living, but of all created things, and, with the exception of Him who put all things under Him, Jesus is Lord of all, and His elect, in Him, are raised to a dominion wider than that of the first Adam, as shall be more clearly seen at His coming. Well might the psalmist wonder at the singular exaltation of man in the scale of being, when he marked his utter nothingness in comparison with the starry universe.

You made him a little lower than the angels—a little lower in nature, since they are immortal, and but a little, because time is short; and when that is over, saints are no longer lower than the angels. The margin reads it, "A little while inferior to." You crowned him. The dominion that God has bestowed on man is a great glory and honor to him; for all dominion is honor, and the highest is that which wears the crown. A full list is given of the subjugated creatures, to show that all the dominion lost by sin is restored in Christ Jesus.

Let none of us permit the possession of any earthly creature to be a snare to us, but let us remember that we are to reign over them, and not to allow them to reign over us. Under our feet we must keep the world, and we must shun that base spirit which is content to let worldly cares and pleasures sway the empire of the immortal soul.

Psalm 8:9 O LORD our Lord, *how excellent is thy name in all the earth!*

EXPOSITION: **Verse 9.** Here, like a good composer, the poet returns to his key note, falling back, as it were, into his first state of wondering adoration. What he started with as a proposition in the first verse, he closes with as a well proven conclusion, with a sort of *quod erat demonstrandum*.[19] O for grace to walk worthy of that excellent name which has been named upon us, and which we are pledged to magnify!

---

19. Latin: "that which was to be demonstrated"

PSALM 9

PSALM 9:1–9:20

Psalm 9:1 *I will praise thee, O Lord, with my whole heart; I will shew forth all thy marvellous works.*

EXPOSITION: **Verse 1.** With a holy resolution the songster begins his hymn; *I will praise thee, O Lord.* It sometimes needs all our determination to face the foe, and bless the Lord in the teeth of His enemies; vowing that whoever else may be silent we will bless His name; here, however, the overthrow of the foe is viewed as complete, and the song flows with sacred fullness of delight. It is our duty to praise the Lord; let us perform it as a privilege. Observe that David's praise is all given to the Lord. Praise is to be offered to God alone; we may be grateful to the intermediate agent, but our thanks must have long wings and mount aloft to Heaven.

With my whole heart. Half heart is no heart. *I will show forth.* There is true praise to the thankful telling forth to others of our heavenly Father's dealings with us; this is one of the themes upon which the godly should speak often to one another, and it will not be casting pearls before swine if we make even the ungodly hear of the loving-kindness of the Lord to us. *All thy marvelous works.* Gratitude for one mercy refreshes the memory as to thousands of others.

One silver link in the chain draws up a long series of tender remembrances. Here is eternal work for us, for there can be no end to the showing forth of all His deeds of love. If we consider our own sinfulness and nothingness, we must feel that every work of preservation, forgiveness, conversion, deliverance, sanctification, etc., which the Lord has wrought for us, or in us is a marvelous work. Even in Heaven, divine loving-kindness will doubtless be as much a theme of surprise as of rapture.

Psalm 9:2 *I will be glad and rejoice in thee: I will sing praise to thy name, O thou most High.*

EXPOSITION: Verse 2. Gladness and joy are the appropriate spirit in which to praise the goodness of the Lord. Birds extol the Creator in notes of overflowing joy, the cattle low forth His praise with tumult of happiness, and the fish leap up in His worship with excess of delight. Moloch may be worshipped with shrieks of pain, and Juggernaut may be honored by dying groans and inhuman yells, but He whose name is Love is best pleased with the holy mirth, and sanctified gladness of His people. Daily rejoicing is an ornament to the Christian character, and a suitable robe for God's choristers to wear. God loveth a cheerful giver, whether it be the gold of his purse or the gold of his mouth which he presents upon His altar. "I will sing praise to thy name, O thou most high." Songs are the fitting expression of inward thankfulness, and it is well if we indulge ourselves and honor our Lord with more of them. Mr. P.B. Power[20] has well said:

> The sailors give a cheery cry as they weigh anchor, the ploughman whistles in the morning as he drives his team; the milkmaid sings her rustic song as she sets about her early task; when soldiers are leaving friends behind them, they do not march out to the tune of the "Dead March in Saul," but to the quick notes of some lively air.

---

20. English clergyman and author.

A praising spirit would do for us all that their songs and music do for them; and if only we could determine to praise the Lord, we should surmount many a difficulty which our low spirits never would have been equal to, and we should do double the work which can be done if the heart be languid in its beating, if we be crushed and trodden down in soul.

As the evil spirit in Saul yielded in olden time to the influence of the harp of the son of Jesse, so would the spirit of melancholy often take flight from us, if only we would take up the song of praise.

Psalm 9:3 *When mine enemies are turned back, they shall fall and perish at thy presence.*

EXPOSITION: Verse 3. God's presence is evermore sufficient to work the defeat of our most furious foes, and their ruin is so complete when the Lord takes them in hand, that even flight cannot save them; they fall to rise no more when He pursues them. We must be careful, like David, to give all the glory to Him whose presence gives the victory. If we have here the exulting of our conquering Captain, let us make the triumphs of the Redeemer the triumphs of the redeemed, and rejoice with Him at the total discomfiture of all His foes.

Psalm 9:4 *For thou hast maintained my right and my cause; thou satest in the throne judging right.*

EXPOSITION: Verse 4. One of our nobility has for his motto, "I will maintain it;" but the Christian has a better and more humble one, *Thou hast maintained it.* God and my right, are united by my faith: while God lives my right shall never be taken from me. If we seek to maintain the cause and honor of our Lord we may suffer reproach and misrepresentation, but it is a rich comfort to remember that He who sits on the throne knows our hearts, and will not leave us to the ignorant and ungenerous judgment of erring man.

Psalm 9:5 *Thou hast rebuked the heathen, thou hast destroyed the wicked, thou hast put out their name for ever and ever.*

EXPOSITION: Verse 5. God rebukes before He destroys, but when He once comes to blows with the wicked He ceases not until He has dashed them in pieces so small that their very name is forgotten, and like a noisome snuff their remembrance is put out forever and ever. How often the word "thou" occurs in this and the former verse, to show us that the grateful strain mounts up directly to the Lord as does the smoke from the altar when the air is still. My soul, send up all the music of all your powers to Him who has been and is your sure deliverance.

Psalm 9:6 *O thou enemy, destructions are come to a perpetual end: and thou hast destroyed cities; their memorial is perished with them.*

EXPOSITION: Verse 6. Here the psalmist exults over the fallen foe. He bends as it were, over his prostrate form, and insults his once-vaunted strength. He plucks the boaster's song out of his mouth, and sings it for him in derision. After this fashion does our Glorious Redeemer ask of death, *Where is thy sting?* and of the grave, *Where is thy victory?* [1 Corinthians 15:55]. The spoiler is spoiled, and he who made captive is led into captivity himself. Let the daughters of Jerusalem go forth to meet their King, and praise Him with timbrel and harp. In the light of the past the future is not doubtful. Since the same Almighty God fills the throne of power, we can with unhesitating confidence, exult in our security for all time to come.

Psalm 9:7 *But the Lord shall endure for ever: he hath prepared his throne for judgment.*

EXPOSITION: **Verse 7.** The enduring existence and unchanging dominion of our Jehovah are the firm foundations of our joy. The enemy and his destructions shall come to a perpetual end, but God and His throne shall endure forever. The eternity of divine sovereignty yields unfailing consolation. By the throne being prepared for judgment, are we not to understand the swiftness of divine justice. In heaven's court suitors are not worn out with long delays. Term-time lasts all the year round in the court of King's Bench above. Thousands may come at once to the throne of the Judge of all the Earth, but neither plaintiff nor defendant shall have to complain that He is not prepared to give their cause a fair hearing.

Psalm 9:8 *And he shall judge the world in righteousness, he shall minister judgment to the people in uprightness.*

EXPOSITION: **Verse 8.** Whatever earthly courts may do, heaven's throne ministers judgment in uprightness. Partiality and respect of persons are things unknown in the dealings of the Holy One of Israel. How the prospect of appearing before the impartial tribunal of the Great King should act as a check to us when tempted to sin, and as a comfort when we are slandered or oppressed.

Psalm 9:9 *The* LORD *also will be a refuge for the oppressed, a refuge in times of trouble.*

EXPOSITION: Verse 9. He, who gives no quarter to the wicked in the Day of Judgment, is the defense and refuge of His saints in the day of trouble. There are many forms of oppression; both from man and from Satan oppression comes to us; and for all its forms, a refuge is provided in the Lord Jehovah. There were cities of refuge under the law; God is our refuge city under the gospel. As the ships when vexed with tempest make for harbor, so do the oppressed hasten to the wings of a just and gracious God. He is a high tower so impregnable, that the hosts of hell cannot carry it by storm, and from its lofty heights faith looks down with scorn upon her enemies.

Psalm 9:10 *And they that know thy name will put their trust in thee: for thou,* LORD, *hast not forsaken them that seek thee.*

EXPOSITION: Verse 10. Ignorance is worst when it amounts to ignorance of God, and knowledge is best when it exercises itself upon the name of God. This most excellent knowledge leads to the most excellent grace of faith. O, to learn more of the attributes and character of God. Unbelief, that hooting night bird, cannot live in the light of divine knowledge; it flies before the sun of God's great and gracious name. If we read this verse literally, there is, no doubt, a glorious fullness of assurance in the names of God. The names of God inspire trust. Jehovah Jireh, Tsidkenu, Rophi, Shammah, Nissi, Elohim, Shaddai, Adonai , etc. By knowing His name is also meant an experimental acquaintance with the attributes of God, and every one of them anchors to hold the soul from drifting in seasons of peril.

The Lord may hide His face for a season from His people, but He never has utterly, finally, really, or angrily forsaken them that seek Him. Let the poor seekers draw comfort from this fact, and let the finders rejoice yet more exceedingly, for what must be the Lord's faithfulness to those who find if He is so gracious to those who seek.

> O hope of every contrite heart,
> O joy of all the meek,
> To those who fall how kind thou art,
> How good to those who seek.
> But what to those who find, ah, this
> Nor tongue nor pen can show
> The love of Jesus what it is,
> None but his loved ones know.[21]

Psalm 9:11 *Sing praises to the LORD, which dwelleth in Zion: declare among the people his doings.*

EXPOSITION: **Verse 11.** Being full of gratitude himself, our inspired author is eager to excite others to join the strain, and praise God in the same manner as he himself vowed to do in the first and second verses. The heavenly spirit of praise is gloriously contagious, and he that has it is never content unless he can excite all who surround him to unite in his sweet employ. Singing and preaching, as means of glorifying God, are here joined together, and it is remarkable that, connected with all revivals of gospel ministry, there has been a sudden outburst of the spirit of song. Luther's psalms and hymns were in all men's mouths, and in the modern revival under Wesley and Whitefield, the

---

21. Hymn: "Jesus, the Very Thought of Thee," words by Bernard of Clairvaux (1090–1153)

strains of Charles Wesley,[22] Cennick,[23] Berridge,[24] Toplady,[25] Hart[26], Newton[27], and many others, were the outgrowth of restored piety.

The singing of the birds of praise fitly accompanies the return of the gracious spring of divine visitation through the proclamation of the truth. Sing on brethren, and preach on, and these shall both be a token that the Lord still dwells in Zion. It will be well for us when coming up to Zion, to remember that the Lord dwells among His saints, and is to be had in peculiar reverence of all those that are about Him.

Psalm 9:12 *When he maketh inquisition for blood, he remembereth them: he forgetteth not the cry of the humble.*

EXPOSITION: **Verse 12.** When an inquest is held concerning the blood of the oppressed, the martyred saints will have the first remembrance; He will avenge His own elect. Those saints who are living shall also be heard; they shall be exonerated from blame, and kept from destruction, even when the Lord's most terrible work is going on; the man with the inkhorn by his side shall mark them all for safety, before the slaughter men are permitted to smite the Lord's enemies. The humble cry of the poorest saints shall neither be drowned by the voice of the thundering justice nor by the shrieks of the condemned.

---

22. Charles Wesley, 1707–1788, poet, preacher, hymn-writer
23. John Cennick, 1716–1793, hymn-writer
24. John Berridge, 1716–1796, hymn-writer
25. Augustus Montague Toplady, 1740–1778, poet, preacher, hymn-writer
26. Joseph Hart, 1712–1768, clergyman, hymn-writer
27. John Newton, 1725–1807, clergyman, hymn-writer

Psalm 9:13 *Have mercy upon me, O LORD; consider my trouble which I suffer of them that hate me, thou that liftest me up from the gates of death.*

EXPOSITION: Verse 13. Memories of the past and confidences concerning the future conducted the man of God to the mercy seat to plead for the needs of the present. Between praising and praying he divided all his time. How could he have spent it more profitably? His first prayer is one suitable for all persons and occasions, it breathes a humble spirit, indicates self-knowledge, appeals to the proper attributes, and to the fitting person.

Have mercy upon me, O Lord. Just as Luther used to call some texts little bibles, so we may call this sentence a little prayer book; for it has in it the soul and marrow of prayer. It is multum in parvo pardon,[28] and like the angelic sword turns every way. The ladder looks to be short, but it reaches from Earth to Heaven. What a noble title is here given to the Most High. *Thou that liftest me up from the gates of death!* What a glorious lift! In sickness, in sin, in despair, in temptation, we have been brought very low, and the gloomy portal has seemed as if it would open to imprison us, but, underneath us were the everlasting arms, and, therefore, we have been uplifted even to the gates of Heaven. Joseph Trapp[29] quaintly says, "He commonly reserveth his hand for a dead lift, and rescueth those who were even talking of their graves."

Psalm 9:14 *That I may shew forth all thy praise in the gates of the daughter of Zion: I will rejoice in thy salvation.*

---

28. Latin for "much in little."
29. Joseph Trapp (1679–1747), English clergyman.

EXPOSITION: **Verse 14.** We must not overlook David's object in desiring mercy, it is God's glory: that I may show forth all your praise. Saints are not so selfish as to look only to self; they desire mercy's diamond that they may let others see it flash and sparkle, and may admire Him who gives such priceless gems to His beloved. The contrast between the gates of death and the gates of the New Jerusalem is very striking; let our songs be excited to the highest and most rapturous pitch by the double consideration of where we are taken, and to what we have been advanced, and let our prayers for mercy be made more energetic and agonizing by a sense of the grace which such a salvation implies. When David speaks of his showing forth all God's praise, he means that, in his deliverance grace in all its heights and depths would be magnified. Just as verse 3 of our hymn by Isaac Watts puts it:

> O the length and breadth of love!
> Jesus, Savior, can it be?
> All thy mercy's height I prove,
> All the depth is seen in me.

Here ends the first part of this instructive psalm, and in pausing awhile we feel bound to confess that we have only flitted over its surface and have not dug into the depths. The verses are singularly full of teaching, and if the Holy Spirit will bless the reader, he may go over this psalm, as the writer has done scores of times, and see on each occasion fresh beauties.

Psalm 9:15 – 16 *The heathen are sunk down in the pit that they made: in the net which they hid is their own foot taken. The LORD is known by the judgment which he executeth: the wicked is snared in the work of his own hands. Higgaion. Selah.*

EXPOSITION: **Verses 15 – 16.** In considering this terrible picture of the Lord's overwhelming judgments of His enemies, we are called upon to ponder and meditate upon it with deep seriousness by the two untranslated words, *Higgaion, Selah.* Meditate, pause. Consider, and tune your instrument. Think and solemnly adjust your hearts to the solemnity which is so well becoming the subject. Let us in a humble spirit approach these verses, and notice, first, that the character of God requires the punishment of sin.

Jehovah is known by the judgment which He executes; His holiness and abhorrence of sin is thus displayed. A ruler who winked at evil would soon be known by all his subjects to be evil himself, and he, on the other hand, who is severely just in judgment reveals his own nature thereby. So long as our God is God, He will not, He cannot spare the guilty; except through that one glorious way in which He is just, and yet the justifier of him that believeth in Jesus. We must notice, secondly, that the manner of His judgment is singularly wise, and indisputably just. He makes the wicked become their own executioners. *The heathen are sunk down in the pit that they made,* etc. Like cunning hunters they prepared a pitfall for the godly and fell into it themselves: the foot of the victim escaped their crafty snares, but the toils surrounded themselves: the cruel snare was laboriously manufactured, and it proved its efficacy by snaring its own maker. Persecutors and oppressors are often ruined by their own malicious projects. "Drunkards kill themselves; prodigals beggar themselves;" the contentious are involved in ruinous costs; the vicious are devoured with fierce diseases; the envious eat their own hearts; and blasphemers curse their own souls. Thus, men may read their sin in their punishment. They sowed the seed of sin, and the ripe fruit of damnation is the natural result.

Psalm 9:17 *The wicked shall be turned into hell, and all the nations that forget God.*

EXPOSITION: Verse 17. The justice which has punished the wicked, and preserved the righteous, remains the same, and therefore in days to come, retribution will surely be meted out. How solemn Psalm 9:17 is, especially in its warning to forgetters of God. The moral who are not devout, the honest who are not prayerful, the benevolent who are not believing, the amiable who are not converted, these must all have their own portion with the openly wicked in the hell which is prepared for the devil and his angels. There are whole nations of such; the forgetters of God are far more numerous than the profane or profligate, and according to the very forceful expression of the Hebrew, the nethermost hell will be the place into which all of them shall be hurled headlong. Forgetfulness seems a small sin, but it brings eternal wrath upon the man who lives and dies in it.

Psalm 9:18 *For the needy shall not always be forgotten: the expectation of the poor shall not perish for ever.*

EXPOSITION: Verse 18. Mercy is as ready to her work as ever justice can be. Needy souls fear that they are forgotten; well, if it be so, let them rejoice that they shall not always be so. Satan tells poor tremblers that their hope shall perish, but they have here the divine assurance that their expectation shall not perish forever. The Lord's people are a humbled people, afflicted, emptied, sensible of need, and driven to a daily attendance on God, daily begging of Him, and living upon the hope of what is promised. Such persons may have to wait, but they shall find that they do not wait in vain.

Psalm 9:19 *Arise, O* LORD; *let not man prevail: let the heathen be judged in thy sight.*

EXPOSITION: **Verse 19.** Prayers are the believer's weapons of war. When the battle is too hard for us, we call in our great ally, who, as it were, lies in ambush until faith gives the signal by crying out, Arise, O Lord. Although our cause is all but lost, it shall be soon won again, if the Almighty does but stir himself. He will not suffer man to prevail over God, but with swift judgments will confound their glorying. In the very sight of God the wicked will be punished, and He who is now all tenderness will have no bowels of compassion for them, since they had no tears of repentance while their day of grace endured.

Psalm 9:20 *Put them in fear, O* LORD: *that the nations may know themselves to be but men. Selah.*

EXPOSITION: **Verse 20.** One would think that men would not grow so vain as to deny themselves to be but men, but it appears to be a lesson which only a divine schoolmaster can teach to some proud spirits. Crowns leave their wearers but men, degrees of eminent learning make their owners not more than men, valor and conquest cannot elevate beyond the dead level of "but men;" and all the wealth of Croesus, the wisdom of Solon, the power of Alexander, the eloquence of Demosthenes, if added together, would leave the possessor but a man. May we ever remember this lest like those in the text, we should be put in fear. Before leaving this psalm, it will be very profitable if the student will peruse it again as the triumphal hymn of the Redeemer, as He devoutly brings the glory of his victories and lays it down at his Father's feet. Let us joy in His joy, and our joy shall be full.

PSALM 10
PSALM 10:1–PSALM 10:18

Psalm 10:1 *Why standest thou afar off, O Lord? why hidest thou thyself in times of trouble?*

EXPOSITION: **Verse 1.** To the tearful eye of the sufferer the Lord seemed to stand still, as if He calmly looked on, and did not sympathize with His afflicted one. More so, the Lord appeared to be afar off, no longer *a very present help in trouble,* [See Psalm 46:1.] but an inaccessible mountain, into which no man would be able to climb. The presence of God is the joy of His people, but any suspicion of His absence is distracting beyond measure. Let us, then, ever remember that the Lord is near us.

The refiner is never far from the mouth of the furnace when His gold is in the fire, and the Son of God is always walking in the midst of the flames when His holy children are cast into them. Yet He that knows the frailty of man will little wonder that when we are sharply exercised, we find it hard to bear the apparent neglect of the Lord when He forbears to work our deliverance.

Why hide yourself in times of trouble? It is not the trouble, but the hiding of our Father's face, which cuts us to the quick. When trial and desertion come together, we are in as perilous a plight as Paul, when his ship fell into a place where two seas met [See Acts 27:41.]. It is but little wonder if we are like the vessel which ran aground, and the forepart stuck fast, and remained unmovable, while the hind part was broken by the violence of the waves.

When our sun is eclipsed, it is dark indeed. If we need an answer to the question, *Why hidest thou thyself?* it is to be found in the fact that there is a "needs be," not only for trial, but for heaviness of heart under trial [See 1 Peter 1:6.]; but how could this be the case, if the Lord would shine upon us while He is afflicting us? Should the parent comfort his child while he is correcting him, where would be the use of the chastening? A smiling face and a rod are not fit companions. God bares the back that the blow may be felt; for it is only felt affliction which can become blest affliction. If we were carried in the arms of God over every stream, where would be the trial, and where the experience, which trouble is meant to teach us?

Psalm 10:2 *The wicked in his pride doth persecute the poor: let them be taken in the devices that they have imagined.*

EXPOSITION: **Verse 2.** The second verse contains the formal indictment against the wicked: The wicked in his pride persecutes the poor. The accusation divides itself into two distinct charges—pride and tyranny; the one the root and cause of the other. The second sentence is the humble petition of the oppressed: Let them be taken in the devices that they have imagined. The prayer is reasonable, just, and natural. Even our enemies themselves being judges, it is but right that men should be done by as they wished to do to others.

We only weigh you on your own scales, and measure your corn with your own bushel. Terrible shall be your day, O persecuting Babylon! When you shall be made to drink of the wine cup which you yourself have filled to the brim with the blood of saints. There are none who will dispute the justice of God, when He shall hang every Haman on his own gallows, and cast all the enemies of His Daniels into their own den of lions.

Psalm 10:3 *For the wicked boasteth of his heart's desire, and blesseth the covetous, whom the LORD abhorreth.*

EXPOSITION: Verse 3. The indictment being read, and the petition presented, the evidence is now heard upon the first count. The evidence is very full and conclusive upon the matter of pride, and no jury could hesitate to give a verdict against the prisoner at the bar. Let us, however, hear the witnesses one by one. The first testifies that he is a boaster.

For the wicked boasteth of his heart's desire. He is a very silly boaster, for he glories in a mere desire: a very brazen-faced boaster, for that desire is villainy; and a most abandoned sinner, to boast of that which is his shame. Bragging sinners are the worst and most contemptible of men, especially when their filthy desires—too filthy to be carried into act—become the theme of their boastings. When Mr. Hate Good and Mr. Heady are joined in partnership, they drive a brisk trade in the devil's wares. This one proof is enough to condemn the prisoner at the bar. Take him away, jailor! But stay, another witness desires to be sworn and heard.

This time, the impudence of the proud rebel is even more apparent; *for he blesseth the covetous, whom the Lord abhorreth.* This is insolence, which is pride unmasked. He is haughty enough to differ from the Judge of all the Earth, and bless the men whom God has cursed. So did the sinful generation in the days of Malachi, who called the proud happy, and set up those that worked wickedness (Malachi 3:15). These base pretenders would dispute with their Maker; they would—

> Snatch from His hand the balance and the rod,
> Rejudge His justice, be the god of God.[30]

How often have we heard the wicked man speaking in terms of honor of the covetous, the grinder of the poor, and the sharp dealer! Our old proverb has it—"I wot [know] well how the world wags; [how the world conducts itself] He is most loved that hath most bags."

Pride meets covetousness, and compliments it as wise, thrifty, and prudent. We say it with sorrow, there are many professors of religion who esteem a rich man, and flatter him, even though they know that he has fattened himself upon the flesh and blood of the poor. The only sinners who are received as respectable are covetous men. If a man is a fornicator, or a drunkard, we put him out of the church; but who ever read of church discipline against that idolatrous wretch—the covetous man? Let us tremble, lest we be found to be partakers of this atrocious sin of pride, "blessing the covetous, whom Jehovah abhorreth."

Psalm 10:4 *The wicked, through the pride of his countenance, will not seek after God: God is not in all his thoughts.*

EXPOSITION: **Verse 4.** The proud boastings and lewd blessings of the wicked have been received in evidence against him, and now his own face confirms the accusation, and his empty closet cries aloud against him. *The wicked, through the pride of his countenance, will not seek after God.* Proud hearts breed proud looks and stiff knees. It is an admirable arrangement that the heart is often written on the countenance, just as the motion of the wheels of a clock find

---

30. From the poem, "An Essay on Man: Epistle I," by Alexander Pope (1688–1744).

their record on its face. A brazen face and a broken heart never go together. We are not quite sure that the Athenians were wise when they ordained that men should be tried in the dark lest their countenances should weigh with the judges; for there is much more to be learned from the motions of the muscles of the face than from the words of the lips. Honesty shines in the face, but villainy peeps out at the eyes. See the effect of pride; it kept the man from seeking God. It is hard to pray with a stiff neck and an unbending knee.

God is not in all his thoughts: he thought much, but he had no thoughts for God. Amid heaps of chaff there was not a grain of wheat. The only place where God is not is in the thoughts of the wicked. This is a damning accusation; for where the God of Heaven is not, the lord of hell is reigning and raging; and if God be not in our thoughts, our thoughts will bring us to perdition.

Psalm 10:5 *His ways are always grievous; thy judgments are far above out of his sight: as for all his enemies, he puffeth at them.*

EXPOSITION: **Verse 5.** *His ways are always grievous.* To himself they are hard. Men go a rough road when they go to hell. God has hedged up the way of sin: O what folly to leap these hedges and fall among the thorns! To others, also, his ways cause much sorrow and vexation; but what cares he? He sits like the idol god upon his monstrous car, utterly regardless of the crowds who are crushed as he rolls along.

Thy judgments are far above out of his sight: he looks high, but not high enough. As God is forgotten, so are his judgments. He is not able to comprehend the things of God; a swine may sooner look through a telescope at the stars than this man study the Word of God to understand the righteousness of the Lord.

As for all his enemies, he puffeth at them. He defies and domineers; and when men resist his injurious behavior, he sneers at them, and threatens to annihilate them with a puff. In most languages there is a word of contempt borrowed from the action of puffing with the lips, and in English we should express the idea by saying, "He cries, Pooh, Pooh!" at His enemies. Ah! There is one enemy who will not be puffed at. Death will puff at the candle of his life and blow it out, and the wicked boaster will find it grim work to brag in the tomb.

Psalm 10:6 *He hath said in his heart, I shall not be moved: for I shall never be in adversity.*

EXPOSITION: **Verse 6.** The testimony of the sixth verse concludes the evidence against the prisoner upon the first charge of pride, and certainly it is conclusive in the highest degree. The present witness has been prying into the secret chambers of the heart, and has come to tell us what he has heard.

He hath said in his heart, I shall not be moved: for I shall never be in adversity. O impertinence runs to seed! The man thinks himself immutable and omnipotent too, for he is never to be in adversity. He counts himself a privileged man. He sits alone, and shall see no sorrow. His nest is in the stars, and he dreams not of a hand that shall pluck him away. But let us remember that this man's house is built upon the sand, upon a foundation no more substantial than the rolling waves of the sea. He that is too secure is never safe.

Boastings are not buttresses, and self-confidence is a sorry bulwark. This is the ruin of fools, that when they succeed they become too big, and swell with self-conceit, as if their summer would last forever, and their flowers bloom on eternally. Be humble, O man! For you are mortal, and your lot is mutable. The second crime is now to be proved. The fact that the man is proud and arrogant may go a long way to prove that he is vindictive and cruel. Haman's pride was the father of a cruel design to murder all the Jews. Nebuchadnezzar builds an idol; in pride he commands all men to bow before it; and then cruelly stands ready to heat the furnace seven times hotter for those who will not yield to his imperious will. Every proud thought is twin brother to a cruel thought. He who exalts himself will despise others, and one step further will make him a tyrant.

Psalm 10:7 *His mouth is full of cursing and deceit and fraud: under his tongue is mischief and vanity.*

EXPOSITION: Verse 7. Let us now hear the witnesses in court. Let the wretch speak for himself, for out of his own mouth he will be condemned. His mouth is full of cursing and deceit and fraud. There is not only a little evil there, but his mouth is full of it. A three-headed serpent has stowed away its coils and venom within the den of its black mouth. There is cursing which he spits against both God and men, deceit with which he entraps the unwary, and fraud by which, even in his common dealings, he robs his neighbors. Beware of such a man: have no sort of dealing with him: none but the silliest of geese would go to the fox's sermon, and none but the most foolish will put themselves into the society of knaves. But we must proceed. Let us look under this man's tongue as well as in his mouth; under his tongue is mischief and vanity. Deep in his throat are the unborn words which shall come forth as mischief and iniquity.

Psalm 10:8 *He sitteth in the lurking places of the villages: in the secret places doth he murder the innocent: his eyes are privily set against the poor.*

EXPOSITION: **Verse 8.** Despite the bragging of this base wretch, it seems that he is as cowardly as he is cruel. *He sitteth in the lurking places of the villages: in the secret places doth he murder the innocent: his eyes are privily set against the poor.* He acts the part of the highwayman, who springs upon the unsuspecting traveler in some desolate part of the road. There are always bad men lying in wait for the saints. This is a land of robbers and thieves; let us travel well armed, for every bush conceals an enemy. Everywhere there are traps laid for us, and foes thirsting for our blood. There are enemies at our table as well as across the sea. We are never safe, save when the Lord is with us.

Psalm 10:9 *He lieth in wait secretly as a lion in his den: he lieth in wait to catch the poor: he doth catch the poor, when he draweth him into his net.*

EXPOSITION: **Verse 9.** The picture becomes blacker, for here is the cunning of the lion, and of the huntsman, as well as the stealthiness of the robber. Surely there are some men who come up to the very letter of this description. With watching, perversion, slander, whispering, and false swearing, they ruin the character of the righteous, and murder the innocent; or, with legal quibbles, mortgages, bonds, writs, and the like, they catch the poor, and draw them into a net.

Chrysostom[31] was peculiarly severe upon this last phase of cruelty, but assuredly not more so than was richly merited. Take care, brethren, for there are other traps besides these. Hungry lions are crouching in every den, and fowlers spread their nets in every field. Quarles[32] well pictures our danger in those memorable lines:

---

31. John Chrysostom (347–407), Archbishop of Constantinople
32. Francis Quarles (1592–1644), English poet

The close pursuers busy hands do plant
Snares in thy substance; snares attend thy want;
Snares in thy credit; snares in thy disgrace;
Snares in thy high estate; snares in thy base;
Snares tuck thy bed; and snares surround thy board;
Snares watch thy thoughts; and snares attack thy word;
Snares in thy quiet; snares in thy commotion;
Snares in thy diet; snares in thy devotion;
Snares lurk in thy resolves; snares in thy doubt;
Snares lie within thy heart; and snares without;
Snares are above thy head, and snares beneath;
Snares in thy sickness; snares are in thy death.

O Lord! Keep your servants, and defend us from all our enemies!

Psalm 10:10 *He croucheth, and humbleth himself, that the poor may fall by his strong ones.*

EXPOSITION: Verse 10. *He croucheth and humbleth himself, that the poor may fall by his strong ones.* Seeming humility is often armor-bearer to malice. The lion crouches that he may leap with the greater force, and bring down his strong limbs upon his prey. When a wolf was old, and had tasted human blood, the old Saxon cried, "Ware, wolf!" and we may cry, "Ware fox!" They who crouch to our feet are longing to make us fall. Be very careful of fawners; for friendship and flattery are deadly enemies.

Psalm 10:11 *He hath said in his heart, God hath forgotten: he hideth his face; he will never see it.*

EXPOSITION: Verse 11. As upon the former count, so upon this one; a witness is forthcoming, who has been

127

listening at the keyhole of the heart. Speak up, friend, and let us hear your story. *He hath said in his heart, God hath forgotten: he hideth his face; he will never see it.* This cruel man comforts himself with the idea that God is blind, or, at least, forgetful: a fond and foolish fancy, indeed. Men doubt Omniscience when they persecute the saints. If we had a sense of God's presence with us, it would be impossible for us to ill-treat His children. In fact, there can scarcely be a greater preservation from sin than the constant thought "God sees me." Thus has the trial proceeded. The case has been fully stated; and now it is but little wonder that the oppressed petitioner lifts up the cry for judgment, which we find in the following verse.

Psalm 10:12 *Arise, O Lord; O God, lift up thine hand: forget not the humble.*

EXPOSITION: Verse 12. With what bold language will faith address its God, and yet what unbelief is mingled with our strongest confidence. Fearlessly the Lord is stirred up to arise and lift up His hand, yet timidly He is begged not to forget the humble; as if Jehovah could ever be forgetful of His saints. This verse is the incessant cry of the Church, and she will never refrain from speaking it until her Lord shall come in His glory to avenge her of all her adversaries.

Psalm 10:13 *Wherefore doth the wicked contemn God? he hath said in his heart, Thou wilt not require it.*

EXPOSITION: Verse 13. In these verses the description of the wicked is condensed, and the evil of his character traced to its source, viz., atheistical ideas with regard to the government of the world. We may at once perceive that this is intended to be another urgent plea with the Lord to show His power, and reveal His justice. When the wicked call God's righteousness in question, we may well beg Him to teach them terrible things in righteousness. In Psalm 10:13, the hope of the infidel and his heart wishes are laid bare. He despises the Lord, because he will not believe that sin will meet with punishment: *He has said in his heart, Thou will not require it.* If there were no hell for other men, there ought to be one for those who question the justice of it.

Psalm 10:14 *Thou hast seen it; for thou beholdest mischief and spite, to requite it with thy hand: the poor committeth himself unto thee; thou art the helper of the fatherless.*

EXPOSITION: **Verse 14.** This vile suggestion receives its answer in Psalm 10:14. *Thou hast seen it; for thou beholdest mischief and spite, to requite it with thy hand.* God is all eye to see, and all hand to punish His enemies. From Divine oversight there is no hiding, and from Divine justice there is no fleeing. Wanton mischief shall meet with woeful misery, and those who harbor spite shall inherit sorrow. Verily there is a God that judges in the Earth. Nor is this the only instance of the presence of God in the world; for while He chastises the oppressor, He befriends the oppressed.

The poor committeth himself unto thee. They give themselves up entirely into the Lord's hands. Resigning their judgment to His enlightenment, and their wills to His supremacy, they rest assured that He will order all things for the best. Nor does He deceive their hope. He preserves them in times of need, and causes them to rejoice in His goodness. *Thou art the helper of the fatherless.* God is the parent of all orphans. When the earthly father sleeps beneath the sod, a heavenly Father smiles from above. By some means or other, orphan children are fed, and well they may when they have such a Father.

Psalm 10:15 *Break thou the arm of the wicked and the evil man: seek out his wickedness till thou find none.*

EXPOSITION: **Verse 15.** In this verse we hear again the burden of the psalmist's prayer: *Break thou the arm of the wicked and the evil man.* Let the sinner lose his power to sin; stop the tyrant, arrest the oppressor, weaken the loins of the mighty, and dash in pieces the terrible. They deny your justice: let them feel it to the full. Indeed, they shall feel it; for God shall hunt the sinner forever: so long as there is a grain of sin in him it shall be sought out and punished. It is not a little worthy of note, that very few great persecutors have ever died in their beds: the curse has manifestly pursued them, and their fearful sufferings have made them own that divine justice at which they could at one time launch defiance. God permits tyrants to arise as thorn hedges to protect His Church from the intrusion of hypocrites, and that He may teach His backsliding children by them, as Gideon did the men of Succoth with the briers of the wilderness; but He soon cuts up these Herods, like the thorns, and casts them into the fire. Thales, the Milesian, one of the wise men of Greece, being asked what he thought to be the greatest rarity in the world, replied, "To see a tyrant live to be an old man." See how the Lord breaks, not only the arm, but the neck of proud oppressors! To the men who had neither justice nor mercy for the saints there shall be rendered justice to the full, but not a grain of mercy.

Psalm 10:16–18 *The* LORD *is King for ever and ever: the heathen are perished out of his land.* LORD, *thou hast heard the desire of the humble: thou wilt prepare their heart, thou wilt cause thine ear to hear: To judge the fatherless and the oppressed, that the man of the earth may no more oppress.*

EXPOSITION: Verses 16–18. The psalm ends with a song of thanksgiving to the great and everlasting King, because He has granted the desire of His humble and oppressed people, has defended the fatherless, and punished the heathen who trampled upon His poor and afflicted children. Let us learn that we are sure to speed well, if we carry our complaint to the King of kings. Rights will be vindicated, and wrongs redressed, at his throne. His government neglects not the interests of the needy, nor does it tolerate oppression in the mighty. Great God, we leave ourselves in your hand; to you we commit your Church afresh. Arise, O God, and let the man of the earth—the creature of a day—be broken before the majesty of your power. Come, Lord Jesus, and glorify your people. Amen and Amen.

Psalm 11

Psalm 11:1–11:7

Psalm 11:1 *In the Lord put I my trust: how say ye to my soul, Flee as a bird to your mountain?*

EXPOSITION: **Verse 1.** These verses contain an account of a temptation to distrust God, with which David was, upon some unmentioned occasion, greatly exercised. It may be that in the days when he was in Saul's court, he was advised to flee at a time when this flight would have been charged against him as a breach of duty to the king, or a proof of personal cowardice. His case was like that of Nehemiah, when his enemies, under the garb of friendship, hoped to entrap him by advising him to escape for

his life. Had he done so, they could then have found a ground of accusation. Nehemiah bravely replied, *Shall such a man as I flee?* [See Nehemiah 6:11.]. David, in a like spirit, refuses to retreat, exclaiming, in Psalm 11:1, *In the Lord put I my trust: how say ye to my soul, Flee as a bird to your mountain?*

When Satan cannot overthrow us by presumption, how craftily will he seek to ruin us by distrust! He will employ our dearest friends to argue us out of our confidence, and he will use such plausible logic, that unless we once for all assert our immovable trust in Jehovah, he will make us like the timid bird which flies to the mountain whenever danger presents itself.

Psalm 11:2 *For, lo, the wicked bend their bow, they make ready their arrow upon the string, that they may privily shoot at the upright in heart.*

EXPOSITION: **Verse 2.** How forcibly the case is put! The bow is bent, the arrow is fitted to the string: "Flee, flee, you defenseless bird, your safety lies in flight; fly away, for your enemies will send their shafts into your heart; haste, haste, for soon you will be destroyed!" David seems to have felt the force of the advice, for it came home to his soul; but yet he would not yield, but would rather dare the danger than exhibit a distrust in the Lord his God. Doubtless the perils which encompassed David were great and imminent; it was quite true that his enemies were ready to ambush and shoot at him.

Psalm 11:3 *If the foundations be destroyed, what can the righteous do?*

EXPOSITION: **Verse 3.** It was equally correct that the very foundations of law and justice were destroyed under Saul's unrighteous government: but what were all these things to the man whose trust was in God alone? He could brave the dangers, could escape the enemies, and defy the injustice which surrounded him. His answer to the question, *what can the righteous do?* would be the counter-question,

"What cannot they do?"

When prayer engages God on our side, and when faith secures the fulfillment of the promise, what cause can there be for flight, however cruel and mighty our enemies? With a sling and a stone, David had smitten a giant before whom the whole hosts of Israel were trembling, and the Lord, who delivered him from the uncircumcised Philistine, could surely deliver him from King Saul and his myrmidons.[33] There is no such word as "impossibility" in the language of faith; that martial grace knows how to fight and conquer, but she knows not how to flee.

Psalm 11:4 *The LORD is in his holy temple, the LORD's throne is in heaven: his eyes behold, his eyelids try, the children of men.*

EXPOSITION: Verse 4. David here declares the great source of his unflinching courage. He borrows his light from Heaven—from the great central orb of deity. The God of the believer is never far from him; He is not merely the God of the mountain vastnesses, but of the dangerous valleys and battle plains.

Jehovah is in His holy temple. The heavens are above our heads in all regions of the Earth, and so is the Lord ever near to us in every state and condition. This is a very strong reason why we should not adopt the vile suggestions of distrust. There is one who pleads His precious blood in our behalf in the temple above, and there is one upon the throne who is never deaf to the intercession of His Son. Why then, should we fear? What plots can men devise which Jesus will not discover?

Satan has doubtless desired to have us, that he may sift us as wheat [See Luke 22:31.], but Jesus is in the temple

---

33. Followers

praying for us, and how can our faith fail? What attempts can the wicked make which Jehovah shall not behold? And since He is in His holy temple, delighting in the sacrifice of His Son, will He not defeat every device, and send us a sure deliverance?

Jehovah's throne is in the heavens; He reigns supreme. Nothing can be done in Heaven, or Earth, or hell, which He does not ordain and overrule. He is the world's great Emperor. Why, then, should we flee? If we trust this King of kings, is not this enough? Cannot He deliver us without our cowardly retreat? Yes, blessed be the Lord our God, we can salute Him as Jehovah-nissi;[34] in His name we set up our banners, and instead of flight, we once more raise the shout of war.

His eyes behold. The eternal Watcher never slumbers; His eyes never know a sleep. His eyelids try the children of men: he narrowly inspects their actions, words, and thoughts. As men, when intently and narrowly inspecting some very minute object, almost close their eyelids to exclude every other object, so will the Lord look all men through and through. God sees each man as much and as perfectly as if there were no other creature in the universe. He sees us always; He never removes His eyes from us; He sees us entirely, reading the recesses of the soul as readily as the glancing of the eye. Is not this a sufficient ground of confidence, and an abundant answer to the solicitations of despondency? My danger is not hid from Him; He knows my extremity, and I may rest assured that He will not suffer [allow] me to perish while I rely alone on Him. Why then, should I take wings of a timid bird, and flee from the dangers which beset me?

---

34. Jehovah-nissi: The LORD our Banner.

Psalm 11:5 *The LORD trieth the righteous: but the wicked and him that loveth violence his soul hateth.*

EXPOSITION: Verse 5. *The Lord trieth the righteous.* He does not hate them, but only tries them. They are precious to Him, and therefore He refines them with afflictions. None of the Lord's children may hope to escape from trial, nor, indeed, in our right minds, would any of us desire to do so, for trial is the channel of many blessings.

> It is my happiness below
> Not to live without the Cross;
> But the Saviour's power to know,
> Sanctifying every loss.
> Trials make the promise sweet;
> Trials give new life to prayer;
> Trials bring me to his feet—and
> Lay me low, and keep me there.
> Did I meet no trials here—
> No chastisement by the way—
> Might I not, with reason,
> fear I should prove a cast-away?
> Bastards may escape the rod,
> Sunk in earthly vain delight;
> But the true born child of God
> Must not—would not, if he might.
> —William Cowper[35]

Is not this a very cogent reason why we should not distrustfully endeavor to shun a trial? For in so doing we are seeking to avoid a blessing.

---

35. Verses 1–3 of a hymn called "Welcome Cross," written by William Cowper (1731–1800).

Psalm 11:6 *Upon the wicked he shall rain snares, fire and brimstone, and an horrible tempest: this shall be the portion of their cup.*

EXPOSITION: Verse 6. But the wicked and him that loves violence His soul hates: why, then, shall I flee from these wicked men? If God hates them, I will not fear them. Haman was very great in the palace until he lost favor, but when the king abhorred him, how bold were the meanest attendants to suggest the gallows for the man at whom they had often trembled!

Look at the black mark upon the faces of our persecutors, and we shall not run away from them. If God is in the quarrel as well as ourselves, it would be foolish to question the result, or avoid the conflict. Sodom and Gomorrah perished by a fiery hail, and by a brimstone shower from Heaven; so shall all the ungodly. They may gather together like Gog and Magog to battle, but the Lord will rain upon them *an overflowing rain, and great hailstones, fire, and brimstone* (Ezekiel 38:22). Some expositors think that in the term *horrible tempest,* there is in the Hebrew an allusion to that burning, suffocating wind, which blows across the Arabian deserts, and is known by the name of Simoom. "A burning storm," Lowth calls it, while another great commentator reads it "wrath wind;" in either version the language is full of terrors.

What a tempest will that be which shall overwhelm the despisers of God! Oh! What a shower will that be which shall pour out itself forever upon the defenseless heads of impenitent sinners in hell! Repent, you rebels, or this fiery deluge shall soon surround you. Hell's horrors will be your inheritance, your entailed estate, the portion of your cup. The dregs of that cup you shall wring out, and drink forever. A drop of hell is terrible, but what must a full cup of torment be?

Think of it—a cup of misery, but not a drop of mercy. O people of God, how foolish it is to fear the faces of men who shall soon be a bundle of sticks in the fire of hell! Think of their end, their fearful end, and all fear of them must be changed into contempt of their threatening, and pity for their miserable estate.

Psalm 11:7 *For the righteous* LORD *loveth righteousness; his countenance doth behold the upright.*

EXPOSITION: **Verse 7.** The delightful contrast of the last verse is most worthy of our observation, and it affords another overwhelming reason why we should be steadfast, unmovable, not carried away with fear, or led to adopt carnal expedients in order to avoid trial.

For the righteous Lord loves righteousness. It is not only His office to defend it, but His nature to love it. He would deny himself if He did not defend the just. It is essential to the very being of God that He should be just; fear not, then, the end of all your trials, but "be just, and fear not." God approves, and, if men oppose, what does it matter? His countenance beholds the upright. We need never be out of countenance, for God countenances us. He observes, He approves, and He delights in the upright. He sees His own image in them, an image of His own fashioning, and therefore with complacency He regards them.

Shall we dare to put forth our hand unto iniquity in order to escape affliction? Let us be done with byways and short turnings, and let us keep to that fair path of right along which Jehovah's smile shall light us. Are we tempted to put our light under a bushel, to conceal our religion from our neighbors? Is it suggested to us that there are ways of avoiding the Cross, and shunning the reproach of Christ? Let us not hearken to the voice of the charmer, but seek an increase of faith, that we may wrestle with principalities and powers, and follow the Lord, fully going outside the camp, bearing His reproach.

Mammon, the flesh, the devil, will all whisper in our ear, "Flee as a bird to your mountain;" but let us come forth and defy them all. *Resist the devil, and he will flee from you* [James 4:7]. There is no room or reason for retreat. Advance! Let the vanguard push on! To the front all you powers and passions of our soul! On! On! In God's name, on! For *the Lord of hosts is with us; the God of Jacob is our refuge* [Psalm 46:7].

PSALM 12

PSALM 12:1–PSALM 12:8

Psalm 12:1 *Help, Lord; for the godly man ceaseth;*
for the faithful fail from among the children of men.

EXPOSITION: Verse 1. Help, Lord. A short but sweet,
suggestive, seasonable, and serviceable prayer; a kind of
angel's sword, to be turned every way, and to be used on
all occasions. Ainsworth says the word rendered "help," is
largely used for all manner of saving, helping, delivering,
preserving, etc. Thus it seems that the prayer is very full
and instructive. The psalmist sees the extreme danger of his
position, for a man had better be among lions than among
liars; he feels his own inability to deal with such sons of
Belial, for *he who shall touch them must be fenced with
iron* [See 2 Samuel 23:7.]. He therefore turns himself to his
all-sufficient Helper, the Lord, whose help is never denied
to His servants, and whose aid is enough for all their needs.

"Help, Lord," is a very useful exclamation on which we
may dart up to Heaven on occasions of emergency, whether
in labor, learning, suffering, fighting, living, or dying. As small
ships can sail into harbors which larger vessels, drawing more
water, cannot enter, so our brief cries and short petitions
may trade with Heaven when our soul is wind-bound, and
business-bound, as to longer exercises of devotion, and when
the stream of grace seems at too low an ebb to float a more
laborious supplication.

For the godly man ceases; the death, departure, or decline
of godly men should be a trumpet call for more prayer. They

say that fish smell first at the head, and when godly men decay, the whole commonwealth will soon go rotten. We must not, however, be rash in our judgment on this point, for Elijah erred in counting himself the only servant of God alive, when there were thousands whom the Lord held in reserve. The present times always appear to be peculiarly dangerous, because they are nearest to our anxious gaze, and whatever evils are rife are sure to be observed, while the faults of past ages are further off, and are more easily overlooked. Yet we expect that in the latter days, *because iniquity shall abound, the love of many shall wax cold* [Matthew 24:12.], and then we must the more thoroughly turn from man, and address ourselves to the Church, Lord, by whose help the gates of hell shall be kept from prevailing against us. The faithful fail from among the children of men; when godliness goes, faithfulness inevitably follows; without fear of God, men have no love of truth. Common honesty is no longer common; when common irreligiousness leads to universal godlessness.

Psalm 12:2 *They speak vanity every one with his neighbour: with flattering lips and with a double heart do they speak.*

EXPOSITION: **Verse 2.** *They speak vanity every one with his neighbor.* They utter that which is vain to hear, because of its frivolous, foolish, want of worth; vain to believe, because it was false and lying; vain to trust to, since it was deceitful and flattering; vain to regard, for it lifted up the hearer, filling him with proud conceit of himself. It is a sad thing when it is the fashion to talk vanity. "Call me, and I will call thee" is the old Scotch proverb; give me a high-sounding character, and I will give you one. Compliments and fawning congratulations are hateful to honest men; they know that if they accept them they must give them, and they scorn to do either. These accommodation bills are most admired by those who are bankrupt in character. The times are bad when every man flatters and deceives his neighbor.

With flattering lips and with a double heart do they speak. He, who puffs up another's heart, has nothing better than wind in his own. If a man extols me to my face, he only shows me one side of his heart, and the other is black with contempt for me, or foul with intent to cheat me. Flattery is the sign of the tavern where duplicity is the host. The Chinese consider a man of two hearts to be a very base man, and we shall be safe in reckoning all flatteries to be such.

Psalm 12:3−4 *The LORD shall cut off all flattering lips, and the tongue that speaketh proud things: Who have said, With our tongue will we prevail; our lips are our own: who is lord over us?*

EXPOSITION: Verses 3−4. Total destruction shall overwhelm the lovers of flattery and pride, but meanwhile how they bully and fume! Well did the apostle call them *raging waves of the sea, foaming out their own shame* [Jude 1:13]. Freethinkers are generally very free talkers, and they are never more at ease than when railing at God's dominion, and taking unto themselves unbounded license. Strange it is that the easy yoke of the Lord should so gall the shoulders of the proud, while the iron bands of Satan they bind about themselves as chains of honor; as they boastfully cry unto God, "Who is lord over us?" And hear not the hollow voice of the evil one, who cries from the infernal lake, "I am your lord, and right faithfully do you serve me."

Alas, poor fools, their pride and glory shall be cut off like a fading flower! May God grant that our soul may not be gathered with them. It is worthy of observation that flattering lips, and tongues speaking proud things, are classed together: the fitness of this is clear, for they are guilty of the same vice, the first flatters another, and the second flatters himself, in both cases a lie is in their right hands. One generally imagines that flatterers are such mean parasites, so cringing and fawning, that they cannot be proud; but the wise man will tell you that while all pride is truly meanness, there is in the very lowest meanness no small degree of pride.

Caesar's horse is even more proud of carrying Caesar, than Caesar is of riding him. The mat on which the emperor wiped his shoes, boasts vain gloriously, crying out, "I cleaned the imperial boots." None are so detestably domineering as the little creatures who creep into office by cringing to the great; those are bad times, indeed, in which these obnoxious beings are numerous and powerful. No wonder the justice of God in cutting off such injurious persons is matter for a psalm; for both Earth and Heaven are weary of such provoking offenders, whose presence is a very plague to the people afflicted by them. Men cannot tame the tongues of such boastful flatterers; but the Lord's remedy is sharp and sure, and is an unanswerable answer to their swelling words of vanity.

Psalm 12:5 *For the oppression of the poor, for the sighing of the needy, now will I arise, saith the* LORD; *I will set him in safety from him that puffeth at him.*

EXPOSITION: **Verse 5.** In due season the Lord will hear His elect ones, who cry day and night unto Him, and though He bears long with their oppressors, yet He will avenge them speedily. Observe that the mere oppression of saints, however silently they bear it, is in itself a cry to God: Moses was heard at the Red Sea, though he said nothing;

and Hagar's affliction was heard despite her silence. Jesus feels with His people, and their misery and pain are mighty orators with Him. By and by, however, they begin to sigh and express their misery, and then relief comes post-haste. Nothing moves a father like the cries of his children; he rouses himself, wakes up his manhood, overthrows the enemy, and sets his beloved in safety. A puff is too much for the child to bear, and the foe is so haughty, that he laughs the little one to scorn; but the father comes, and then it is the child's turn to laugh, when he is set above the rage of his tormentor

What virtue is there in a poor man's sighs, that they should move the Almighty God to arise from His throne? The needy did not dare to speak, and could only sigh in secret, but the Lord heard, and could rest no longer, but girded on His sword for the battle. It is a fair day when our soul brings God into her quarrel, for when His bare arm is seen, Philistia shall rue the day. The darkest hours of the Church's night are those which precede the break of day. Man's extremity is God's opportunity. Jesus will come to deliver just when His needy ones shall sigh, as if all hope had gone forever.

O Lord, set your now near at hand, and rise up speedily to our help. If the afflicted reader is able to lay hold upon the promise of this verse, let him gratefully fetch a fullness of comfort from it. Gurnall[36] says,

> As one may draw out the wine of a whole hogshead at one tap, so may a poor soul derive the comfort of the whole covenant to himself through one promise, if he be able to apply it.

He, who promises to set us in safety, means thereby preservation on Earth, and eternal salvation in Heaven.

---

36. William Gurnall (1617–1679), English clergyman and author.

Psalm 12:6 *The words of the LORD are pure words: as silver tried in a furnace of earth, purified seven times.*

EXPOSITION: **Verse 6.** What a contrast between the vain words of man, and the pure words of Jehovah. Man's words are yea and nay, but the Lord's promises are yea and amen. For truth, certainty, holiness, faithfulness, the words of the Lord are pure as well-refined silver. In the original there is an allusion to the most severely purifying process known to the ancients, through which silver was passed when the greatest possible purity was desired; the dross was all consumed, and only the bright and precious metal remained; so clear and free from all alloy of error or unfaithfulness is the Book of the Words of the Lord.

The Bible has passed through the furnace of persecution, literary criticism, philosophic doubt, and scientific discovery, and has lost nothing but those human interpretations which clung to it as alloy to precious ore. The experience of saints has tried it in every conceivable manner, but not a single doctrine or promise has been consumed in the most excessive heat. What God's Words are, the words of His children should be. If we would be Godlike in conversation, we must watch our language, and maintain the strictest purity of integrity and holiness in all our communications.

Psalm 12:7 *Thou shalt keep them, O LORD, thou shalt preserve them from this generation for ever.*

EXPOSITION: **Verse 7.** To fall into the hands of an evil generation, so as to be baited by their cruelty, or polluted by their influence, is an evil to be dreaded beyond measure; but it is an evil foreseen and provided for in the text. In life many a saint has lived a hundred years before his age, as though he had darted his soul into the brighter future, and escaped the mists of the beclouded present.

He has gone to his grave without reverence and misunderstood, and as generations come and go, all of a sudden the hero is unearthed, and lives in the admiration and love of the excellent of the Earth; preserved forever from the generation which condemned him as a sower of sedition, or burned him as a heretic.

It should be our daily prayer that we may rise above our age as the mountain tops above the clouds, and may stand out as a Heaven pointing pinnacle high above the mists of ignorance and sin which roll around us. O Eternal Spirit, fulfill in us the faithful saying of this verse! Our faith believes those two assuring words, and cries, "Thou shalt," "thou shalt."

Psalm 12:8 *The wicked walk on every side, when the vilest men are exalted.*

EXPOSITION: **Verse 8.** Here we return to the fount of bitterness, which first made the psalmist run to the wells of salvation, namely, the prevalence of wickedness. When those in power are vile, their underlings will be no better. As a warm sun brings out noxious flies, so does a sinner in honor foster vice everywhere. Our turf would not so swarm with the abominable if those who are styled honorable did not give their countenance to the craft. I pray to God that the glory and triumph of our Lord Jesus would encourage us to walk and work on every side; as like acts upon like, since an exalted sinner encourages sinners, our exalted Redeemer must surely excite, cheer, and stimulate His saints. Nerved by a sight of His reigning power we shall meet the evils of the times in the spirit of holy resolution, and shall the more hopefully pray, "Help, Lord."

PSALM 13
PSALM 13:1–PSALM 13:6

Psalm 13:1 *How long wilt thou forget me, O Lord? for ever? how long wilt thou hide thy face from me?*

EXPOSITION: Verse 1. *How long?* This question is repeated no less than four times. It shows a very intense desire for deliverance, and great anguish of heart. And what if there is some impatience mingled therein; is this not a truer portrait of our own experience? It is not easy to prevent desire from degenerating into impatience. O for grace that, while we wait on God, we may be kept from indulging a murmuring spirit! *How long?* Does not the often repeated cry become a very *howling?* And what if grief should find no other means of utterance? Even then, God is not far from the voice of our roaring; for He does not regard the music of our prayers, but His own Spirit's work in them in exciting desire and inflaming the affections. *How long?* Ah! How long do our days appear when our soul is cast down within us! Time flies with full-fledged wing in our summer days, but in our winters he flutters painfully. A week within prison walls is longer than a month at liberty. Long sorrow seems to argue abounding corruption; for the gold which is long in the fire must have had much dross to be consumed, hence the question "how long?" may suggest a deep searching of the heart.

How long wilt thou forget me? Ah, David, how like a fool you speak! Can God forget? Can omniscience[37] fail in

---

37. Infinite knowledge.

memory? Above all, can Jehovah's heart forget His own beloved child? Brethren, let us drive away the thought, and hear the voice of our covenant God by the mouth of the prophet,

> *But Zion said, The Lord hath forsaken me, and my Lord hath forgotten me* [Isaiah 49:14]. *Can a woman forget her sucking child, that she should not have compassion on the son of her womb? yea, they may forget, yet will I not forget thee. Behold, I have graven thee upon the palms of my hands; thy walls are continually before me* [See Isaiah 49:15–16.].

Forever? Oh, dark thought! It was surely bad enough to suspect a temporary forgetfulness, but shall we ask the ungracious question, and imagine that the Lord will forever cast away His people? No, His anger may endure for a night, but His love shall abide eternally.

How long wilt thou hide thy face from me? This is a far more rational question, for God may hide His face, and yet He may still remember. A hidden face is no sign of a forgetful heart. It is in love that His face is turned away; yet to a real child of God, this hiding of His Father's face is terrible and he will never be at ease until, once more he has seen his Father's smile.

Psalm 13:2 *How long shall I take counsel in my soul, having sorrow in my heart daily? how long shall mine enemy be exalted over me?*

EXPOSITION: **Verse 2.** *How long shall I take counsel, in my soul, having sorrow in my heart daily?* There is in the original the idea of "laying up" counsels in his heart, as if his devices had become innumerable but unavailing. Herein we have often been like David, for we have considered and reconsidered day after day, but have not discovered the happy device by which to escape from our trouble. Such storing of counsels is a sad sore. Ruminating upon trouble is bitter work. Children fill their mouths with bitterness when they rebelliously chew the pill which they ought obediently to have taken at once.

How long shall my enemy be exalted over me? This is like wormwood in the gall, to see the wicked enemy exulting while our soul is bowed down within us. The laughter of a foe grates horribly on the ears of grief. For the devil to make mirth of our misery is the last ounce of our complaint, and quite breaks down our patience; therefore let us make it one chief argument in our plea with mercy.

Thus the careful reader will remark that the question "how long?" is put in four shapes. The writer's grief is viewed, as it seems to be, as it is, as it affects himself within, and his foes without. We are all prone to play most on the worst string. We set up monumental stones over the graves of our joys, but who thinks of erecting monuments of praise for mercies received? We write four books of Lamentations and only one of Canticles, and are far more at home in wailing out a Miserere.[38]

Psalm 13:3 *Consider and hear me, O LORD my God: lighten mine eyes, lest I sleep the sleep of death.*

EXPOSITION: Verse 3. But now prayer lifts up her voice, like the watchman who proclaims the daybreak. Now will the tide turn, and the weeper shall dry his eyes. The mercy seat is the life of hope and the death of despair. The gloomy thought of God's having forsaken him is still upon the psalmist's soul, and he therefore cries, *Consider and hear*

---

38. Miserere: A psalm usually appointed for penitential acts. Psalm 50 in the Latin starts with the word *Miserere.*

me. He remembers at once the root of his woe, and cries aloud that it may be removed. The final absence of God is Tophet's[39] fire, and his temporary absence brings his people into the very suburbs of hell. God is here entreated to see and hear, so that He may be doubly moved to pity. What should we do if we had no God to turn to in the hour of wretchedness? Note the cry of faith, O Lord My God! Is it not a very glorious fact that our interest in our God is not destroyed by all our trials and sorrows? We may lose our gourds, but not our God. The title deed of Heaven is not written in the sand, but in eternal brass.

Lighten my eyes: that is, let the eye of my faith be clear, that I may see my God in the dark; let my eye of watchfulness be wide open, lest I be entrapped, and let the eye of my understanding be illuminated to see the right way. Perhaps, too, here is an allusion to that cheering of the spirits so frequently called the enlightening of the eyes because it causes the face to brighten and the eyes to sparkle. Well may we use the prayer, "Lighten our darkness, we beseech thee, O Lord!" for in many respects we need the Holy Spirit's illuminating rays.

Lest I sleep the sleep of death. Darkness engenders sleep, and despondency is not slow in making the eyes heavy. From this faintness and dimness of vision, caused by despair, there is but a step to the iron sleep of death. David feared that his trials would end his life, and he rightly uses his fear as an argument with God in prayer; for deep distress has in it a kind of claim upon compassion, not a claim of right, but a plea which has power with grace. Under the pressure of heart sorrow, the psalmist does not look forward to the sleep of death with hope and joy, as assured believers do, but he shrinks from it with dread, from which we gather that bondage from fear of death is no new thing.

---

39. A synonym for hell.

Psalm 13:4 *Lest mine enemy say, I have prevailed against him; and those that trouble me rejoice when I am moved.*

EXPOSITION: Verse 4. Another plea is urged in the fourth verse, and it is one the tried believer may handle well when on his knees. We make use of our archenemy for once, and compel him, like Samson, to grind in our mill while we use his cruel arrogance as an argument in prayer. It is not the Lord's will that the great enemy of our souls should overcome His children. This would dishonor God, and cause the evil one to boast. It is well for us that our salvation and God's honor are so intimately connected, that they stand or fall together. Our covenant God will complete the confusion of all our enemies, and if for awhile we become their scoff and jest, the day is coming when the shame will change sides, and the contempt shall be poured on those to whom it is due.

Psalm 13:5 *But I have trusted in thy mercy; my heart shall rejoice in thy salvation.*

EXPOSITION: Verse 5. What a change is here! Lo, the rain is over and gone, and the time of the singing of birds is come. The mercy seat has so refreshed the poor weeper, that he clears his throat for a song. If we have mourned with him, let us now dance with him. David's heart was more often out of tune than his harp, He begins many of his psalms sighing, and ends them singing; and others he begins in joy and ends in sorrow; "so that one would think," says Peter Moulin,[40] "that those Psalms had been composed by two men of a contrary humor." It is worthy to be observed that the joy is all the greater because of the previous sorrow, as calm is all

---

40. Peter du Mulin (1601–1684), French-English Anglican clergyman and author.

153

the more delightful in recollection of the preceding tempest. "Sorrows remembered sweeten present joy."[41] Here is his avowal of his confidence:

But I have trusted in thy mercy. For many a year it had been his desire to make the Lord his castle and tower of defense, and he smiles from behind the same bulwark still. He is sure of his faith, and his faith makes him sure; had he doubted the reality of his trust in God, he would have blocked up one of the windows through which the sun of Heaven delights to shine. Faith is now in exercise, and consequently is readily discovered; there is never a doubt in our heart about the existence of faith while it is in action: when the hare or partridge is quiet we see it not, but let the same be in motion and we soon perceive it.

All the powers of his enemies had not driven the psalmist from his stronghold. As the shipwrecked mariner clings to the mast, so did David cling to his faith; he neither could nor would give up his confidence in the Lord his God. O that we may profit by his example and hold by our faith as by our very life! Now hearken to the music which faith makes in his soul. The bells of the mind are all ringing,

My heart shall rejoice in thy salvation. There is joy and feasting within doors, for a glorious guest has come, and the fatted calf is killed. Sweet is the music which sounds from the strings of the heart. But this is not all; the voice joins itself in the blessed work, and the tongue keeps tune with the soul, while the writer declares, *I will sing unto the Lord.*

> I will praise thee every day,
> Now thine anger's past away;
> Comfortable thoughts arise
> From the bleeding sacrifice.[42]

---

41. Quote from Robert Pollok (1798–1827), Scottish poet.
42. Hymn by William Cowper called, "O Lord I Will Praise Thee."

Psalm 13:6 *I will sing unto the* LORD, *because he hath dealt bountifully with me.*

EXPOSITION: **Verse 6.** The psalm closes with a sentence which is a refutation of the charge of forgetfulness which David had uttered in the first verse, *He hath dealt bountifully with me.* So shall it be with us if we wait awhile. The complaint which in our haste we utter shall be joyfully retracted, and we shall witness that the Lord has dealt bountifully with us.

PSALM 14
PSALM 14:1–PSALM 14:7

Psalm 14:1 *The fool hath said in his heart, There is no God. They are corrupt, they have done abominable works, there is none that doeth good.*

EXPOSITION: **Verse 1.** *The fool.* The Atheist is the fool preeminently, and a fool universally. He would not deny God if he were not a fool by nature, and having denied God it is no marvel that he becomes a fool in practice. Sin is always folly, and as it is the height of sin to attack the very existence of the Most High, so it is also the greatest imaginable folly. To say there is no God is to belie the plainest evidence, which is obstinacy; to oppose the common consent of mankind, which is stupidity; to stifle consciousness, which is madness.

If the sinner could by his atheism destroy the God whom he hates then there would be some sense, although much wickedness, in his infidelity; but as denying the existence of fire does not prevent its burning a man who is in it, so doubting the existence of God will not stop the Judge of all the Earth from destroying the rebel who breaks His laws. No, this atheism is a crime which much provokes Heaven, and will bring down terrible vengeance on the fool who indulges it. The proverb says, "A fool's tongue cuts his own throat," and in this instance it kills both soul and body forever. I pray to God the mischief stopped even there, but alas, one fool makes hundreds, and a noisy blasphemer spreads his horrible doctrines as lepers spread the plague! Ainsworth, in his *Annotations*, tells us that the word here used is nabal which has the signification of fading, dying, or falling away, as a withered leaf or flower; it is a title given to the foolish man as having lost the juice and sap of wisdom, reason, honesty, and godliness. Trapp hits the mark when he calls him "that sapless fellow, that carcass of a man, that walking sepulchre of himself, in whom all religion and right reason is withered and wasted, dried up and decayed." Some translate it the apostate, and others the wretch. With what earnestness should we shun the appearance of doubt as to the presence, activity, power and love of God, for all such mistrust is of the nature of folly, and who among us would wish to be ranked with the fool in the text?

Yet let us never forget that all unregenerate men are more or less such fools. The fool "has said in his heart." May a man with his mouth profess to believe, and yet in heart say the reverse? Had he hardly become audacious enough to utter his folly with his tongue? Did the Lord look upon his thoughts as being in the nature of words to Him though not to man? Is this where man first becomes an unbeliever?—in his heart, not in his head? And when he talks atheistically, is it a foolish heart speaking, and endeavoring to clamor down the voice of conscience? We think so.

If the affections were set upon truth and righteousness, the understanding would have no difficulty in settling the question of a present personal Deity, but as the heart dislikes the good and the right, it is no wonder that it desires to be rid of Elohim, who is the great moral Governor, the Patron of rectitude and the Punisher of iniquity. While men's hearts remain what they are, we must not be surprised at the prevalence of skepticism; a corrupt tree will bring forth corrupt fruit.

"Every man," says Dickson,[43] "so long as he lies unrenewed

43. David Dickson (1780–1842), clergyman

and unreconciled to God is nothing in effect but a madman." What wonder then if he raves? Such fools as those we are now dealing with are common to all time, and all countries; they grow without watering, and are found all the world over. The spread of mere intellectual enlightenment will not diminish their number, for since it is an affair of the heart, this folly and great learning will often dwell together. To answer skeptical objections will be labor lost until grace enters to make the mind willing to believe; fools can raise more objections in an hour than wise men can answer in seven years, indeed they find it humorous to set stools for wise men to stumble over.

Let the preacher aim at the heart, and preach the all-conquering love of Jesus, and he will by God's grace win more doubters to the faith of the Gospel than any hundred of those who reason and only direct their arguments to the head. *The fool hath said in his heart, There is no God.* So monstrous is the assertion that the man hardly dared to put it as a positive statement, but went very near to doing so. Calvin seems to regard this saying, "no God," as hardly amounting to a syllogism,[44] scarcely reaching to a positive, dogmatical declaration; but Dr. Alexander[45] clearly shows that it does. It is not merely the wish of the sinner's corrupt nature, and the hope of his rebellious heart, but he manages after a fashion to bring himself to assert it, and at certain seasons he thinks that he believes it. It is a solemn reflection that some who worship God with their lips may in their hearts be saying, "no God."

It is worthy of observation that he does not say there is no Jehovah, but there is no Elohim; Deity in the abstract is not so much the object of attack, as the covenant, personal,

---

44. Deductive reasoning
45. Dr. William Lindsay Alexander (1808–1884), English clergyman.

ruling and governing presence of God in the world. God as ruler, lawgiver, worker, Savior, is the butt at which the arrows of human wrath are shot. How impotent the malice! How mad the rage which raves and foams against Him in whom we live and move and have our being! How horrible the insanity which leads a man who owes his all to God to cry out, "No God"! How terrible the depravity which makes the whole race adopt this as their hearts' desire, "no God!"

They are corrupt. This refers to all men, and we have the warrant of the Holy Ghost for so saying; see the third chapter of the epistle to the Romans. Where there is enmity to God, there is deep, inward depravity of mind. The words are rendered by eminent critics in an active sense, "they have done corruptly:" this may serve to remind us that sin is not only in our nature passively as the source of evil, but we ourselves actively fan the flame and corrupt ourselves, making that blacker still which was black as darkness itself already. We rivet our own chains by habit and continuance.

They have done abominable works. When men begin with renouncing the Most High God, who shall tell where they will end? When the Master's eyes are put out, what will not the servants do? Observe the state of the world before the flood, as portrayed in Genesis 6:12, and remember that human nature is unchanged. He who would see a terrible photograph of the world without God must read that most painful of all inspired Scriptures, the first chapter of the epistle to the Romans. Learned Hindus have confessed that the description is literally correct in Hindustan at the present moment; and were it not for the restraining grace of God, it would be so in England. Alas, it is even here but too correct a picture of things which are done of men in secret. Things loathsome to God and man are sweet to some palates.

There is none that doeth good. Sins of omission must abound where transgressions are rife. Those who do the things which they ought not to have done, are sure to leave undone, those things which they ought to have done. What a picture of our race is this! Save only where grace reigns, there is none that doeth good; humanity, fallen and debased, is a desert without an oasis, a night without a star, a dunghill without a jewel, a hell without a bottom.

Psalm 14:2 *The* LORD *looked down from heaven upon the children of men, to see if there were any that did understand, and seek God.*

EXPOSITION: **Verse 2.** *The Lord looked down from heaven upon the children of men.* As from a watchtower, or other elevated place of observation, the Lord is represented as gazing intently upon men. He will not punish blindly, nor like a tyrant command an indiscriminate massacre because a rumor of rebellion has come up to His ears. What condescending interest and impartial justice are here imaged! The case of Sodom, visited before it was overthrown, illustrates the careful manner in which Divine Justice beholds the sin before it avenges it, and searches out the righteous that they perish not with the guilty. Behold then the eyes of Omniscience ransacking the globe, and prying among every people and nation, to see if there were any that did understand and seek God. He who is looking down knows the good, is quick to discern it, would be delighted to find it; but as He views all the unregenerate children of men His search is fruitless, for of all the race of Adam, no unrenewed soul is other than an enemy to God and goodness. The objects of the Lord's search are not wealthy men, great men, or learned men; these, with all they can offer, cannot meet the demands of the great Governor: at the same time, He is not looking for superlative eminence in virtue, He seeks for any that understand themselves, their state, their duty, their destiny, their happiness; He looks for any that seek God, who, if there be a God, are willing and anxious to find Him out.

Surely this is not too great a matter to expect; for if men have not yet known God, if they have any right understanding, they will seek Him. Alas! even this low degree of good is not to be found even by Him who sees all things: but men love the hideous negation of "No God," and with their backs to their Creator, who is the sun of their life, they journey into the dreary region of unbelief and alienation, which is a land of darkness as darkness itself, and of the shadow of death without any order and where the light is as darkness.

Psalm 14:3 *They are all gone aside, they are all together become filthy: there is none that doeth good, no, not one.*

EXPOSITION: Verse 3. *They are all gone aside.* Without exception, all men have apostatized from the Lord their Maker, from His laws, and from all the eternal principles of right. Like stubborn heifers they have sturdily refused to receive the yoke, like errant sheep they have found a gap and left the right field. The original speaks of the race as a whole, as a totality; and humanity as a whole has become depraved in heart and defiled in life.

They are altogether become filthy; as a whole they are spoiled and soured like corrupt leaven, or, as some put it, they have become putrid and even stinking. The only reason why we do not more clearly see this foulness is because we are accustomed to it, just as those who work daily among offensive odors at last cease to smell them. The miller does not observe the noise of his own mill, and we are slow to discover our own ruin and depravity. But are there no special cases, are all men sinful? "Yes," says the psalmist, in a manner not to be mistaken, "they are." He has put it positively, he repeats it negatively, *There is none that doeth good, no, not one.* The Hebrew phrase is an utter denial concerning any mere man that he of himself does good. What can be more sweeping? This is the verdict of the all-seeing Jehovah, who cannot exaggerate or mistake. As if no hope of finding a solitary specimen of a good man among the unrenewed human family might be harbored for an instant. The Holy Spirit is not content with saying all and altogether, but adds the crushing threefold negative, "none, no, not one." What say the opponents to the doctrine of natural depravity to this? Rather what do we feel concerning it? Do we not confess that we by nature are corrupt, and do we not bless the sovereign grace which has renewed us in the spirit of our minds, that sin may no more have dominion over us, but that grace may rule and reign?

Psalm 14:4 *Have all the workers of iniquity no knowledge? who eat up my people as they eat bread, and call not upon the LORD.*

EXPOSITION: Verse 4. Hatred of God and corruptness of life are the motive forces which produce persecution. Men who having no saving knowledge of divine things, enslave themselves to become workers of iniquity, have no heart to cry to the Lord for deliverance, but seek to amuse themselves with devouring the poor and despised people of God.

It is hard bondage to be a worker of iniquity; a worker at the galleys. A worker in the mines of Siberia is not more truly degraded and wretched; the toil is hard and the reward dreadful: those who have no knowledge choose such slavery, but those who are taught of God cry to be rescued from it. The same ignorance which keeps men bondsmen to evil makes them hate the freeborn sons of God. Therefore, they seek to eat them up as they eat bread—daily, ravenously, as though it were an ordinary, usual, everyday matter to oppress the saints of God. As pikes in a pond eat up little fish, as eagles prey on smaller birds, as wolves rend the sheep of the pasture, so sinners naturally and as a matter of course, persecute, malign, and mock the followers of the Lord Jesus. While preying upon the saints of God they reject all prayer completely, for how could they hope to be heard while their hands are full of blood?

Psalm 14:5 *There were they in great fear: for God is in the generation of the righteous.*

EXPOSITION: Verse 5. Oppressors do not have it all their own way; they have their fits of trembling and their appointed seasons of overthrow. There–where they denied God and hectored against His people; there—where they thought of peace and safety, they were made to quail. *There where they* loudmouthed—these very loud-mouthed, iron-handed, proud-hearted like Nimrods and Herod, those heady, high-minded sinners—were *in great fear.* A panic terror seized them: "they feared a fear," as the Hebrew puts it; an indefinable, horrible, mysterious dread crept over them. The most hardened of men have their periods when conscience casts them into a cold sweat of alarm. As cowards are cruel, so all cruel men are cowards at heart. The ghost of past sin is a terrible specter to haunt any man, and though unbelievers may boast as loudly as they will, a sound is in their ears which makes them ill at ease.

For God is in the generation of the righteous. This makes the company of godly men irksome to the wicked because they perceive that God is with them. Shut their eyes as they may, they cannot but perceive the image of God in the character of His truly gracious people, nor can they fail to see that He works for their deliverance. Like Haman, they instinctively feel a trembling when they see God's Mordecai's.

Even though the saint may be in a lowly position, mourning at the gate where the persecutor rejoices in state, the sinner feels the influence of the believer's true nobility and quails before it, for God is there. Let scoffers beware, for they persecute the Lord Jesus when they molest His people; the union is very close between God and His people, it amounts to a mysterious indwelling, *for God is in the generation of the righteous.*

Psalm 14:6 *Ye have shamed the counsel of the poor, because the LORD is his refuge.*

EXPOSITION: Verse 6. Notwithstanding their real cowardice, the wicked put on the lion's skin and lord it over the Lord's poor ones. Though fools themselves, they mock at the truly wise as if the folly were on their side; but this is what might be expected, for how should brutish minds appreciate excellence, and how can those who have owl's eyes admire the sun? The special point and butt of their jest seems to be the confidence of the godly in their Lord. What can your God do for you now? Who is that God who can deliver out of our hand? Where is the reward of all your praying and beseeching?

Taunting questions of this sort they thrust into the faces of weak but gracious souls, and tempt them to feel ashamed of their refuge. Let us not be laughed out of our confidence by them, let us scorn their scorning and defy their jeers; we shall need to wait but a little, and then the Lord our refuge will avenge His own elect, and ease himself of His adversaries, who once made so light of Him and of His people.

Psalm 14:7 *Oh that the salvation of Israel were come out of Zion! when the LORD bringeth back the captivity of his people, Jacob shall rejoice, and Israel shall be glad.*

EXPOSITION: **Verse 7.** Natural enough is this closing prayer, for what would so effectually convince atheists, overthrow persecutors, stay sin, and secure the godly, as the manifest appearance of Israel's great Salvation? The coming of Messiah was the desire of the godly in all ages, and though He has already come with a sin offering to purge away iniquity, we look for Him to come a second time, to come without a sin offering unto salvation.

O that these weary years would have an end! Why does He tarry so long? He knows that sin abounds and that His people are down trodden; why does He not come to the rescue? His glorious advent will restore His ancient people from literal captivity, and His *spiritual* seed from *spiritual* sorrow. Wrestling Jacob and prevailing Israel shall alike rejoice before Him when He is revealed as their salvation. O that He would soon come! What happy, holy, halcyon, heavenly days should we then see! But let us not count Him slack, for behold He comes, He comes quickly! Blessed are all they that wait for Him.

PSALM 15
PSALM 15:1–PSALM 15:5

Psalm 15:1 *Lord, who shall abide in thy tabernacle? who shall dwell in thy holy hill?*

EXPOSITION: **Verse 1.** The question, Jehovah, High and holy One: who shall be permitted to have fellowship with you? The heavens are not pure in your sight, and you charge your angels with folly, who then of mortal mold shall dwell with you, for you are a dread consuming fire? A sense of the glory of the Lord and of the holiness which becomes His house, His service, and His attendants, excites the humble mind to ask the solemn question before us. Where angels bow with veiled faces, how shall man be able to worship at all? The unthinking many imagine it to be a very easy matter to approach the Most High, and when professedly engaged in His worship they have no questionings of heart as to their fitness for it; but truly humbled souls often shrink under a sense of utter unworthiness, and would not dare to approach the throne of the God of Holiness if it were not for Him, our Lord, our Advocate, who can abide in the heavenly temple, because His righteousness endures forever. *Who shall abide in thy tabernacle?* Who shall be admitted to be one of the household of God, to sojourn under His roof and enjoy communion with himself?

Who shall dwell in thy holy hill? Who shall be a citizen of Zion, and an inhabitant of the heavenly Jerusalem? The question is raised, because it is a question. All men have not this privilege, no; even among professors there are aliens from the commonwealth, who have no secret communication with God. On the grounds of law no mere man can dwell with God, for there is not one upon Earth who answers to the just requirements mentioned in the succeeding verses. The questions in the text are asked of the Lord, as if none but the Infinite Mind could answer them so as to satisfy the unquiet conscience. We must know from the Lord of the tabernacle what the qualifications for His service are, and when we have been taught of Him, we shall clearly see that only our spotless Lord Jesus, and those who are conformed unto His image, can ever stand with acceptance before the Majesty on high.

Impertinent curiosity frequently desires to know who and how many shall be saved; if those who ask the question, *Who shall dwell in thy holy hill?* would make it a soul-searching enquiry in reference to themselves they would act much more wisely. Members of the visible Church, which is God's tabernacle of worship, and hill of eminence, should diligently see to it that they have the preparation of heart which fits them to be residents of the house of God. Without the wedding dress of righteousness in Christ Jesus, we have no right to sit at the banquet of communion. Without uprightness of walk we are not fit for the imperfect Church on Earth, and certainly we must not hope to enter the perfect Church above.

Psalm 15:2 *He that that walketh uprightly, and worketh righteousness, and speaketh the truth in his heart.*

EXPOSITION: **Verse 2.** The Answer: The Lord in answer to the question informs us by His Holy Spirit of the character of the man who alone can dwell in His holy hill. In perfection this holiness is found only in the Man of Sorrows, but in a measure it is wrought in all His people by the Holy

Ghost. Faith and the graces of the Spirit are not mentioned, because this is a description of outward character, and where fruits are found the root may not be seen, but it is surely there. Observe the accepted man's walk, work, and word.

He that walketh uprightly, he keeps himself erect as those do who traverse high ropes; if they lean on one side over they must go, or as those who carry precious but fragile ware in baskets on their heads, who lose all if they lose their perpendicular. True believers do not cringe as flatterers, wriggle as serpents, bend double as earth grubbers, or crook on one side as those who have sinister aims; they have the strong backbone of the vital principle of grace within, and being themselves upright, they are able to walk uprightly. Walking is of far more importance than talking. He only is right who is upright in walk and downright in honesty.

And worketh righteousness. His faith shows itself by good works, and therefore is no dead faith. God's house is a hive for workers, not a nest for drones. Those who rejoice that everything is done for them by another, even the Lord Jesus, and therefore hate legality, are the best doers in the world upon gospel principles. If we are not positively serving the Lord, and doing His holy will to the best of our power, we may seriously debate our interest in divine things, for trees which bear no fruit must be hewn down and cast into the fire.

And speaketh the truth in his heart. The fool in the last psalm spoke falsely in his heart; observe both here and elsewhere in the two psalms, the striking contrast. Saints not only desire to love and speak truth with their lips, but they seek to be true within; they will not lie even in the closet of their hearts, for God is there to listen; they scorn double meanings, evasions, equivocations, white lies, flatteries, and deceptions.

Though truths, like roses, have thorns about them, good men wear them in their bosoms. Our heart must be the sanctuary and refuge of truth, for if it were banished from all the world and hunted for among men; we must, at all risk, entertain the angel of truth, for truth is God's daughter. We must be careful that the heart is really fixed and settled in principle, for tenderness of conscience toward truthfulness; like the bloom on a peach, needs gentle handling, and once lost it is hard to regain it. Jesus was the mirror of sincerity and holiness. Oh, to be more and more fashioned after His similitude!

Psalm 15:3 *He that backbiteth not with his tongue, nor doeth evil to his neighbour, nor taketh up a reproach against his neighbour.*

EXPOSITION: Verse 3. After the positive comes the negative. *He that backbiteth not with his tongue.* Here is a sinful way of backbiting with the heart when we think too critically of a neighbor, but it is the tongue which does the mischief. Some men's tongues bite more than their teeth. The tongue is not steel, but it cuts, and its wounds are very hard to heal; its worst wounds are not with its edge to our face, but with its back when our head is turned. Under the law, a night hawk was an unclean bird, and its human image is abominable everywhere. All slanderers are the devil's bellows to blow up contention, but those are the worst which blow at the back of the fire.

Nor doeth evil to his neighbour. He who bridles his tongue will not give a license to his hand. Loving our neighbor as ourselves will make us jealous of his good name, careful not to injure his estate, or by ill example to corrupt his character.

Nor taketh up a reproach against his neighbour. He is a fool if not a knave who picks up stolen goods and harbors them; in slander as well as robbery, the receiver is as bad as the thief. If there were not gratified hearers of ill reports, there would be an end of the trade of spreading them. The English Puritan, John Trapp, says in his commentary: "the tale bearer carrieth the devil in his tongue, and the tale hearer carries the devil in his ear." The original may be translated, "endureth;" implying that it is a sin to endure or tolerate tale-bearers.

"Show that man out!" we should say of a drunkard, yet it is very questionable if his unmanly behavior will do us so much mischief as the tale-bearers' insinuating story. "Call for a policeman!" we say if we see a thief at his business; should we feel no indignation when we hear a gossip at their work? Mad dog! mad dog!! is a terrible hue and cry, but there are few curs whose bite is so dangerous as a busybody's tongue. Fire! fire!! is an alarming note, but the tale-bearer's tongue is set on fire of hell, and those who indulge it had better mend their manners, or they may find that there is fire in hell for unbridled tongues. Our Lord spoke evil of no man, but breathed a prayer for His foes; we must be like Him, or we shall never be with Him.

Psalm 15:4 *In whose eyes a vile person is contemned; but he honoureth them that fear the LORD. He that sweareth to his own hurt, and changeth not.*

EXPOSITION: **Verse 4.** *In whose eyes a vile person is contemned; but he honoureth them that fear the Lord.* We must be as honest in paying respect as in paying our bills. Honor to whom honor is due. To all good men we owe a debt of honor, and we have no right to hand over what is their due to vile persons who happen to be in high places. When base men are in office, it is our duty to respect the office; but we cannot so violate our consciences as to do otherwise than contemn the men; and on the other hand, when true saints are in poverty and distress, we must sympathize with their afflictions and honor the men none the less. We may honor the roughest cabinet for the sake of the jewels, but we must not prize false gems because of their setting. A sinner in a gold chain and silken robes is no more to be compared with a saint in rags than a rush light in a silver candlestick with the sun behind a cloud. The proverb says, that "ugly women, finely dressed, are the uglier for it," and so mean men in high estate are the more mean because of it.

He that sweareth to his own hurt, and changeth not. Scriptural saints under the New Testament rule "swear not at all," but their word is as good as an oath: those men of God who think it right to swear, are careful and prayerful lest they should even seem to overshoot the mark. When engagements have been entered into which turn out to be unprofitable, *the saints are men of honour still.* Our blessed Surety swore to His own hurt, but how gloriously He stood to His suretyship! What a comfort to us that He changes not, and what an example to us to be scrupulously and precisely exact in fulfilling our covenants with others! The most far-seeing trader may enter into engagements which turn out to be serious losses, but whatsoever else he loses, if he keeps his honor, his losses will be bearable; if that be lost all is lost.

Psalm 15:5 *He that putteth not out his money to usury, nor taketh reward against the innocent. He that doeth these things shall never be moved.*

EXPOSITION: **Verse 5.** *He that putteth not out his money to usury.* Usury was and is hateful both to God and man. That a lender should share with the borrower in gains made by his money is most fitting and proper; but that the man of property should eat up the poor wretch who unfortunately obtained a loan of him is abominable. Those who grind poor tradesmen, needy widows, and such like, by charging them interest at intolerable rates, will find that their gold and their silver are cankered. The man who shall ascend into the hill of the Lord must shake off this sin as Paul shook the viper into the fire.

Nor taketh reward against the innocent. Bribery is a sin both in the giver and the receiver. It was frequently practiced in Eastern courts of justice; that form of it is now under our excellent judges almost an unheard of thing; yet the sin survives in various forms, which the reader needs not that we should mention; and under every shape it is loathsome to the true man of God. He remembers that Jesus instead of taking reward against the innocent died for the guilty.

He that doeth these things shall never be moved. No storm shall tear him from his foundations, drag him from his anchorage, or uproot him from his place. Like the Lord Jesus, whose dominion is everlasting, the true Christian shall never lose his crown. He shall not only be on Zion, but like Zion, fixed and firm. He shall dwell in the tabernacle of the Most High, and neither death nor judgment shall remove him from his place of privilege and blessedness.

Let us therefore, take ourselves to prayer and self-examination, for this psalm is as fire for the gold, and as a furnace for silver. Can we endure its testing power?

PSALM 16
PSALM 16:1–PSALM 16:11

Psalm 16:1 *Preserve me, O God: for in thee do I put my trust.*

EXPOSITION: Verse 1. *Preserve me,* keep, or save me, or as Horsley[46] thinks, "guard me," even as bodyguards surround their monarch, or as shepherds protect their flocks. Tempted in all points like as we are, the manhood of Jesus needed to be preserved from the power of evil; and though in itself pure, the Lord Jesus did not confide in that purity of nature, but as an example to His followers, looked to the Lord, His God, for preservation. One of the great names of God is *"the Preserver of men,"* [Job 7:20] and this gracious office the Father exercised towards our Mediator and Representative. It had been promised to the Lord Jesus in express words, that He should be preserved in Isaiah 49:7a–8a, *Thus saith the Lord, the Redeemer of Israel and his Holy One, to him whom man despiseth, to him whom the nation abhorreth, I will preserve thee, and give thee for a covenant of the people.*

This promise was to the letter fulfilled, both by providential deliverance and sustaining power, in the case of our Lord. Being preserved himself, He is able to restore the preserved of Israel, for we are *preserved in Christ Jesus and called* [See Jude 1:1.]. As one with Him, the elect were preserved in His preservation, and we may view this mediatorial supplication as the petition of the Great High Priest for all those who are in Him. The intercession recorded in John 17:1–26 is but an

---

46. Samuel Horsley (1733–1806), English clergyman and author.

175

amplification of this cry, *Holy Father, keep through thine own name those whom thou hast given me, that they may be one, as we are.* When He says, *preserve me,* He means His members, His mystical body, himself, and all in Him.

But while we rejoice in the fact that the Lord Jesus used this prayer for His members, we must not forget that He employed it most surely for himself; He had so emptied himself, and so truly taken upon Him the form of a servant, that as man He needed divine keeping even as we do, and often cried unto the strong One for strength. Frequently on the mountaintop He breathed forth this desire, and on one occasion in almost the same words, He publicly prayed, *Father, save me from this hour* (John 12:27). If Jesus looked out of himself for protection, how much more must we, His erring followers, do so!

O God. The word for God here used is El, by which name the Lord Jesus, when under a sense of great weakness, as for instance when upon the Cross, addressed the Mighty God, the Omnipotent Helper of His people. We, too, may turn to El, the Omnipotent One, in all hours of peril, with the confidence that He who heard the strong crying and tears of our faithful High Priest is both able and willing to bless us in Him. It is well to study the name and character of God, so that in our straits we may know how and by what title to address our Father who is in Heaven. For in you do I put my trust, or, I have taken shelter in you. As chickens run beneath the hen, so do I take myself to you. You are my great overshadowing Protector, and I have taken refuge beneath your strength. This is a potent argument in pleading, and our Lord knew not only how to use it with God, but how to yield to its power when wielded by others upon himself.

According to thy faith be it done unto thee [Matthew 8:13] is a great rule of Heaven in dispensing favor, and when we can sincerely declare that we exercise faith in the Mighty God with regard to the mercy which we seek, we may rest assured that our plea will prevail. Faith, like the sword of Saul, never returns empty; it overcomes Heaven when held in the hand of prayer. As the Savior prayed, so let us pray, and as He became more than a conqueror, so shall we also through Him; let us when buffeted by storms right bravely cry to the Lord as He did: *in thee do I put my trust.*

Psalm 16:2 *O my soul, thou hast said unto the* LORD, *Thou art my Lord: my goodness extendeth not to thee.*

EXPOSITION: **Verse 2.** *O my soul, thou hast said unto the Lord, Thou art my Lord.* In His inmost heart the Lord Jesus bowed himself to do service to His Heavenly Father, and before the throne of Jehovah His soul vowed allegiance to the Lord for our sakes. We are like Him when our soul, truly and constantly in the presence of the heart searching God, declares her full consent to the rule and government of the Infinite Jehovah, saying, *Thou art my Lord.*

To avow this with the lip is little, but for the soul to say it, especially in times of trial, is a gracious evidence of spiritual health; to profess it before men is a small matter, but to declare it before Jehovah himself is of far more consequence. This sentence may also be viewed as the utterance of appropriating faith, laying hold upon the Lord by personal covenant and enjoyment; in this sense may it be our daily song in the house of our pilgrimage.

My goodness extendeth not to thee. The work of our Lord Jesus was not needful on account of any necessity in the Divine Being. Jehovah would have been inconceivably glorious had the human race perished, and had no atonement been offered. Although the life work and death agony of the

Son did reflect unparalleled luster upon every attribute of God, yet the Most Blessed and Infinitely Happy God stood in no need of the obedience and death of His Son; it was for our sakes that the work of redemption was undertaken, and not because of any lack or want on the part of the Most High. How modestly does the Savior here estimate His own goodness! What overwhelming reasons have we for imitating His humility! *If thou be righteous, what givest thou him? or what receiveth he of thine hand?* (Job 35:7).

Psalm 16:3 *But to the saints that are in the earth, and to the excellent, in whom is all my delight.*

EXPOSITION: **Verse 3.** *But to the saints that are in the earth.* These sanctified ones, although still upon the Earth, partake of the results of Jesus' mediatorial work, and by His goodness are made what they are. The peculiar people, zealous for good works, and hallowed to sacred service, are arrayed in the Savior's righteousness and washed in His blood, and so receive of the goodness treasured up in Him. These are the persons who are profited by the work of the man Christ Jesus; but that work added nothing to the nature, virtue, or happiness of God, who is blessed for evermore.

How much more forcibly is this true of us, poor unworthy servants not fit to be mentioned in comparison with the faithful Son of God! Our hope must ever be that haply some poor child of God may be served by us, for the Great Father can never need our aid. Well may we sing the verses of Dr. Isaac Watts' hymn, "Preserve Me Lord in Time of Need":

> Oft have my heart and tongue confessed
> How empty and how poor I am;
> My praise can never make thee blest,
> Nor add new glories to thy name.

> Yet, Lord, thy saints on earth may reap
> Some profit by the good we do;
> These are the company I keep,
> These are the choicest friends I know.

Poor believers are God's receivers, and have a warrant from the Crown to receive the revenue of our offerings in the King's name. Saints departed we cannot bless; even prayer for them is of no service; but while they are here we should, in practice, prove our love to them, even as our Master did, for they are the excellent of the Earth. Despite their infirmities, their Lord thinks highly of them, and reckons them to be as nobles among men. The title of "His Excellency" more properly belongs to the meanest saint than to the greatest governor. The true aristocracies are believers in Jesus. They are the only Right Honorable ones. Stars and Garters[47] are poor distinctions compared with the graces of the Spirit. He who knows them best says of them, *in whom is all my delight*. They are His Hephzibah and His Beulah land, and before all worlds His delights were with these chosen sons of men.

Their own opinion of themselves is far less than their Beloved's opinion of them; they count themselves to be less than nothing, yet He makes much of them, and sets His heart towards them. What wonders the eyes of Divine Love can see where the Hands of Infinite Power have been graciously at work. It was this quick-sighted affection which led Jesus to see in us a recompense for all His agony, and sustained Him under all His sufferings by the joy of redeeming us from going down into the pit.

---

47. The name "Star and Garter" originates from an abbreviation of the name of the insignia belonging to the Order of the Garter, which is the oldest British Order of Chivalry, founded by Edward III in 1348. The Order consists of the King and twenty-five knights drawn from men who have held public office, who have made a contribution to national life, or who have served the King personally.

Psalm 16:4 *Their sorrows shall be multiplied that hasten after another god: their drink offerings of blood will I not offer, nor take up their names into my lips.*

EXPOSITION: **Verse 4.** The same loving heart which opens towards the chosen people is fast closed against those who continue in their rebellion against God. Jesus hates all wickedness, and especially the high crime of idolatry. The text, while it shows our Lord's abhorrence of sin, shows also the sinner" greediness after it. Professed believers are often slow towards the true Lord, but sinners hasten after another god. They run like madmen where we creep like snails. Let their zeal rebuke our tardiness. Yet theirs is a case in which the more they hurry, the worse they speed, for their sorrows are multiplied by their diligence in multiplying their sins.

Matthew Henry pithily says, "They that multiply gods multiply griefs to themselves; for whosoever thinks one god too little, will find two too many, and yet hundreds not enough." The cruelties and hardships which men endure for their false gods is wonderful to contemplate; our missionary reports are a noteworthy comment on this passage; but perhaps our own experience is an equally vivid exposition; for when we have given our heart to idols, sooner or later we have had to smart for it.

Near the roots of our self-love all our sorrows lie, and when that idol is overthrown, the sting is gone from grief. Moses broke the golden calf and ground it to powder, and cast it into the water of which he made Israel drink, and so shall our cherished idols become bitter portions for us, unless we at once forsake them. Our Lord had no selfishness; He served but one Lord, and served Him only. As for those who turn aside from Jehovah, He was separate from them, bearing their reproach outside the camp. Sin and the Savior had no communion. He came to destroy, not to patronize or be allied with the works of the devil. Therefore, He refused the testimony of unclean spirits as to His divinity, for in nothing would He have fellowship with darkness. We should be careful above measure not to connect ourselves in the remotest degree with falsehood in religion; even the most solemn of Popish rites we must abhor.

Their drink offerings of blood will I not offer. The old proverb says, "It is not safe to eat at the devil's mess, though the spoon be never so long." The mere mentioning of ill names it is well to avoid—nor take up their names into my lips. If we allow poison upon the lip, it may before long penetrate into the body, and it is well to keep out of the mouth that which we would shut out from the heart.

If the Church wants to enjoy union with Christ, she must break all the bonds of impiety, and keep herself pure from all the pollutions of carnal will worship, which now pollute the service of God. Some professors are guilty of great sin in remaining in the communion of Popish churches, where God is as much dishonored as in Rome herself, only in a craftier manner.

Psalm 16:5 *The* LORD *is the portion of mine inheritance and of my cup: thou maintainest my lot.*

EXPOSITION: **Verse 5.** *The Lord is the portion of mine inheritance and of my cup.* With what confidence and bounding joy does Jesus turn to Jehovah, whom His soul possessed and delighted in! Content beyond measure with His portion in the Lord His God, He had not a single desire with which to hunt after other gods; His cup was full, and His heart was full too; even in His sorest sorrows He still laid hold with both His hands upon His Father, crying, "My God, my God." He had not so much as a thought of falling down to worship the prince of this world, although tempted with an *all these will I give thee* [See Matthew 4:9.].

We, too, can make our boast in the Lord; He is the meat and the drink of our souls. He is our portion, supplying all our necessities, and our cup yielding royal luxuries; our cup in this life, and our inheritance in the life to come. As children of the Father who is in Heaven, we inherit, by virtue of our joint heirship with Jesus, all the riches of the covenant of grace; and the portion which falls to us sets upon our table the bread of Heaven and the new wine of the kingdom. Who would not be satisfied with such dainty diet? Our shallow cup of sorrow we may well drain with resignation, since the deep cup of love stands side by side with it, and will never be empty.

Thou maintainest my lot. Some tenants have a covenant in their leases that they themselves shall maintain and uphold, but in our case Jehovah himself maintains our lot. Our Lord Jesus delighted in this truth, that the Father was on His side, and would maintain His right against all the wrongs of men. He knew that His elect would be reserved for Him, and that almighty power would preserve them as His lot and reward forever. Let us also be glad, because the Judge of all the Earth will vindicate our righteous cause.

Psalm 16:6 *The lines are fallen unto me in pleasant places; yea, I have a goodly heritage.*

EXPOSITION: Verse 6. Jesus found the way of obedience to lead into pleasant places. Notwithstanding all the sorrows which marred His countenance, He exclaimed, *Lo, I come; in the volume of the book it is written of me, I delight to do thy will, O my God: yea, thy law is within my heart* [Psalm 40:7–8]. It may seem strange, but while no other man was ever so thoroughly acquainted with grief, it is our belief that no other man ever experienced so much joy and delight in service, for no other served so faithfully and with such great results in view as His recompense of reward. The joy which was set before Him must have sent some of its beams of splendor down the rugged places where He *endured the cross, despising the shame* [Hebrews 12:2], and must have made them in some respects pleasant places to the generous heart of the Redeemer.

At any rate, we know that Jesus was well content with the blood-bought portion which the lines of electing love marked off as His spoil with the strong and His portion with the great. Therein He solaced himself on Earth, and delights himself in Heaven; and He asks no more *goodly heritage* than that His own beloved may be with Him where He is and behold His glory [See John 17:24.]. All the saints can use the language of this verse, and the more thoroughly they can enter into its contented, grateful, joyful spirit the better for themselves and the more glorious to their God.

Our Lord was poorer than we are, for He had *not where to lay his head* [Matthew 8:20], and yet when He mentioned His poverty He never used a word of murmuring; discontented spirits are as unlike Jesus as the croaking raven is unlike the cooing dove. Martyrs have been happy in dungeons. "From the delectable orchard of the Leonine prison the Italian martyr dated his letter, and the presence of God made the gridiron of Laurence pleasant to him." Mr. Greenham [48]was bold enough to say, "They never felt God's love, or tasted forgiveness of sin, who are discontented." Some divines think that discontent was the first sin, the rock which wrecked our race in paradise; certainly there can be no paradise where this evil spirit has power, its slime will poison all the flowers of the garden.

---

48. Richard Greenham (1535–1594), Elizabethan pastor in England

Psalm 16:7 *I will bless the* LORD, *who hath given me counsel: my reins also instruct me in the night seasons.*

EXPOSITION: **Verse 7.** *I will bless the Lord, who hath given me counsel.* Praise as well as prayer was presented to the Father by our Lord Jesus, and we are not truly His followers unless our resolve be, "I will bless the Lord." Jesus is called Wonderful, Counselor, but as man He spoke not of himself, but as His Father had taught Him. Read in confirmation of this, John 7:16; 8:28; far-seeing 12:49–50; and the prophecy concerning Him in Isaiah 11:2–3. It was our Redeemer's desire to always look to His Father for direction, and having received it, He blessed Him for giving Him counsel. It would be well for us if we would follow His example of lowliness, cease from trusting in our own understanding, and seek to be guided by the Spirit of God.

My reins also instruct me in the night seasons. By the reins understand the inner man, the affections and feelings. The communion of the soul with God brings to it an inner spiritual wisdom which in still seasons is revealed to it. Our Redeemer spent many nights alone upon the mountain, and we may readily conceive that together with His fellowship with Heaven, He carried on a profitable commerce with himself; reviewing His experience, forecasting His work, and considering His position. Great generals fight their battles in their own mind long before the trumpet sounds, and so did our Lord win our battle on His knees before He gained it on the Cross. It is a gracious habit after taking counsel from above to take counsel within. Wise men see more with their eyes shut by night than fools can see by day with their eyes open. He who learns from God and so gets the seed, will soon find wisdom within himself growing in the garden of his soul; thine ears *shall hear a voice behind thee, saying, This is the way, walk ye in it, when ye turn to the right hand*

and when ye turn to the left [Isaiah 30:21].The night season which the sinner chooses for his sins is the hallowed hour of quiet when believers hear the soft still voices of Heaven, and of the heavenly life within themselves.

Psalm 16:8 *I have set the LORD always before me: because he is at my right hand, I shall not be moved.*

EXPOSITION: Verse 8. The fear of death at one time cast its dark shadow over the soul of the Redeemer, and we read that, *he was heard in that he feared* [See Hebrews 5:7.]. There appeared unto Him an angel, strengthening Him; perhaps the heavenly messenger reassured Him of His glorious resurrection as His people's surety, and of the eternal joy into which He would admit the flock redeemed by blood. Then hope shone full upon our Lord's soul, and, as recorded in these verses, He surveyed the future with holy confidence because He had a continued eye to Jehovah, and enjoyed His perpetual presence. He felt that, thus sustained, He could never be driven from His life's grand design; nor was He, for He stayed not His hand until He could say, *It is finished* [John 19:30]. What an infinite mercy was this for us! In this immovableness, caused by simple faith in the divine help, Jesus is to be viewed as our exemplar; to recognize the presence of the Lord is the duty of every believer;

I have set the Lord always before me; and to trust the Lord as our champion and guard is the privilege of every saint; *because he is at my right hand, I shall not be moved.* The apostle translates this passage, *I foresaw the Lord always before my face* (Acts 2:25); the eye of Jesus' faith could discern beforehand the continuance of divine support to His suffering Son, in such a degree that He would never be moved from the accomplishment of His purpose of redeeming His people. By the power of God at His right hand He foresaw that He would smite through all who rose up against Him, and on that power He placed the firmest reliance.

Psalm 16:9 *Therefore my heart is glad, and my glory rejoiceth: my flesh also shall rest in hope.*

EXPOSITION: Verse 9. He clearly foresaw that He must die, for He speaks of His flesh resting, and of His soul in the abode of separate spirits; death was full before His face, or He would not have mentioned corruption; but such was His devout reliance upon His God, that He sang over the tomb, and rejoiced in vision of the sepulcher. He knew that the visit of His soul to Sheol, or the invisible world of disembodied spirits, would be a very short one, and that His body in a very brief space would leave the grave, uninjured by its sojourn there; all this made Him say, my heart is glad, and moved His tongue, the glory of His frame, to rejoice in God, the strength of His salvation. Oh, for such holy faith in the prospect of trial and of death! It is the work of faith, not merely to create a peace which passes all understanding, but to fill the heart full of gladness until the tongue, which, as the organ of an intelligent creature, is our glory, bursts forth in notes of harmonious praise. Faith gives us living joy, and bestows dying rest. My flesh also shall rest in hope.

Psalm 16:10 *For thou wilt not leave my soul in hell; neither wilt thou suffer thine Holy One to see corruption.*

EXPOSITION: Verse 10. Our Lord Jesus was not disappointed in His hope. He declared His Father's faithfulness in the words, *For thou wilt not leave my soul in hell,* and that faithfulness was proven on the resurrection morning. Among the departed and disembodied Jesus was not left; He had believed in the resurrection, and He received it on the third day, when His body rose in glorious life, according as He had said in joyous confidence, *neither wilt thou suffer thine Holy One to see corruption.*

Into the outer prison of the grave His body might go, but into the inner prison of corruption He could not enter. He who in soul and body was preeminently God's Holy One, was loosed from the pains of death, because it was not possible that He would be held by it.

This is noble encouragement to all the saints; die they must, but rise they shall, and though in their case they shall see corruption, yet they shall rise to everlasting life. Christ's resurrection is the cause, the earnest, the guarantee, and the emblem of the rising of all His people. Let them, therefore, go to their graves as to their beds, resting their flesh among the clods as they now do upon their couches.

> Since Jesus is mine, I will not fear undressing,
> But gladly put off these garments of clay;
> To die in the Lord is a covenant blessing,
> Since Jesus to glory through death led the way.[49]

Wretched will that man be who, when the Philistines of death invade his soul, shall find that, like Saul, he is forsaken of God; but blessed is he who has the Lord at his right hand, for he shall fear no ill, but shall look forward to an eternity of bliss.

Psalm 16:11 *Thou wilt shew me the path of life: in thy presence is fulness of joy; at thy right hand there are pleasures for evermore.*

EXPOSITION: Verse 11. *Thou wilt shew me the path of life.* To Jesus first this way was shown, for He is the first

---

49. Note left by a dying child.

begotten from the dead, the firstborn of every creature. He himself opened up the way through His own flesh, and then trod it as the forerunner of His own redeemed. The thought of being made the path of life to His people, gladdened the soul of Jesus.

In thy presence is fulness of joy. Christ being raised from the dead ascended into glory, to dwell in constant nearness to God, where joy is at its full forever: the foresight of this urged Him onward in His glorious but grievous toil. To bring His chosen to eternal happiness was the high ambition which inspired Him, and made Him wade through a sea of blood. O God, when a worldling's mirth has all expired, forever with Jesus may we dwell at your right hand, where there are pleasures for evermore; and meanwhile, may we have an earnest by tasting your love below. Joseph Trapp's note on the heavenly verse which closes the psalm is a sweet morsel, which may serve for a contemplation, and yield a foretaste of our inheritance. He writes,

> "Here is as much said as can be, but words are too weak to utter it. For quality there is in heaven joy and pleasures; for quantity, a fullness, a torrent whereat they drink without let or loathing; for constancy, it is at God's right hand, who is stronger than all, neither can any take us out of his hand; it is a constant happiness without intermission: and for perpetuity it is for evermore. Heaven's joys are without measure, mixture, or end."

PSALM 17
PSALM 17:1–PSALM 17:15

Psalm 17:1 *Hear the right, O Lord, attend unto my cry, give ear unto my prayer, that goeth not out of feigned lips.*

EXPOSITION: **Verse 1.** *Hear the right, O Lord.* He that has the worst cause makes the most noise; hence the oppressed soul is apprehensive that its voice may be drowned, and therefore pleads in this one verse for a hearing no less than three times. The troubled heart craves for the ear of the great Judge, persuaded that with Him to hear is to redress. If our God could not or would not hear us, our state would be deplorable indeed; and yet some who profess their Christianity set such small store by the mercy seat, that God does not hear them for the simple reason that they neglect to plead. Without the mercy seat we would always be defending our own cause and never going to God.

There is more fear that we will not hear the Lord than that the Lord will not hear us. *Hear the right;* it is well if our case is good in itself and can be urged as a right one, for right shall never be wronged by our righteous Judge; but if our suit is marred by our infirmities, it is a great privilege that we may make mention of the righteousness of our Lord Jesus, which is ever prevalent on high. Right has a voice which Jehovah always hears; and if my wrongs clamor against me with great force and fury, I will pray the Lord to hear that still louder and mightier voice of the right, and the rights of His dear Son. "Hear, O God, the Just One;" i.e., "hear the

Messiah," is a rendering adopted by Jerome, and admired by Bishop Horsley, whether correct or not as a translation, it is proper enough as a plea. Let the reader plead it at the throne of the righteous God, even when all other arguments are unavailing.

Attend unto my cry. This shows the vehemence and earnestness of the petitioner; he is no mere talker, he weeps and laments. Who can resist a cry? A real hearty, bitter, piteous cry, might almost melt a rock, there can be no fear of its prevalence with our heavenly Father. A cry is our earliest utterance, and in many ways the most natural of human sounds; if our prayer should like the infant's cry be more natural than intelligent, and more earnest than elegant, it will be none the less eloquent with God. There is a mighty power in a child's cry to prevail with a parent's heart.

Give ear unto my prayer. Some repetitions are not vain. The reduplication here used is neither superstition nor tautology, but is like the repeated blow of a hammer hitting the same nail on the head to fix it the more effectually, or the continued knocking of a beggar at the gate that cannot be denied alms.

That goeth not out of feigned lips. Sincerity is a *sine qua non* [prerequisite] in prayer. Lips of deceit are detestable to man and much more to God. In communion so hallowed as that of prayer, hypocrisy even in the remotest degree is as fatal as it is foolish. Hypocritical piety is double iniquity. He who would feign and flatter had better try his craft with a fool like himself, for to deceive the all-seeing One is as impossible as to take the moon in a net, or to lead the sun into a snare. He who would deceive God is himself already most grossly deceived. Our sincerity in prayer has no merit in it, any more than the earnestness of a mendicant [beggar] in the street; but at the same time the Lord has regard to it, through Jesus, and will not long refuse His ear to an honest and fervent petitioner.

Psalm 17:2 *Let my sentence come forth from thy presence; let thine eyes behold the things that are equal.*

EXPOSITION: **Verse 2.** *Let my sentence come forth from your presence.* The psalmist has now grown bold by the strengthening influence of prayer, and he now entreats the Judge of all the Earth to give sentence upon His case. He has been libeled, basely and maliciously libeled; and having brought his action before the highest court, he, like an innocent man, has no desire to escape the enquiry, but even invites and sues for judgment. He does not ask for secrecy, but wants the result to come forth to the world. He wants the sentence pronounced and executed without delay.

In some matters we may venture to be as bold as this; but unless we can plead something better than our own supposed innocence, it would be a terrible presumption to challenge the judgment of a sin hating God. With Jesus as our complete and all glorious righteousness we need not fear, though the Day of Judgment may begin at once, and hell open her mouth at our feet, but might joyfully prove the truth of our hymn writer's holy boast—

> Bold shall I stand in that great day;
> For who aught to my charge shall lay?
> While, through thy blood, absolved I am,
> From sin's tremendous curse and shame.

Let thine eyes behold the things that are equal. Believers do not desire any other judge than God, or to be excused from judgment, or even to be judged on principles of partiality. No; our hope does not lie in the prospect of favoritism from God, and the consequent suspension of His law; we expect to be judged on the same principals as other men, and through the blood and righteousness of our Redeemer we shall pass the ordeal unscathed. The Lord will weigh us in the scales of justice fairly and justly. He will not use false weights to permit us to escape, but with the sternest equity those balances will be used upon us as well as upon others; and with our blessed Lord Jesus as our all in all we tremble not, for we shall not be found wanting. In David's case, he felt his cause to be so right that he simply desired the Divine eyes to rest upon the matter, and he was confident that equity would give him all that he needed.

Psalm 17:3 *Thou hast proved mine heart; thou hast visited me in the night; thou hast tried me, and shalt find nothing; I am purposed that my mouth shall not transgress.*

EXPOSITION: **Verse 3.** *Thou hast proved mine heart.* Like Peter, David uses the argument, *Thou knowest all things, thou knowest that I love thee* [John 21:17]. It is a most assuring thing to be able to appeal at once to the Lord, and call upon our Judge to be a witness for our defense. *Beloved, if our heart condemn us not, then have we confidence toward God* [1 John 3:21].

Thou hast visited me in the night. As if he had said, "Lord, you have entered my house at all hours; and you have seen me when no one else was near; you have come upon me unawares and marked my unrestrained actions, and you know whether or not I am guilty of the crimes laid at my door." Happy is the man who can remember the omniscient eye, and the omnipresent visitor, and find comfort in the remembrance. We hope we have had our midnight visits from our Lord, and truly they are sweet; so sweet that the recollection of them sets us longing for more of such condescending communing. Lord, if indeed, we were hypocrites, would we have had such fellowship, or feel such hungering after a renewal of it?

Thou hast tried me, and shalt find nothing. Surely the psalmist means nothing hypocritical or wicked in the sense in which his slanderers accused him; for if the Lord would put the best of His people into the crucible, the dross would be a fearful sight, and would make penitence open her sluices wide. Assayers very soon detect the presence of alloy, and when the chief of all assayers shall, at the last, say of us He has found nothing, it will be a glorious hour indeed—*They are without fault before the throne of God* [See Revelation 14:5.]. Even here, as viewed in our covenant Head, the Lord sees no sin in Jacob, nor perverseness in Israel; even the all detecting glance of Omniscience can see no flaw where the great Substitute covers all with beauty and perfection.

I am purposed that my mouth shall not transgress. Oh those sad lips of ours! We would need goal-directed sense purpose if we would keep them from exceeding their bounds. The number of diseases of the tongue is as many as the diseases of all the rest of the man put together, and they are more inveterate [habitual]. Hands and feet one may bind, but who can fetter the lips? Iron bands may hold a madman, but what chains can restrain the tongue? It needs more than a purpose to keep this nimble offender within its proper range. Lion-taming and serpent-charming are not to be mentioned in the same category as tongue-taming, for the tongue can no man tame. Those who have to suffer from the falsehoods of others should be all the more jealous over themselves. Perhaps this led the psalmist to register this holy resolution; and, furthermore, he may have intended thereby to aver [affirm] that if he had said too much in his own defense, it was not intentional, for he desired in all respects to tune his lips to the sweet and simple music of truth. Notwithstanding all this David was slandered, as if to show us that the purest innocence will be stained by malice. There is no sunshine without a shadow, no ripe fruit not pecked by the birds.

Psalm 17:4 *Concerning the works of men, by the word of thy lips I have kept me from the paths of the destroyer.*

EXPOSITION: **Verse 4.** *Concerning the works of men.* While we are in the midst of men we will have their works before our eyes and in our ears on a daily basis, and we will be compelled to keep a corner of our diary headed "concerning the works of men." To be quite clear from the dead works of carnal humanity is the devout desire of souls who are quickened by the Holy Spirit.

By the word of thy lips I have kept me from the paths of the destroyer. He had kept the highway of Scripture, and not chosen the paths of malice. We would imitate the example of the worst of men if the grace of God did not use the Word of God as the great preservative from evil. The paths of the destroyer have often tempted us; we have been prompted to become destroyers too, when we have been sorely provoked, and resentment has grown warm. But we have remembered the example of our Lord, who would not call fire from Heaven upon His enemies, but meekly prayed, *Father, forgive them* [Luke 23:34].

All the ways of sin are the paths of Satan—the Apollyon [Destroyer] or Abaddon, [angel of the bottomless pit] both of which words signify the destroyer. Foolish indeed are those who give their hearts to the old murderer, because for only a time does he pander to their evil desires. That heavenly Book which lies neglected on many a shelf is the only guide for those who would avoid the enticing and entangling mazes of sin; and it is the best means of preserving the youthful pilgrim from ever treading those dangerous ways. We must follow one or the other; the Book of Life, or the way of death; the Word of the Holy Spirit, or the suggestion of the Evil Spirit. David could urge as the proof of his sincerity that he had no part or lot with the ungodly in their ruinous ways. How can we venture to plead our cause with God, unless we also can wash our hands clean of all connection with the enemies of the Great King?

Psalm 17:5 *Hold up my goings in thy paths, that my footsteps slip not.*

EXPOSITION: **Verse 5.** Under trial it is not easy to behave ourselves rightly; a candle is not easily kept lit when many envious mouths are puffing at it. In evil times prayer is peculiarly needful, and wise men resort to it at once. Plato said to one of his disciples, "When men speak ill of thee, live so that no one will believe them;" good enough advice, but he did not tell us how to carry it out. We have a precept here incorporated in an example; if we want to be preserved, we must cry to the Preserver, and enlist divine support upon our side.

Hold up my goings—as a careful driver holds up his horse when going downhill. We have all sorts of paces, both fast and slow, and the road is never long of one sort, but with God to hold up our goings, nothing in the pace or in the road can cast us down. He who has been down once and cut his knees sadly, even to the bone, had need to redouble his zeal when using this prayer; and all of us, since we are so weak on our legs through Adam's fall, have need to use it every hour of the day. If a perfect father fell, how shall an imperfect son dare to boast?

In thy paths. Forsaking Satan's paths, he prayed to be upheld in God's paths. We cannot keep from evil without keeping to good. If the bushel is not full of wheat, it may soon be once more full of chaff. In all the appointed ordinances and duties of our most holy faith, may the Lord enable us to run through His upholding grace!

That my footsteps slip not. What, slip in God's ways? Yes, the road is good, but our feet are evil, and therefore slip, even on the King's highway. Who would be surprised if carnal men slide and fall in ways of their own choosing, which like the vale [valley] of Siddim, are full of deadly slime pits? One may trip over an ordinance as well as over a temptation. Jesus Christ himself is a stumbling block to some, and the doctrines of grace have been the occasion of offence to many. Grace alone can hold up our goings in the paths of truth.

Psalm 17:6 *I have called upon thee, for thou wilt hear me, O God: incline thine ear unto me, and hear my speech.*

EXPOSITION: Verse 6. *I have called upon thee, for thou wilt hear me, O God.* You have always heard me, O my Lord, and therefore I have the utmost confidence in again approaching your altar. Experience is a blessed teacher. He, who has tried the faithfulness of God in hours of need, has great boldness in laying his case before the throne. The well of Bethlehem, from which we drew such cooling draughts in years gone by, our souls long for still; nor will we leave it for the broken cisterns of Earth.

Incline thine ear unto me, and hear my speech. Stoop out of Heaven and put your ear to my mouth; give me your ear all to myself, as men do when they lean over to catch every word from their friend. The psalmist here comes back to his first prayer, and thus sets us an example of asking again and again, until we have a full assurance that we have succeeded.

Psalm 17:7 *Shew thy marvellous lovingkindness, O thou that savest by thy right hand them which put their trust in thee from those that rise up against them.*

EXPOSITION: Verse 7. *Shew thy marvellous lovingkindness.* Marvelous in its antiquity, its distinguishing character, its faithfulness, its immutability, and above all, marvelous in the wonders which it works. That marvelous grace, which has redeemed us with the precious blood of God's only begotten, is here invoked to come to the rescue. That grace is sometimes hidden; the text says, *Shew it.* Present enjoyments of divine love are matchless cordials to support fainting hearts. Believer, what a prayer is this!

Consider it well. O Lord, *shew thy marvellous lovingkindness;* show it to my intellect, and remove my ignorance; show it to my heart, and revive my gratitude; show it to my faith, and renew my confidence; show it to my experience, and deliver me from all my fears. The original word here used is the same which in Psalm 4:3, is rendered set apart, and it has the force of—Distinguish your mercies, set them out, and set apart the choicest to be bestowed upon me in this hour of my severest affliction.

O thou that savest by thy right hand them which put their trust in thee from those that rise up against them. The title here given to our gracious God is eminently consolatory. He is the God of salvation; it is His present and perpetual habit to save believers; He puts forth His best and most glorious strength, using His right hand of wisdom and might, to save all those, of whatsoever rank or class, who trust themselves to Him.

Happy is the faith that secures the omnipotent protection of Heaven! Blessed God, to be this gracious to unworthy mortals, when they have but grace to rely upon you! The right hand of God is interposed between the saints and all harm; God is never at a loss for means; His own bare hand is enough. He works without tools as well as with them.

Psalm 17:8 *Keep me as the apple of the eye, hide me under the shadow of thy wings.*

EXPOSITION: **Verse 8.** *Keep me as the apple of the eye.* No part of the body more precious, more tender, and more carefully guarded than the eye; and of the eye, no portion more peculiarly to be protected than the central apple, the pupil, or as the Hebrew calls it, "the daughter of the eye." The all wise Creator has placed the eye in a well-protected position; it stands surrounded by projecting bones like Jerusalem encircled by mountains. Moreover, its great Author has surrounded it with many tunics of inward covering, besides the hedge of the eyebrows, the curtain of the eyelids, and the fence of the eyelashes. In addition to this, He has given to every man so high a value for his eyes, and so quick an apprehension of danger, that no member of the body is more faithfully cared for than the organ of sight. Thus, Lord, keep me, for I trust I am one with Jesus, and so a member of His mystical body.

Hide me under the shadow of thy wings. Even as the parent bird completely shields her brood from evil, and meanwhile cherishes them with the warmth of her own heart, by covering them with her wings, do so with me also, most condescending God, for I am your offspring, and you have a parent's love in perfection. This last clause is in the Hebrew in the future tense, as if to show that what the writer had asked for but a moment before he was now sure would be granted to him. Confident expectations should keep pace with earnest supplication.

Psalm 17:9 *From the wicked that oppress me, from my deadly enemies, who compass me about.*

EXPOSITION: **Verse 9.** *From the wicked that oppress me, from my deadly enemies, who compass me about.* The foes from whom David sought to be rescued were wicked men. It is hopeful for us when our enemies are God's enemies. They were deadly enemies, whom nothing but His death would satisfy. The foes of a believer's soul are mortal foes most emphatically, for they who war against our faith aim at the very life of our life. Deadly sins are deadly enemies, and what sin is there which has not death in its bowels? These foes oppressed David, they laid his spirit waste, as invading armies ravage a country, or as wild beasts desolate a land. He likens himself to a besieged city, and complains that his foes compass him about. It may well quicken our business upward, when all around us, every road, is blockaded by deadly foes. This is our daily position, for all around us dangers and sins are lurking. O God, do protect us from them all.

Psalm 17:10 *They are inclosed in their own fat: with their mouth they speak proudly.*

EXPOSITION: **Verse 10.** *They are inclosed in their own fat.* Luxury and gluttony beget vainglorious fatness of heart, which shuts up its gates against all compassionate emotions and reasonable judgments. The old proverb says that full bellies make empty skulls, and it is yet truer that they frequently make empty hearts. The most profuse weeds grow out of the fattest soil. Riches and self-indulgence are the fuel upon which some sins feed their flames. Pride and fullness of bread were Sodom's twin sins. [See Ezekiel 16:49.]

Well-fed hawks forget their masters; and the moon at its fullest is furthest from the sun. Eglon[50] was very fat and a

---

50. King of the Moabites. "Eglon was a very fat man" (Judges 3:17).

notable example that a well-fed corporation is no security to life, when a sharp message comes from God, addressed to the inward vitals of the body. With their mouth they speak proudly.

He, who adores himself, will have no heart to adore the Lord. Full of selfish pleasure within his heart, the wicked man fills his mouth with boastful and arrogant expressions. Prosperity and vanity often lodge together. Woe to the well-fed ox when it bellows at its owner, the poleax is not far off.

Psalm 17:11 *They have now compassed us in our steps: they have set their eyes bowing down to the earth.*

EXPOSITION: **Verse 11.** *They have now compassed us in our steps.* The fury of the ungodly is aimed not at one believer alone, but at all the band; they have compassed us. All the race of the Jews was but a morsel for Haman's hungry revenge, and all because of one Mordecai. The prince of darkness hates all the saints for their Master's sake. The Lord Jesus is one of us, and herein is our hope. He is the Breaker, and will clear a way for us through the hosts which environ us. The hatred of the powers of evil is continuous and energetic, for they watch every step, hoping that the time may come when they shall catch us by surprise. If our spiritual adversaries thus compass every step, how anxiously should we guard all our movements, lest by any means we should be betrayed into evil!

They have set their eyes bowing down to the earth. Joseph Trapp wittily explains this metaphor by an allusion to a bull about to run at his victim; he lowers his head, looks downward, and then concentrates all his force in the dash which he makes. It most probably denotes the malicious jealousy with which the enemy watches the steps of the righteous; as if they studied the ground on which they trod, and searched after some wrong footmark to accuse them for the past, or some stumbling stone to cast in their future path to trip them in days to come.

Psalm 17:12 *Like as a lion that is greedy of his prey, and as it were a young lion lurking in secret places.*

EXPOSITION: Verse 12. Lions are not greedier, nor are their ways more cunning than Satan and his helpers when engaged against the children of God. The adversary thirsts after the blood of souls, and all his strength and craft are exerted to the utmost to satisfy his detestable appetite. We are weak and foolish like sheep; but we have a Shepherd wise and strong, who knows the old lion's wiles, and is more than a match for his force; therefore we will not fear, but rest in safety in the fold. Let us beware, however, of our lurking foe; and in those parts of the road where we feel most secure, let us look about us lest our foe should take the advantage and leap upon us.

Psalm 17:13 *Arise, O LORD, disappoint him, cast him down: deliver my soul from the wicked, which is thy sword.*

EXPOSITION: Verse 13. *Arise, O Lord.* The more furious the attack, the more fervent the psalmist's prayer. His eye rests singly upon the Almighty, and he feels that God has but to rise from the seat of His patience, and the work will be performed at once. Let the lion spring upon us, if Jehovah steps between we need no better defense. When God meets our foe face to face in battle, the conflict will soon be over.

Disappoint him. Be beforehand with him, outwit and outrun him. Appoint it otherwise than he has appointed, and so disappoint him.

Cast him down. Prostrate him. Make him sink upon his knees. Make him bow as the conquered bows before the conqueror. What a glorious sight will it be to behold Satan prostrate beneath the foot of our glorious Lord! Haste, glorious day!

Deliver my soul from the wicked, which is thy sword. He recognizes the most profane and oppressive as being under the providential rule of the King of kings, and used as a sword in the divine hand. What can a sword do unless it is wielded by a hand? No more could the wicked annoy us, unless the Lord permitted them so to do. Most translators are, however, agreed that this is not the correct reading, but that it should be as Calvin puts it, "Deliver my soul from the ungodly man by thy sword." Thus David contrasts the sword of the Lord with human aids and reliefs, and rests assured that he is safe enough under the patronage of Heaven.

Psalm 17:14 *From men which are thy hand, O LORD, from men of the world, which have their portion in this life, and whose belly thou fillest with thy hid treasure: they are full of children, and leave the rest of their substance to their babes.*

EXPOSITION: Verse 14. Almost every word of this verse has furnished matter for discussion to scholars, for it is very obscure. We will, therefore, rest content with the common version, rather than distract the reader with diverse translations.

From men which are thy hand. Having styled the ungodly a sword in his Father's hand, he now likens them to that hand itself, to set forth his conviction that God could as easily remove their violence as a man moves his own hand. He will never slay His child with His own hand.

From men of the world, mere earthworms; not men of the world to come, but mere dwellers in this narrow sphere of mortality; having no hopes or wishes beyond the ground on which they tread.

Which have their portion in this life. Like the prodigal, they have their portion, and are not content to wait their Father's time. Like Passion in the *Pilgrim's Progress,* they have their best things first, and revel during their little hour. Martin Luther was always afraid lest he should have his portion here, and therefore frequently gave away sums of money which had been presented to him. We cannot have Earth and Heaven too for our choice and portion; wise men choose that which will last the longest.

Whose belly thou fillest with thy hid treasure. Their sensual appetite gets the gain which it craved for. God gives to these swine the husks which they hunger for. A generous man does not deny dogs their bones; and our generous God gives even His enemies enough to fill them, if they were not so unreasonable as never to be content. Gold and silver which are locked up in the dark treasuries of the Earth are given to the wicked liberally, and they therefore roll in all manner of carnal delights. Every dog has his day, and they have theirs, and a bright summer's day it seems; but how soon it ends in night! *They are full of children.* This was their fondest hope, that a race from their loins would prolong their names far down the page of history, and God has granted them this also; so that they have all that heart can wish. What enviable creatures they seem, but it only seems!

They are full of children, and leave the rest of their substance to their babes. They were fat housekeepers, and yet leave no lean wills. Living and dying they lacked for nothing but grace and alas that lack spoils everything! They had a fair portion within the little circle of time, but eternity entered not into their calculations. They were penny-wise, but pound-foolish; they remembered the present, and forgot the future; they fought for the shell, and lost the kernel. How fine a description have we here of many a successful merchant, or popular statesman; and it is, at first sight, very showy and tempting, but in contrast with the glories of the world to come, what are these paltry molehill joys. Self, self, self, all these joys begin and end in basest selfishness; but oh, our God, how rich are those who begin and end in you! From all the contamination and injury which association with worldly men is sure to bring us, deliver us, O God!

Psalm 17:15 *As for me, I will behold thy face in righteousness: I shall be satisfied, when I awake, with thy likeness.*

EXPOSITION: **Verse 15.** *As for me.* I neither envy nor covet these men's happiness, but partly have and partly hope for a far better. To behold God's face and to be changed by that vision into His image, so as to partake in His righteousness, this is my noble ambition; and in the prospect of this I cheerfully waive all my present enjoyments. My satisfaction is to come; I do not look for it as yet. I shall sleep awhile, but I shall wake at the sound of the trumpet; wake to everlasting joy, because I arise in your likeness, O my God and King! Glimpses of glory good men have here below to stay their sacred hunger, but the full feast awaits them in the upper skies. Compared with this deep, ineffable, eternal fullness of delight, the joys of the worldlings are as a glowworm to the sun, or the drop of a bucket to the ocean.

PSALM 18
PSALM 18:1–PSALM 18:50

Psalm 18:1 *I will love thee, O Lord, my strength.*

EXPOSITION: Verse 1. *I will love thee, O Lord.* With strong, hearty affection I will cling to you; as a child to its parent, or a spouse to her husband. The word is intensely forcible; the love is of the deepest kind: "I will love heartily, with my inmost bowels." Here is a fixed resolution to abide in the nearest and most intimate union with the Most High. Our triune God deserves the warmest love of all our hearts. Father, Son and Spirit have each a claim upon our love. The solemn purpose never to cease loving naturally springs from present fervor of affection. It is wrong to make rash resolutions, but this when made in the strength of God is most wise and fitting.

My strength. Our God is the strength of our life, our graces, our works, our hopes, our conflicts, our victories. This verse is not found in 2 Samuel 22:1-51, and is a most precious addition, placed above all and after all to form the pinnacle of the temple, the apex of the pyramid. Love is still the crowning grace.

Psalm 18:2 *The LORD is my rock, and my fortress, and my deliverer; my God, my strength, in whom I will trust; my buckler, and the horn of my salvation, and my high tower.*

EXPOSITION: Verse 2. *The Lord is my rock and my fortress.* Dwelling among the crags and mountain fastnesses of Judea, David had escaped the malice of Saul, and here he compares his God to such a place of concealment and security. Believers are often hidden in their God from the strife of tongues and the fury of the storm of trouble. The clefts of the Rock of Ages are safe abodes. *"My deliverer,"* interposing in my hour of peril. When almost captured, the Lord's people are rescued from the hand of the mighty by Him who is mightier still. This title of "deliverer" has many sermons in it, and is well worthy of the study of all experienced saints. *My God;* this is all good things in one. There is a boundless wealth in this expression; it means my perpetual, unchanging, infinite, eternal good. He who can say truly "my God," may well add, "my Heaven, my all." *My strength;* this word is really my rock, in the sense of strength and immobility. My sure, unchanging, eternal confidence and support. Thus the word rock occurs twice, but it is not tautology, for the first time it is a rock for concealment, but here a rock for firmness and immutability.

In whom I will trust. Faith must be exercised, or the preciousness of God is not truly known; and God must be the object of faith, or faith is mere presumption. *My buckler,* warding off the blows of my enemy, shielding me from arrow or sword. The Lord furnishes His warriors with weapons both offensive and defensive. Our armory is completely stored so that none need go to battle unarmed. *The horn of my salvation,* enables me to push down my foes, and to triumph over them with holy exultation. *My high tower,* a citadel high planted on a rocky eminence beyond the reach of my enemies, from the heights of which I look down upon their fury without alarm, and survey a wide landscape of mercy reaching even unto the goodly land beyond Jordan. Here are many words, but none too many; we might profitably examine each one of them had we the time, but summing up the whole, we may conclude with Calvin, that David here equips the faithful from head to foot.

Psalm 18:3 *I will call upon the LORD, who is worthy to be praised: so shall I be saved from mine enemies.*

EXPOSITION: **Verse 3.** In this verse the happy poet resolves to invoke the Lord in joyful song, believing that in all future conflicts his God would deal as well with him as in the past. It is well to pray to God as to one who deserves to be praised, for then we plead in a happy and confident manner. If I feel that I can and do bless the Lord for all His past goodness, I am bold to ask great things of Him. That word has so much in it. To be saved singing is to be saved indeed. Many are saved mourning and doubting; but David had such faith that he could fight singing, and win the battle with a song still upon his lips. How happy a thing to receive fresh mercy with a heart already enjoying mercy and to anticipate new trials with a confidence based upon past experiences of divine love!

> No fearing or doubting with Christ on our side,
> We hope to die shouting, "The Lord will provide."[51]

Psalm 18:4 *The sorrows of death compassed me, and the floods of ungodly men made me afraid.*

EXPOSITION: **Verses 4-19.** In most poetical language the psalmist now describes his experience of Jehovah's delivering power. Poesy has in all her treasures no gem more lustrous than the sonnet of the following verses; the sorrow, the cry, the descent of the Divine One, and the rescue of the

---

51. Hymn: "Though Troubles Assail," verse 7, by John Newton (1725–1807).

afflicted, are here set to a music worthy of the golden harps. The Messiah, our Savior, is evidently, over and beyond David or any other believer, the main and chief subject of this song; and while studying it we have grown more and surer that every line here has its deepest and profoundest fulfillment in Him. But as we are desirous not to extend our comment beyond moderate bounds, we must leave it with the devout reader to make the very easy application of the passage to our once distressed but now triumphant Lord.

Verse 4. *The sorrows of death compassed me.* Death like a cruel conqueror seemed to twist round about him the cords of pain. He was environed and hemmed in with threatening deaths of the most appalling sort. He was like a mariner broken by the storm and driven upon the rocks by dreadful breakers, white as the teeth of death. Sad plight for the man after God's own heart, but thus it is that Jehovah deals with His sons.

The floods of ungodly men made me afraid. Torrents of ungodliness threatened to swamp all religion, and to hurry away the godly man's hope as a thing to be scorned and despised; so far was this threat fulfilled, that even the hero who slew Goliath began to be afraid. The most seaworthy bark is sometimes hard put to it when the storm fiend is abroad. The most courageous man, who as a rule hopes for the best, may sometimes fear the worst. Beloved reader, he who pens these lines has known better than most men what this verse means, and feels inclined to weep, and yet to sing, while he writes upon a text so descriptive of his own experience.

On the night of the lamentable accident at the Surrey Music Hall, the floods of Belial were let loose, and the subsequent remarks of a large portion of the press were exceedingly malicious and wicked; our soul was afraid as we stood encompassed with the sorrows of death and the blasphemies of the cruel. But oh, what mercy there was in it all, and what honey of goodness was extracted by our Lord out of this lion of affliction! Surely God has heard me! Are you in an ill plight? Dear friend, learn from our experience to trust in the Lord Jehovah, who forsakes not His chosen.

Psalm 18:5 *The sorrows of hell compassed me about: the snares of death prevented me.*

EXPOSITION: Verse 5. *The sorrows of hell compassed me about.* From all sides the hell hounds barked furiously. A cordon of devils hemmed in the hunted man of God; every way of escape was closed up. Satan knows how to blockade our coasts with the iron warships of sorrow, but, blessed be God, the port of all prayer is still open, and grace can run the blockade bearing messages from Earth to Heaven, and blessings in return from Heaven to Earth.

The snares of death prevented me. The old enemy hunts for his prey, not only with the dogs of the infernal kennel, but also with the snares of deadly craft. The nets were drawn closer and closer until the contracted circle completely prevented the escape of the captive:

> About me the cords of hell were wound,
> And snares of death my footsteps bound.[52]

Thus hopeless was the case of this good man, as hopeless as a case could be, so utterly desperate that none but an almighty arm could be of any service. According to the four metaphors which he employs, he was bound like a malefactor for execution; overwhelmed like a shipwrecked mariner; surrounded and standing at bay like a hunted stag; and

---

52. From *The Book of Psalms in an English Metrical Version* by Bishop Richard Mant (London: Oxford, 1824), 49.

captured in a net like a trembling bird. What more of terror and distress could meet upon one poor defenseless head?

Psalm 18:6 *In my distress I called upon the LORD, and cried unto my God: he heard my voice out of his temple, and my cry came before him, even into his ears.*

EXPOSITION: Verse 6. *In my distress I called upon the Lord, and cried unto my God.* Prayer is that postern [rear] gate which is left open even when the city is badly besieged by the enemy; it is that way upward from the pit of despair to which the spiritual miner flies at once when the floods from beneath break forth upon him. Observe that he calls, and then cries; prayer grows in intensity as it proceeds. Note also that he first invokes his God under the name of Jehovah, and then advances to a more familiar name, my God. Thus faith increases by exercise, and He whom we at first viewed as Lord is soon seen to be our God in covenant. It is never an ill time to pray; no distress should prevent us from using the divine remedy of supplication. Above the noise of the raging billows of death, or the barking dogs of hell, the feeblest cry of a true believer will be heard in Heaven.

He heard my voice out of his temple, and my cry came before him, even into his ears. Far up within the jeweled walls, and through the gates of pearl, the cry of the suffering supplicant was heard. Music of angels and harmony of seraphs availed not to drown or even to impair the voice of that humble call. The King heard it in His palace of light insufferable, and lent a willing ear to the cry of His own beloved child. O honored prayer, to be able through Jesus' blood to penetrate the very ears and heart of Deity. The voice and the cry are themselves heard directly by the

Lord, and not made to pass through the medium of saints and intercessors. My cry came before Him; the operation of prayer with God is immediate and personal. We may cry with confident and familiar importunity, while our Father himself listens.

Psalm 18:7 *Then the earth shook and trembled; the foundations also of the hills moved and were shaken, because he was wroth.*

EXPOSITION: **Verse 7.** There was no great space between the cry and its answer. The Lord is not slack concerning His promise, but is swift to rescue His afflicted. David has in his mind's eye the glorious manifestations of God in Egypt, at Sinai, and on different occasions to Joshua and the judges; and he considers that his own case exhibits the same glory of power and goodness, and therefore, he may accommodate the descriptions of former displays of the divine majesty into his hymn of praise.

Then the earth shook and trembled. Observe how the most solid and immovable things feel the force of supplication. Prayer has shaken houses, opened prison doors, and made stout hearts to quail. Prayer rings the alarm bell, and the Master of the house arises to the rescue, shaking all things beneath His tread.

The foundations also of the hills moved and were shaken, because He was wroth. He who fixed the world's pillars can make them rock in their sockets, and can lift the cornerstones of creation. The huge roots of the towering mountains are torn up when the Lord bestirs himself in anger to smite the enemies of His people. How shall puny man be able to face it out with God when the very mountains quake with fear? Let not the boaster dream that his present false confidence will support him in the dread day of wrath.

Psalm 18:8 *There went up a smoke out of his nostrils, and fire out of his mouth devoured: coals were kindled by it.*

EXPOSITION: Verse 8. *There went up a smoke out of his nostrils*—a violent oriental method of expressing fierce wrath. Since the breath from the nostrils is heated by strong emotion, the figure portrays the Almighty Deliverer as pouring forth smoke in the heat of His wrath and the impetuousness of His zeal. Nothing makes God so angry as an injury done to His children. He that touches you touches the apple of mine eye. God is not subject to the passions which govern His creatures, but acting as He does with all the energy and speed of one who is angry, He is here aptly set forth in poetic imagery suitable to human understandings. The opening of His lips is sufficient to destroy His enemies.

And fire out of His mouth devoured. This fire was no temporary one but steady and lasting. *Coals were kindled by it.* The whole passage is intended to depict God's descent to the help of His child, attended by earthquake and tempest: at the majesty of His appearing the Earth rocks, the clouds gather like smoke, and the lightning as flaming fire devours, setting the world on a blaze. What grandeur of description is here! Bishop Mant[53] very admirably rhymes the verse thus:

> Smoke from his heated nostrils came,
> And from his mouth devouring flame;
> Hot burning coals announced his ire,
> And flashes of careering fire.

---

53. Bishop Richard Mant (1776–1848), English clergyman, well-protected hymn-writer, well-protected translator.
From *The Book of Psalms in an English Metrical Version*, 51.

Psalm 18:9 *He bowed the heavens also, and came down: and darkness was under his feet.*

EXPOSITION: Verse 9. Amid the terror of the storm Jehovah the Avenger descended, bending beneath His foot the arch of Heaven. *He bowed the heavens also, and came down.* He came in haste, and spurned everything which impeded his rapidity. The thickest gloom concealed His splendor.

And darkness was under his feet. He fought within the dense vapors, as a warrior in clouds of smoke and dust, and found out the hearts of His enemies with the sharp falchion [a short medieval sword] of His vengeance. Darkness is no impediment to God; its densest gloom He makes His tent and secret pavilion. See how prayer moves Earth and Heaven, and raises storms to overthrow in a moment the foes of God's Israel. Things were bad for David before he prayed, but they were much worse for his foes as soon as the petition had gone up to Heaven. A trustful heart, by enlisting the divine aid, turns the tables on its enemies. If I must have an enemy let him not be a man of prayer, or he will soon get the better of me by calling in his God into the quarrel.

Psalm 18:10 *And he rode upon a cherub, and did fly: yea, he did fly upon the wings of the wind.*

EXPOSITION: Verse 10. There is inimitable grandeur in this verse. Under the Mosaic system the cherubim are frequently represented as the chariot of God; hence Milton, in *Paradise Lost,* writes of the Great Father, "He on the wings of cherubim Uplifted, in paternal glory rode Far into chaos."

Without speculating upon the mysterious and much-disputed subject of the cherubim, it may be enough to remark that angels are doubtless our guards and ministering friends, and all their powers are enlisted to expedite the rescue of the afflicted.

He rode upon a cherub, and did fly. Nature also yields all her agents to be our helpers, and even the powers of the air are subservient: *yea, he did fly upon the wings of the wind.* The Lord comes flying when mercy is His errand, but He lingers long when sinners are being wooed to repent. The flight here pictured is as majestic as it is swift; "flying all abroad" is Sternhold's[54] word, and he is not far from correct. As the eagle soars in easy grandeur with wings outspread, without violent flapping and exertion, so comes the Lord with majesty of omnipotence to aid His own.

Psalm 18:11 *He made darkness his secret place; his pavilion round about him were dark waters and thick clouds of the skies.*

EXPOSITION: Verse 11. *He made darkness his secret place; his pavilion round about him were dark waters and thick clouds of the skies.* The storm thickened, and the clouds pouring forth torrents of rain combined to form the secret chamber of the invisible but wonder working God. "Pavilioned in impervious shade" faith saw Him, but no other eye could gaze through the thick clouds of the skies. Blessed is the darkness which curtains my God; if I may not see Him, it is sweet to know that He is working in secret for my eternal good. Even fools can believe that God is abroad in the sunshine and the calm, but faith is wise, and discerns Him in the terrible darkness and threatening storm.

Psalm 18:12 *At the brightness that was before him his thick clouds passed, hail stones and coals of fire.*

---

54. Thomas Sternhold (1500–1549), English courtier and author of *The First English Version of the Metrical Psalms.*

EXPOSITION: **Verse 12.** *At the brightness that was before him his thick clouds passed, hail stones and coals of fire.* Suddenly the terrible artillery of Heaven was discharged; the brightness of lightning lit up the clouds as with a glory proceeding from Him who was concealed within the cloudy pavilion; and volleys of hailstones and coals of fire were hurled forth upon the enemy. The lightning seemed to separate the clouds and kindle them into a blaze, and then hailstones and flakes of fire with flashes of terrific grandeur terrified the sons of men.

Psalm 18:13 *The LORD also thundered in the heavens, and the Highest gave his voice; hail stones and coals of fire.*

EXPOSITION: **Verse 13.** Over all this splendor of tempest pealed the dread thunder. *The Lord also thundered in the heavens, and the Highest gave His voice.* Fit accompaniment for the flames of vengeance. How will men bear to hear it at the last when addressed to them in proclamation of their doom, for even now their hearts are in their mouths if they do but hear it muttering from afar? In all this terror David found a theme for song, and thus every believer finds even in the terrors of God a subject for holy praise.

Hail stones and coals of fire are twice mentioned to show how certainly they are in the divine hand, and are the weapons of Heaven's vengeance. Horne[55] remarks that "every thunderstorm should remind us of that exhibition of power and vengeance, which is hereafter to accompany the general resurrection;" may it not also assure us of the real power of Him who is our Father and our friend, and tend to assure us of our safety while He fights our battles for us.

---

55. Bishop George Horne (1730–1792), English clergyman, writer, university administrator.

The prince of the power of the air is soon dislodged when the cherubic chariot is driven through his dominions; therefore let not the legions of hell cause us dismay. He who is with us is greater than all they that are against us.

Psalm 18:14 *Yea, he sent out his arrows, and scattered them; and he shot out lightnings, and discomfited them.*

EXPOSITION: Verse 14. *Yea, he sent out his arrows, and scattered them; and he shot out lightnings, and discomfited them.* The lightning darted forth as forked arrows upon the hosts of the foe, and speedily scattered them. Boastful sinners prove to be great cowards when Jehovah enters the lists with them. They despise His words, and are very tongue valiant, but when it comes to blows they fly quickly. The glittering flames and the fierce bolts of fire discomfited them. God is never at a loss for weapons. Woe be unto him that contends with His Maker! God's arrows never miss their aim; they are feathered with lightning, and barbed with everlasting death. Fly, O sinner, to the rock of refuge before these arrows stick fast in thy soul.

Psalm 18:15 *Then the channels of waters were seen, and the foundations of the world were discovered at thy rebuke, O Lord, at the blast of the breath of thy nostrils.*

EXPOSITION: Verse 15. So tremendous was the shock of God's assault in arms that the order of nature was changed, and the bottoms of rivers and seas were laid bare. The channels of waters were seen; and the deep cavernous bowels of the Earth were raised up until the foundations of the world were discovered. *Then the channels of waters* *were seen, and the foundations of the world were discovered at thy rebuke, O LORD, at the blast of the breath of thy nostrils.* What will not Jehovah's rebuke do? If the blast of the breath of your nostrils, O Lord, is so terrible, what must your arm be? Vain are the attempts of men to conceal anything from Him whose word opens the deep, and lifts the doors of Earth from their hinges! Vain are all hopes of resistance, for a whisper of His voice makes the whole earth quail in abject terror.

Psalm 18:16 *He sent from above, he took me, he drew me out of many waters.*

EXPOSITION: Verse 16. Now comes the rescue. The Author is divine, *He sent from above,* the work is heavenly, from above; the deliverance is marvelous, *He drew me out of many waters.* Here David was like another Moses, drawn from the water; and thus are all believers like their Lord, whose baptism in many waters of agony and in His own blood has redeemed us from the wrath to come. Torrents of evil shall not drown the man whose God sits upon the floods to restrain their fury.

Psalm 18:17 *He delivered me from my strong enemy, and from them which hated me: for they were too strong for me.*

EXPOSITION: Verse 17. When we have been rescued, we must take care to ascribe all the glory to God by confessing our own weakness, and remembering the power of the conquered enemy. God's power derives honor from all the incidents of the conflict. Our great spiritual adversary is a "strong enemy" indeed, much too strong for poor, weak creatures like ourselves, but we have been delivered yesterday, today, and shall be even to the end. Our weakness is a reason for divine help; note the force of the word *"for"* in the text.

Psalm 18:18 *They prevented me in the day of my calamity: but the LORD was my stay.*

EXPOSITION: Verse 18. It was an ill day, a day of calamity, of which evil foes took cruel advantage, while they used crafty means to utterly ruin him, yet, David could say *but the Lord is my stay.* What a blessed *but* which cuts the Gordian knot[56] and slays the hundred headed hydra! There is no fear of deliverance when our stay is in Jehovah.

Psalm 18:19 *He brought me forth also into a large place; he delivered me, because he delighted in me.*

EXPOSITION: Verse 19. *He brought me forth also into a large place.* After pining awhile in the prison house Joseph reached the palace, and from the cave of Adullam David mounted to the throne. Sweet is pleasure after pain. Enlargement is the more delightful after a season of pinching poverty and sorrowful confinement. Besieged souls delight in the broad fields of the promise when God drives off the enemy and sets open the gates of the environed city. The Lord does not leave His work half done, for having routed the foe He leads out the captive into liberty. Large indeed is the possession and place of the believer in Jesus; there need be no limit to his peace, for there is no bound to his privilege.

He delivered me, because he delighted in me. Free grace lies at the foundation. Rest assured, if we go deep enough, sovereign grace is the truth which lies at the bottom of every

---

56. A legendary knot tied by Gordius, King of Phrygia, said in Greek and Roman mythology to have been cut by a swift cut of the sword of Alexander the Great.

well of mercy. Deep sea fisheries in the ocean of divine bounty always bring the pearls of electing, discriminating love to light. Why Jehovah should delight in us is a question without an answer, and a mystery which angels cannot solve; but that He does delight in His beloved is certain, and is the fruitful root of favors as numerous as they are precious. Believer, sit down, and inwardly digest the instructive sentence now before us, and learn to view the uncaused love of God as the cause of all the loving-kindness of which we are the partakers.

Psalm 18:20 *The LORD rewarded me according to my righteousness; according to the cleanness of my hands hath he recompensed me.*

EXPOSITION: Verse 20. *The Lord rewarded me according to my righteousness.* Viewing this psalm as prophetical of the Messiah, these strongly expressed claims to righteousness are readily understood, for His garments were as white as snow; but considered as the language of David they have perplexed many. Yet the case is clear, and if the words are not strained beyond their original intention, no difficulty need occur. Albeit that the dispensations of divine grace are to the fullest degree sovereign and irrespective of human merit, yet in the dealings of Providence there is often discernible a rule of justice by which the injured are at length avenged, and the righteous ultimately delivered. David's early troubles arose from the wicked malice of envious Saul, who no doubt prosecuted his persecutions under cover of charges brought against the character of *the man after God's own heart.* [See 1 Samuel 13:14.] These charges David declares to have been utterly false, and asserts that he possessed a grace given righteousness which the Lord had graciously rewarded in defiance of all his calumniators [slanderers].

Before God the man after God's own heart was a humble

219

sinner, but before his slanderers he could with unblushing face speak of the cleanness of his hands and the righteousness of his life. He knows little of the sanctifying power of divine grace who is not at the bar of human equity able to plead innocence. There is no self-righteousness in an honest man knowing that he is honest, nor even in his believing that God rewards him in providence because of his honesty, for such is often a most evident matter of fact; but it would be self-righteousness indeed if we transferred such thoughts from the region of providential government into the spiritual kingdom, for there grace reigns not only supreme but sole in the distribution of divine favors.

It is not at all an opposition to the doctrine of salvation by grace, and no sort of evidence of a Pharisaic spirit, when a gracious man, having been slandered, stoutly maintains his integrity, and vigorously defends his character. A godly man has a clear conscience, and knows himself to be upright; is he to deny his own consciousness, and to despise the work of the Holy Ghost, by hypocritically making himself out to be worse than he is? A godly man prizes his integrity very highly, or else he would not be a godly man at all; is he to be called proud because he will not readily lose the jewel of a reputable character?

A godly man can see that in divine providence uprightness and truth are in the long run sure to bring their own reward; may he not, when he sees that reward bestowed in his own case, praise the Lord for it? Must he rather not show forth the faithfulness and goodness of his God? Read the cluster of expressions in this and the following verses as the song of a good conscience, after having safely ridden out a storm of false accusations, persecution, and abuse, and there will be no fear of our upbraiding the writer as one who sets too high a price upon his own moral character.

Psalm 18:21 *For I have kept the ways of the LORD, and have not wickedly departed from my God.*

EXPOSITION: Verse 21. Here the assertion of purity is repeated, both in a positive and a negative form. There is I have and I have not, both of which must be blended in a truly sanctified life; constraining and restraining grace must each take its share. The words of this verse refer to the saint as a traveler carefully keeping to the ways of the Lord, and not wickedly, that is, designedly, willfully, persistently, defiantly forsaking the ordained pathway in which God favors the pilgrim with his presence. Observe how it is implied in the expression, *and have not wickedly departed from my God,* that David lived habitually in communion with God, and knew Him to be His own God, whom he might speak of as "my God." God never departs from His people; let them take heed of departing from Him.

Psalm 18:22 *For all his judgments were before me, and I did not put away his statutes from me.*

EXPOSITION: Verse 22. *For all his judgments were before me.* The word, the character, and the actions of God should be evermore before our eyes; we should learn, consider, and reverence them. Men forget what they do not wish to remember, but the excellent attributes of the Most High are objects of the believer's affectionate and delighted admiration. We should keep the image of God so constantly before us that we become in our measure conformed unto it. This inner love to the right must be the main spring of Christian integrity in our public walk. The fountain must be filled with love to holiness, and then the streams which issue from it will be pure and gracious.

I did not put away his statutes from me. To put away the Scriptures from the mind's study is the certain way to prevent their influencing the outward conversation. Backsliders begin with dusty Bibles, and go on to filthy garments.

Psalm 18:23 *I was also upright before him, and I kept myself from mine iniquity.*

EXPOSITION: Verse 23. *I was also upright before him.* Sincerity is here claimed; sincerity, such as would be accounted genuine before the bar of God. Whatever evil men might think of him, David felt that he had the good opinion of his God. Moreover, freedom from his one great besetting sin he ventures also to plead, *I kept myself from mine iniquity.* It is a very gracious sign when the most violent parts of our nature have been well guarded. If the weakest link in the chain is not broken, the stronger links will be safe enough. David's impetuous temper might have led him to slay Saul when he had him within his power, but grace enabled him to keep his hands clean of the blood of his enemy; but what a wonder it was, and how well worthy of such a grateful record as these verses afford! It will be a sweet cordial to us one of these days to remember our self-denials, and to bless God that we were able to exhibit them.

Psalm 18:24 *Therefore hath the LORD recompensed me according to my righteousness, according to the cleanness of my hands in his eyesight.*

EXPOSITION: Verse 24. God first gives us holiness, and then rewards us for it. We are His workmanship; vessels made unto honor; and when made, the honor is not withheld from the vessel; though, in fact, it all belongs to the Potter upon whose wheel the vessel was fashioned. The prize is awarded to the flower at the show, but the gardener reared it; the child wins the prize from the schoolmaster, but the real honor of his schooling lies with the master, although instead of receiving he gives the reward.

Psalm 18:25 *With the merciful thou wilt shew thyself merciful; with an upright man thou wilt shew thyself upright.*

EXPOSITION: Verse 25. The dealings of the Lord in His own case cause the grateful sinner to remember the usual rule of God's moral government; He is just in His dealings with the sons of men, and metes out to each man according to His measure.

With the merciful thou wilt shew thyself merciful; with an upright man thou wilt shew thyself upright. Every man shall have his meat weighed in his own scales, his corn meted in his own bushel, and his land measured with his own rod. No rule can be more fair, to ungodly men more terrible, or to the generous man more honorable. How would men throw away their light weights, and break their short yards, if they could but believe that they themselves are sure to be in the end the losers by their knavish tricks! Note that even the merciful need mercy; no amount of generosity to the poor, or forgiveness to enemies, can set us beyond the need of mercy. Lord, have mercy upon me, a sinner.

Psalm 18:26 *With the pure thou wilt shew thyself pure; and with the froward thou wilt shew thyself froward.*

EXPOSITION: Verse 26. *With the pure thou wilt shew thyself pure; and with the froward thou wilt shew thyself* *froward*. The sinner's frowardness[57] is sinful and rebellious, and the only sense in which the term can be applied to the Most Holy God is that of judicial opposition and sternness, in which the Judge of all the Earth will act at purposes with the offender, and let him see that all things are not to be made subservient to wicked whims and willful fancies. John Calvin very forcibly says, "This brutish and monstrous stupidity in men compels God to invent new modes of expression, and as it were to clothe himself with a different character."

There is a similar sentence in Leviticus 26:21–24, where God says, "and if ye walk contrary unto (or perversely with) me, then I will also walk contrary unto (or perversely, or roughly, or at random with) you." As if He had said that their obstinacy and stubbornness would make Him on His part forget His accustomed forbearance and gentleness, and cast himself recklessly or at random against them. We see then what the stubborn at length gain by their obduracy;[58] it is this, that God hardens himself still more to break them in pieces, and if they are of stone, He causes them to feel that He has the hardness of iron. The Jewish tradition was that the manna tasted according to each man's mouth; certainly God shows himself to each individual according to his character.

Psalm 18:27 *For thou wilt save the afflicted people; but wilt bring down high looks.*

EXPOSITION: **Verse 27.** *For thou wilt save the afflicted people.* This is a comforting assurance for the poor in spirit whose spiritual griefs admit of no sufficient solace from any other than a divine hand. They cannot save themselves nor can others do it, but God will save them.

But will bring down high looks. Those who look down on

---

57. Disobedience and opposition.
58. Unyieldingness and inflexibility.

others with scorn shall be looked down upon with contempt before long. The Lord abhors a proud look. What a reason for repentance and humiliation! How much better to be humble than to provoke God to humble us in His wrath! A considerable number of clauses occur in this passage in the future tense; how forcibly are we thus brought to remember that our present joy or sorrow is not to have so much weight with us as the great and eternal future!

Psalm 18:28 For thou wilt light my candle: the LORD my God will enlighten my darkness.

EXPOSITION: **Verse 28.** For thou wilt light my candle. Even the children of the day sometimes need candlelight. In the darkest hour light will arise; a candle shall be lit, it will be comfort such as we may fittingly use without dishonesty—it will be our own candle; yet God himself will find the holy fire with which the candle shall burn; our evidences are our own, but their comfortable light is from above. Candles which are lit by God, the devil cannot blow out. All candles are not shining, and so there are some graces which yield no present comfort; but it is well to have candles which may by and by be lit, and it is well to possess graces which may yet afford us cheering evidences.

The metaphor of the whole verse is founded upon the dolorous [sorrowful] nature of darkness and the delightfulness of light; Truly the light is sweet, and a pleasant thing it is for the eyes to behold the sun [Ecclesiastes 11:7] and even so the presence of the Lord removes all the gloom of sorrow, and enables the believer to rejoice with exceeding great joy. The lighting of the lamp is a cheerful moment in the winter's evening, but the lifting up of the light of God's countenance is far happier. It is said that the poor in Egypt will stint themselves of bread to buy oil for the lamp, so that they may not sit in darkness; we could well afford to part with all earthly comforts if the light of God's love could but constantly gladden our souls

---

Psalm 18:29 *For by thee I have run through a troop; and by my God have I leaped over a wall.*

EXPOSITION: **Verses 29-45.** Some repetitions are not vain repetitions. Second thoughts upon God's mercy should be and often are the best. Like wines on the lees our gratitude grows stronger and sweeter as we meditate upon divine goodness. The verses which we have now to consider are the ripe fruit of a thankful spirit; they are apples of gold as to matter, and they are placed in baskets of silver as to their language. They describe the believer's victorious career and his enemies' confusion.

Verse 29. *For by thee have I run through a troop; and by my God have I leaped over a wall.* Whether we meet the foe in the open field or leap upon them while they lurk behind the battlements of a city, we shall by God's grace defeat them in either case; if they hem us in with living legions, or environ us with stone walls, we shall with equal certainty obtain our liberty. Such feats we have already performed, hewing our way at a run through hosts of difficulties, and scaling impossibilities at a leap. God's warriors may expect to have a taste of every form of fighting, and must by the power of faith determine to quit themselves like men; but it behooves them to be very careful to lay all their laurels at Jehovah's feet, each one of them saying, "by my God" have I wrought this valiant deed. Our *spolia optima*[59] we hereby dedicate to the God of Battles, and ascribe to Him all glory and strength.

---

59. The trophies of our conflicts.

Psalm 18:30 *As for God, his way is perfect: the word of the* LORD *is tried: he is a buckler to all those that trust in him.*

EXPOSITION: Verse 30. *As for God, his way is perfect.* Far past all fault and error are God's dealings with His people; all His actions are resplendent with justice, truth, tenderness, mercy, and holiness. Every way of God is complete in itself, and all His ways put together are matchless in harmony and goodness. Is it not very consolatory to believe that He who has begun to bless us will perfect His work, for all His ways are "perfect." Nor must the divine "word" be without its song of praise.

The word of the Lord is tried, like silver refined in the furnace. The doctrines are glorious, the precepts are pure, the promises are faithful, and the whole revelation is superlatively full of grace and truth. David had tried it, thousands have tried it, we have tried it, and it has never failed. It was meet[60] that when way and word had been extolled, the Lord himself would be magnified; hence it is added,

He is a buckler to all those that trust in him. No armor of proof or shield of brass so well secures the warrior as the covenant God of Israel protects His warring people. He himself is the buckler of trustful ones; what a thought this is! What peace may every trusting soul enjoy!

Psalm 18:31 *For who is God save the* LORD? *or who is a rock save our God?*

EXPOSITION: Verse 31. Having mentioned his God, the psalmist's heart burns, and his words sparkle; he challenges Heaven and Earth to find another being worthy of adoration or trust in comparison with Jehovah. His God, as Matthew

---

60. Fitting and right.

227

Henry says, "There is None such." The idols of the heathen he scorns to mention, snuffing them all out as mere nothings when Deity is spoken of. *Who is God save the Lord?* Who else creates, sustains, foresees, and overrules? Who but He is perfect in every attribute, and glorious in every act? To whom but Jehovah should creatures bow? Who else can claim their service and their love? *Who is a rock save our God?* Where can lasting hopes be fixed? Where can the soul find rest? Where is stability to be found? Where is strength to be discovered? Surely in the Lord Jehovah alone can we find rest and refuge.

Psalm 18:32 *It is God that girdeth me with strength, and maketh my way perfect.*

EXPOSITION: Verse 32. Surveying all the armor in which he fought and conquered the joyful victor praises the Lord for every part of the panoply [impressive array]. The girdle of his loins earns the first stanza: *It is God that girdeth me with strength, and maketh my way perfect.* Girt about the loins with power from Heaven, the warrior was filled with vigor, far above all created might. Whereas, without this wondrous belt he would have been feeble and effeminate, with relaxed energies and scattered forces, he felt himself, when braced with the girdle of truth, to be compact in purpose, courageous in daring, and concentrated in power. So his course was a complete success, and undisturbed by disastrous defeat as to be called "perfect." Have we been made more than conquerors over sin, and has our life been such as becomes the gospel? Then let us ascribe all the glory to Him who girded us with His own inexhaustible strength, that we might be unconquered in battle and unwearied in pilgrimage.

Psalm 18:33 *He maketh my feet like hinds' feet, and setteth me upon my high places.*

EXPOSITION: **Verse 33.** The conqueror's feet had been by a divine hand, and the next note must, therefore, refer to them. *He maketh my feet like hinds' feet, and setteth me upon my high places.* Pursuing his foes the warrior had been swift of foot as a young roe, but, instead of taking pleasure in the legs of a man, he ascribes the boon of swiftness to the Lord alone.

When our thoughts are nimble, and our spirits rapid, like the chariots of Amminadib, let us not forget that our best Beloved's hand has given us the choice favor. Climbing into impregnable fortresses, David had been preserved from slipping, and made to stand where the wild goat can barely find a footing; herein was preserving mercy manifested. We, too, have had our high places of honor, service, temptation, and danger, but we have been kept from falling. Bring the harp, and let us emulate the psalmist's joyful thanksgiving; had we fallen, our wailings must have been terrible; since we have stood, let our gratitude be fervent.

Psalm 18:34 *He teacheth my hands to war, so that a bow of steel is broken by mine arms.*

EXPOSITION: **Verse 34.** *He teacheth my hands to war.* Martial prowess and skill in the use of weapons are gratefully acknowledged to be the result of divine teaching; no sacrifice is offered at the shrine of self in praise of natural dexterity, or acquired skilfulness; but, regarding all warlike prowess as a gift of heavenly favor, thankfulness is presented to the Giver. The Holy Spirit is the great Drillmaster of heavenly soldiers.

So that a bow of steel is broken by mine arms. A bow of brass is probably meant, and these bows could scarcely be bent by the arms alone, the archer had to gain the assistance of his foot; it was, therefore, a great feat of strength to bend the bow, so far as even to snap it in half. This was meant of the enemies' bow, which he not only snatched from his grasp, but rendered useless by breaking it in pieces.

Jesus not only destroyed the fiery suggestions of Satan, but He broke his arguments with which he shot them, by using Holy Scripture against him; by the same means we may win a like triumph, breaking the bow and cutting the spear in half by the sharp edge of revealed truth. Probably David had by nature a vigorous bodily frame; but it is even more likely that, like Samson, he was at times clothed with more than common strength; at any rate, he ascribes the honor of his feats entirely to his God. Let us never wickedly rob the Lord of His due, but faithfully give unto Him the glory which is due unto His name.

Psalm 18:35 *Thou hast also given me the shield of thy salvation: and thy right hand hath holden me up, and thy gentleness hath made me great.*

EXPOSITION: Verse 35. *Thou hast also given me the shield of thy salvation.* Above all we must take the shield of faith, for nothing else can quench Satan's fiery darts; this shield is of celestial workmanship, and is in all cases a direct gift from God himself; it is the channel, the sign, the guarantee, and the earnest of perfect salvation.

Thy right hand hath holden me up. Secret support is administered to us by the preserving grace of God, and at the same time Providence kindly yields us manifest aid. We are such babes that we cannot stand alone; but when the Lord's right hand upholds us, we are like brazen pillars which cannot be moved.

Thy gentleness hath made me great. There are several readings of this sentence. The word is capable of being translated, "thy goodness hath made me great." David saw much of benevolence in God's action towards him, and he gratefully ascribed all his greatness not to his own goodness, but to the goodness of God. "Thy providence" is another reading, which is indeed nothing more than goodness in action. Goodness is the bud of which providence is the flower; or goodness is the seed of which providence is the harvest. Some render it, "thy help," which is but another word for providence; providence being the firm ally of the saints, aiding them in the service of their Lord.

Certain learned annotators tell us that the text means, "thy humility hath made me great." "Thy condescension" may, perhaps, serve as a comprehensive reading, combining the ideas which we have already mentioned, as well as that of humility. It is God's making himself little which is the cause of our being made great. We are so little that if God should manifest His greatness without condescension, we would be trampled under His feet; but God, who must stoop to view the skies and bow to see what angels do, looks to the lowly and contrite, and makes them great.

While these are the translations which have been given to the adopted text of the original, we find that there are other readings altogether; as for instance, the Septuagint, which reads, "thy discipline"—thy fatherly correction—"hath made me great;" while the Chaldee paraphrase reads, "thy word hath increased me." Still the idea is the same. David ascribes all his own greatness to the condescending goodness and graciousness of his Father in Heaven. Let us all feel this sentiment in our own hearts, and confess that whatever of goodness or greatness God may have put upon us, we must cast our crowns at His feet and cry, "your gentleness has made me great."

Psalm 18:36 *Thou hast enlarged my steps under me, that my feet did not slip.*

EXPOSITION: **Verse 36.** *Thou hast enlarged my steps.* A smooth pathway leading to spacious possessions and camping grounds had been opened up for him. Instead of threading the narrow mountain paths, and hiding in the cracks and corners of caverns, he was able to traverse the plains and dwell under his own vine and fig tree. It is no small mercy to be brought into full Christian liberty and enlargement, but it is a greater favor still to be enabled to walk worthily in such liberty, not being permitted to slip with our feet (. . . *that my feet did not slip*). To stand upon the rocks of affliction is the result of gracious upholding, but that aid is just as much needed in the luxurious plains of prosperity.

Psalm 18:37 *I have pursued mine enemies, and overtaken them: neither did I turn again till they were consumed.*

EXPOSITION: **Verse 37.** *I have pursued mine enemies, and overtaken them: neither did I turn again till they were consumed.* The preservation of the saints is bad news for their adversaries. The Amalekites thought themselves clear away with their booty, but when David's God guided him in the pursuit; they were soon overtaken and cut in pieces. When God is with us sins and sorrows flee, and all forms of evil are consumed before the power of grace. What a noble picture this and the following verses present to us of the victories of our glorious Lord Jesus!

Psalm 18:38 *I have wounded them that they were not able to rise: they are fallen under my feet.*

EXPOSITION: Verse 38. *I have wounded them that they were not able to rise: they are fallen under my feet.* The destruction of our spiritual enemies is complete. We may exult over sin, death, and hell, as disarmed and disabled for us by our conquering Lord; may He graciously give them a like defeat within us.

Psalm 18:39–40 *For thou hast girded me with strength unto the battle: thou hast subdued under me those that rose up against me. Thou hast also given me the necks of mine enemies; that I might destroy them that hate me.*

EXPOSITION: Verses 39–40. *For thou hast girded me with strength unto the battle: thou hast subdued under me those that rose up against me. Thou hast also given me the necks of mine enemies; that I might destroy them that hate me.* It is impossible to be too frequent in the duty of ascribing all our victories to the God of our salvation. It is true that we have to wrestle with our spiritual antagonists, but the triumph is far more the Lord's than ours. We must not boast like the ambitious votaries of vainglory, but we may exult as the willing and believing instruments in the Lord's hands of accomplishing His great designs.

Psalm 18:41 *They cried, but there was none to save them: even unto the LORD, but he answered them not.*

EXPOSITION: Verse 41. *They cried, but there was none to save them; even unto the Lord, but he answered them not.* Prayer is so notable a weapon that even the wicked will take to it in their fits of desperation. Bad men have appealed to God against God's own servants, but all in vain; the Kingdom of Heaven is not divided, and God never helps His foes at the expense of His friends. There are prayers to God which are no better than blasphemy, which bring no comfortable reply, but rather provoke the Lord to greater wrath. Shall I ask a man to wound or slay his own child to gratify my malice? Would he not resent the insult against his humanity? How much less will Jehovah regard the cruel desires of the enemies of the Church, who dare to offer their prayers for its destruction, calling its existence schism, and its doctrine heresy!

Psalm 18:42 *Then did I beat them small as the dust before the wind: I did cast them out as the dirt in the streets.*

EXPOSITION: **Verse 42.** The defeat of the nations who fought with King David was so utter and complete that they were like powders pounded in a mortar; their power was broken into fragments and they became as weak as dust before the wind, and as small as the mire of the roads. *Then did I beat them small as the dust before the wind: I did cast them out as the dirt in the streets.* Thus the enemies of God have now become powerless and base through the victory of the Son of David upon the Cross. Arise, O my soul, and meet your enemies, for they have sustained a deadly blow, and will fall before your bold advance.

> Hell and my sins resist my course,
> But hell and sin are vanquished foes
> My Jesus nailed them to his cross,
> And sung the triumph when he rose.61

---

61. Hymn: "Stand Up, My Soul," verse 2. Written in 1707 by Isaac Watts.

Psalm 18:43 *Thou hast delivered me from the strivings of the people; and thou hast made me the head of the heathen: a people whom I have not known shall serve me.*

EXPOSITION: **Verse 43.** *Thou hast delivered me from the strivings of the people.* Internal strife is very hard to deal with. A civil war is war in its most miserable form; it is a subject for warmest gratitude when harmony rules within. Our poet praises Jehovah for the union and peace which smiled in his dominions, and if we have peace in the three kingdoms of our spirit, soul, and body, we are in duty bound to give Jehovah a song. Unity in a church should assuredly excite like gratitude.

Thou hast made me the head of the heathen; a people whom I have not known shall serve me. The neighboring nations yielded to the sway of Judah's prince. Oh, when shall all lands adore King Jesus, and serve Him with holy joy? Surely there is far more of Jesus than of David here. Missionaries may derive rich encouragement from the positive declaration that heathen lands shall profess the Headship of the Crucified.

Psalm 18:44 *As soon as they hear of me, they shall obey me: the strangers shall submit themselves unto me.*

EXPOSITION: **Verse 44.** *As soon as they hear of me, they shall obey me.* Thus readily did the once-struggling captain become a far-renowned victor, and thus easy shall be our triumphs. We prefer, however, to speak of Jesus. In many cases the gospel is speedily received by hearts apparently unprepared for it. Those who have never heard the gospel before, have been charmed by its first message, and yielded obedience to it; while others who are accustomed to its joyful sound are rather hardened than softened by its teachings. The grace of God sometimes runs like fire among the stubble, and a nation is born in a day. "Love at first sight" is not an uncommon thing when Jesus is the wooer. He can write Caesar's message without boasting, *Veni, vidi, vici;*[62] His gospel is in some cases no sooner heard than believed. What inducements to spread abroad the doctrine of the Cross! *The strangers shall submit themselves unto me.*

Psalm 18:45 *The strangers shall fade away, and be afraid out of their close places.*

EXPOSITION: **Verse 45.** *The strangers shall fade away.* Like sear [dried up] leaves or blasted [shriveled or withered] trees our foes and Christ's foes shall find no sap and stamina remaining in them. Those who are strangers to Jesus are strangers to all lasting happiness; those must soon fade who refuse to be watered from the River of Life.

And be afraid out of their close places. Out of their mountain fastnesses [fortified structures] the heathen crept in fear to own allegiance to Israel's king, and even so, from the castles of self-confidence and the dens of carnal security, poor sinners come bending before the Savior, Christ the Lord. Our sins which have entrenched themselves in our flesh and blood as in impregnable forts, shall yet be driven forth by the sanctifying energy of the Holy Spirit, and we shall serve the Lord in singleness of heart. Thus with remembrance of conquests in the past, and with glad anticipations of victories yet to come, the sweet singer closes the description, and returns to exercise more direct adoration of His gracious God.

---

62. I came, I saw, I conquered.

Psalm 18:46 *The* LORD *liveth; and blessed be my rock; and let the God of my salvation be exalted.*

EXPOSITION: **Verse 46.** *The Lord liveth.* Possessing underived [original], essential, independent and eternal life. We serve no inanimate, imaginary, or dying God. He only has immortality. Like loyal subjects let us cry, "Live on, O God!" Long live the King of kings. By your immortality we dedicate ourselves afresh to you. As the Lord our God lives so should we live to Him.

And blessed be my rock. He is the ground of our hope, and let Him be the subject of our praise. Our hearts bless the Lord, with holy love extolling Him. Jehovah lives, my rock be blessed! Praised be the God who gives me rest!

Let the God of my salvation be exalted. As our Savior, the Lord should more than ever be glorified. We should publish abroad the story of the covenant and the Cross, the Father's election, the Son's redemption, and the Spirit's regeneration. He who rescues us from deserved ruin should be very dear to us. In Heaven they sing, *Unto him that loved us and washed us from our sins in his own blood* [Revelation 1:5]; the like music should be common in the assemblies of the saints below.

Psalm 18:47 *It is God that avengeth me, and subdueth the people under me.*

EXPOSITION: **Verse 47.** *It is God that avengeth me, and subdueth the people under me.* To rejoice in personal revenge is unhallowed and evil, but David viewed himself as the instrument of vengeance upon the enemies of God and His people, and had he not rejoiced in the success accorded to him he would have been worthy of censure. That sinners perish is in itself a painful consideration, but that the Lord's law is avenged upon those who break it is to the devout mind a theme for thankfulness. We must, however, always remember that vengeance is never ours, vengeance belongs unto the Lord, and he is so just and longsuffering in the exercise of it, that we may safely leave its administration in His hands.

Psalm 18:48 *He delivereth me from mine enemies: yea, thou liftest me up above those that rise up against me: thou hast delivered me from the violent man.*

EXPOSITION: Verse 48. From all enemies, and especially from one who was preeminent in violence, the Lord's anointed was preserved, and at the last over the head of Saul and all other adversaries he reigned in honor. The same end awaits every saint, because Jesus who stooped to be lightly esteemed among men is now made to sit far above all principalities and powers.

Psalm 18:49 *Therefore will I give thanks unto thee, O LORD, among the heathen, and sing praises unto thy name.*

EXPOSITION: Verse 49. Paul cites this verse in Romans 15:9: *And that the Gentiles might glorify God for his mercy; as it is written, For this cause I will confess to thee among the Gentiles, and sing unto thy name.* This is clear evidence that David's Lord is here, but David is here too, and is to be viewed as an example of a holy soul making its boast in God even in the presence of ungodly men. Who are the despisers of God that we should stop our mouths for them? We will sing to our God whether they like it or not, and force upon them the knowledge of His goodness. Too much politeness to traitors may be treason to our King.

Psalm 18:50 *Great deliverance giveth he to his king; and sheweth mercy to his anointed, to David, and to his seed for evermore.*

EXPOSITION: Verse 50. This is the winding-up verse into which the writer throws a fullness of expression, indicating the most rapturous delight of gratitude. *Great deliverance.* The word "deliverance" is plural, to show the variety and completeness of the salvation; the adjective "great" is well placed if we consider from what, to what, and how we are saved. All this mercy is given to us in our King, the Lord's Anointed, and those are blessed indeed who as His seed may expect mercy to be built up for evermore. The Lord was faithful to the literal David, and He will not break His covenant with the spiritual David, for that would far more involve the honor of His crown and character. The psalm concludes in the same loving spirit which shone upon its commencement; happy are they who can sing on from love to love, even as the pilgrims marched from strength to strength.

PSALM 19

PSALM 19:1–PSALM 19:14

Psalm 19:1 *The heavens declare the glory of God; and the firmament sheweth his handywork.*

EXPOSITION: **Verse 1.** *The heavens declare the glory of God.* The book of nature has three leaves, Heaven, Earth, and sea, of which Heaven is the first and the most glorious, and by its aid we are able to see the beauties of the other two. Any book without its first page would be sadly imperfect, and especially the great Natural Bible, since its first pages, the sun, moon, and stars, supply light to the rest of the volume, and are thus the keys, without which the writing which follows would be dark and undiscerning. Man walking erect was evidently made to scan the skies, and he who begins to read creation by studying the stars begins the book at the right place.

The heavens are plural for their variety, comprising the watery heavens with their clouds of countless forms, the aerial heavens with their calms and tempests, the solar heavens with all the glories of the day, and the starry heavens with all the marvels of the night. What the Heaven of heavens must be has not entered into the heart of man, but there in, chief of all things, are telling the glory of God. Any part of creation has more instruction in it than human mind will ever exhaust, but the celestial realm is peculiarly rich in spiritual lore.

The heavens declare, or are declaring, for the continuance of their testimony is intended by the participles employed; every moment God's existence, power, wisdom and goodness, are being sounded abroad by the heavenly heralds which shine upon us from above. He who would guess at divine sublimity should gaze upward into the starry vault; and he who would imagine infinity must peer into the boundless expanse. He who desires to see divine wisdom should consider the balancing of the orbs; and he who would know divine fidelity must mark the regularity of the planetary motions. He, who would attain some conceptions of divine power, greatness, and majesty, must estimate the forces of attraction, the magnitude of the fixed stars, and the brightness of the whole celestial train.

It is not merely glory that the heavens declare, but the "glory of God," for they deliver to us such unanswerable arguments for a conscious, intelligent, planning, controlling, and presiding Creator, that no unprejudiced person can remain unconvinced by them. The testimony given by the heavens is no mere hint, but a plain, unmistakable declaration; and it is a declaration of the most constant and abiding kind. Yet for all this, to what avail is the loudest declaration to a deaf man or the clearest showing to one spiritually blind? God the Holy Ghost must illuminate us, or all the suns in the Milky Way never will.

The firmament sheweth his handywork; not handy in the common use of that term, but handwork. The expanse is full of the works of the Lord's skilful, creating hands; hands being attributed to the great creating Spirit to set forth his care and workmanlike action, and to meet the poor comprehension of mortals. It is humbling to find that even when the most devout and elevated minds are desirous to express their loftiest thoughts of God; they must use words and metaphors drawn from the limited language of those on Earth. We are children, and must each confess, "I think as a child, I speak as a child."

In the expanse above us God flies His starry flag to show

that the King is at home, and hangs out His escutcheon [shield] that atheists may see how He despises their denunciations of Him. He who looks up to the firmament and then writes himself down an atheist, brands himself at the same moment as an idiot or a liar. It is strange that some who love God are yet afraid to study the God declaring book of nature. The mock spirituality of some believers, who are too heavenly to consider the heavens, has given color to the vaunts of infidels that nature contradicts revelation. The wisest of men are those who with pious eagerness trace the goings forth of Jehovah as well in creation as in grace; only the foolish have any fears lest the honest study of the one should injure our faith in the other. Dr. James McCosh[63] of Scotland, has well said,

> "We have often mourned over the attempts made to set the works of God against the Word of God, and thereby excite, propagate, and perpetuate jealousies fitted to separate parties that ought to live in closest union. In particular, we have always regretted that endeavors should have been made to depreciate nature with a view of exalting revelation—it has always appeared to us to be nothing else than the degrading of one part of God's work in the hope thereby of exalting and recommending another.
>
> "Let not science and religion be reckoned as opposing citadels, frowning defiance upon each other, and their troops brandishing their armor in hostile attitude. They have too many common foes, if they would but think of it, in ignorance and prejudice, in passion and vice, under all their forms,

---

63. James McCosh (1811–1894), philosopher of the Scottish School of Common Sense and President of Princeton University from 1868–1888.

to admit of their lawfully wasting their strength in a useless warfare with each other.

"Science has a foundation, and so has religion; let them unite their foundations, and the basis will be broader, and they will be two compartments of one great fabric reared to the glory of God. Let one be the outer and the other the inner court. In the one, let all look, and admire and adore; and in the other, let those who have faith kneel, and pray, and praise. Let the one be the sanctuary where human learning may present its richest incense as an offering to God, and the other the holiest of all, separated from it by a veil now rent in twain, and in which, on a blood-sprinkled mercy seat, we pour out the love of a reconciled heart, and hear the oracles of the living God."

Psalm 19:2 *Day unto day uttereth speech, and night unto night sheweth knowledge.*

EXPOSITION: Verse 2. *Day unto day uttereth speech, and night unto night sheweth knowledge.* As if one day took up the story where the other left it, and each night passed over the wondrous tale to the next. The original has in it the thought of pouring out or overflowing with speech; as though days and nights were but as a fountain flowing evermore with Jehovah's praise. Oh to drink often at the celestial well, and learn to utter the glory of God! The witnesses above cannot be slain or silenced; from their elevated seats they constantly preach the knowledge of God, unawed and unbiased by the judgment of men. Even the changes of alternating night and day are mutely eloquent, and light and shade equally reveal the Invisible One. Let the vicissitudes [variations] of our circumstances do the same, and while we bless God for our days of joy, let us also extol Him who gives *songs in the night* [See Job 35:10.].

The lesson of day and night is one which would be well if all men learned. It should be among our day thoughts and night thoughts, to remember the flight of time, the changeful character of earthly things, the brevity both of joy and sorrow, the preciousness of life, our utter powerlessness to recall the hours once flown, and the irresistible approach of eternity. Day bids us labor, night reminds us to prepare for our last time; day bids us work for God, and night invites us to rest in Him; day bids us look for endless day, and night warns us to escape from everlasting night.

Psalm 19:3 *There is no speech nor language, where their voice is not heard.*

EXPOSITION: Verse 3. *There is no speech nor language, where their voice is not heard.* Every man may hear the voices of the stars. Many are the languages of terrestrials, to celestials there is but one, and that one may be understood by every willing mind. The lowest heathen are without excuse, if they do not discover the invisible things of God in the works which He has made. Sun, moon, and stars are God's travelling preachers; they are apostles upon their journey confirming those who regard the Lord and judges on circuit condemning those who worship idols.

The margin[64] gives us another rendering, which is more literal, and involves less repetition; "no speech, no words, their voice is not heard." That is to say, their teaching is not addressed to the ear, and is not uttered in articulate sounds; it

---

64. "margin" refers to the explanatory notes in Spurgeon's Bible, which would have been the Authorized Version (AV), as it is known in England (what Americans know as the King James Version).

is pictorial, and directed to the eye and heart; it touches not the sense by which faith comes, for faith cometh by hearing. Jesus Christ is called the Word, for He is a far more distinct display of Godhead than all the heavens can afford; they are, after all, but dumb instructors; neither star nor sun can arrive at a word, but Jesus is the express image of Jehovah's person, and His name is the Word of God.

Psalm 19:4 *Their line is gone out through all the earth, and their words to the end of the world. In them hath he set a tabernacle for the sun.*

EXPOSITION: Verse 4. *Their line is gone out through all the earth, and their words to the end of the world.* Although the heavenly bodies move in solemn silence, yet in reason's ear they utter precious teachings. They give forth no literal words, but yet their instruction is clear enough to be so described. Horne says that the phrase employed indicates a language of signs, and thus we are told that the heavens speak by their significant actions and operations. Nature's words are like those of the deaf and dumb, but grace tells us plainly of the Father. By their line is probably meant the measure of their domain which, together with their testimony, has gone out to the utmost end of the habitable Earth. No man living beneath the copes [walls] of Heaven dwells beyond the bounds of the diocese of God's Court preachers. It is easy to escape from the light of ministers, who are as stars in the right hand of the Son of Man; but even then men, with a conscience not yet seared, will find a Nathan to accuse them, a Jonah to warn them, and an Elijah to threaten them in the silent stars of night. To gracious souls the voices of the heavens are more influential far, they feel the sweet influences of the Pleiades, and are drawn towards their Father God by the bright bands of Orion.

In them hath he set a tabernacle for the sun. In the heavens the sun encamps, and marches like a mighty monarch on his glorious way. He has no fixed abode, but as a traveler pitches and removes his tent, a tent which will soon be taken down and rolled together as a scroll. As the royal pavilion stood in the centre of the host, so the sun in his place appears like a king in the midst of attendant stars.

Psalm 19:5 *Which is as a bridegroom coming out of his chamber, and rejoiceth as a strong man to run a race.*

EXPOSITION: **Verse 5.** *Which is as a bridegroom coming out of his chamber.* A bridegroom comes forth sumptuously appareled, his face beaming with a joy which he imparts to all around; such, but with a mighty emphasis, is the rising Sun.

And rejoiceth as a strong man to run a race. As a champion girded for running cheerfully addresses himself to the race, so does the sun speed onward with matchless regularity and unwearying swiftness in his appointed orbit. It is but mere play to him; there are no signs of effort, flagging [tiredness], or exhaustion.

No other creature yields such joy to the Earth as her bridegroom the sun; and none, whether they are horse or eagle, can for an instant compare in swiftness with that heavenly champion. But all His glory is but the glory of God; even the sun shines in light borrowed from the Great Father of Lights.

> Thou sun, of this great world both eye and soul,
>
> Acknowledge Him thy greater; sound his praise

Both when you climb, and when high noon
hast gained,

And when you fall.[65]

Psalm 19:6 *His going forth is from the end of the heaven, and his circuit unto the ends of it: and there is nothing hid from the heat thereof.*

EXPOSITION: **Verse 6.** *His going forth is from the end of the heaven, and his circuit unto the ends of it.* He bears His light to the boundaries of the solar heavens, traversing the zodiac with steady motion, denying His light to none who dwell within his range. *And there is nothing hid from the heat thereof.* Above, beneath, around, the heat of the sun exercises an influence. The bowels of the earth are stored with the ancient produce of the solar rays, and even yet earth's inmost caverns feel their power. Where light is shut out, yet heat and other more subtle influences find their way.

There is no doubt a parallel intended to be drawn between the Heaven of grace and the Heaven of nature. God's way of grace is sublime and broad, and full of His glory; in all its displays it is to be admired and studied with diligence; both its lights and its shades are instructive; it has been proclaimed, in a measure, to every people, and in due time shall be yet more completely published to the ends of the Earth. Jesus, like a sun, dwells in the midst of revelation, as a tabernacle among men in all His brightness; rejoicing, as the Bridegroom of His church, to reveal himself to men; and, like a champion, to win unto himself renown.

He makes a circuit of mercy, blessing the remotest corners of the Earth; and there are no seeking souls, however degraded and depraved, who shall be denied the comfortable warmth

---

65. Quote from *Paradise Lost,* by John Milton.

and benediction of His love—even death shall feel the power of His presence, and resign [release] the bodies of the saints, and this fallen Earth shall be restored to its pristine glory.

Psalm 19:7 *The law of the LORD is perfect, converting the soul: the testimony of the LORD is sure, making wise the simple.*

EXPOSITION: In Psalm 19:7–9 we have a brief but instructive hexapla containing six descriptive titles of the word, six characteristic qualities mentioned and six divine effects declared. Names, nature, and effect are well set forth.

Verse 7. *The law of the Lord is perfect;* by which he means not merely the law of Moses but the doctrine of God, the whole run and rule of sacred Writ. The doctrine revealed by God he declares to be perfect, and yet David had but a very small part of the Scriptures, and though a fragment, and because the darkest and most historical portion, is perfect, what must the entire volume be? How more than perfect is the book which contains the clearest possible display of divine love, and gives us an open vision of redeeming grace.

The Gospel is a complete scheme or law of gracious salvation, presenting to the needy sinner everything that his terrible necessities can possibly demand. There are no redundancies and no omissions in the Word of God, and in the plan of grace; why then do men try to paint this lily and gild this refined gold? The Gospel is perfect in all its parts, and perfect as a whole: it is a crime to add to it, treason to alter it, and felony to take from it.

Converting the soul. Making the man to be returned or restored to the place from which sin had cast him. The practical effect of the Word of God is to turn the man to himself, to his God, and to holiness; and the turn or conversion is not outward alone, "the soul" is moved and renewed. The great means of the conversion of sinners is the Word of God, and the more closely we keep to it in our ministry the more likely we are to be successful. It is God's Word rather than man's comment on God's Word which is made mighty with souls. When the law drives and the gospel draws, the action is different but the end is one, for by God's Spirit the soul is made to yield, and cries, "Turn me, and I shall be turned." Try men's depraved nature with philosophy and reasoning, and it laughs your efforts to scorn, but the Word of God soon works a transformation.

The testimony of the Lord is sure. God bears His testimony against sin, and on behalf of righteousness; He testifies of our fall and of our restoration; this testimony is plain, decided, and infallible, and is to be accepted as sure. God's witness in His Word is so sure that we may draw solid comfort from it both for time and eternity, and so sure that no attacks made upon it however fierce or subtle can ever weaken its force. What a blessing that in a world of uncertainties we have something sure to rest upon! We hasten from the quicksand of human speculations to the terra firma of Divine revelation.

Making wise the simple. Humble, candid, teachable minds receive the Word, and are made wise unto salvation. Things hidden from the wise and prudent are revealed unto babes. The persuadable grow wise, but the cavilers[66] continue fools. As a law or plan the Word of God converts, and then as a testimony it instructs; it is not enough for us to be converts, we must continue to be disciples; and if we have felt the power of truth, we must go on to prove its certainty by experience. The perfection of the gospel converts, but its sureness edifies; if we would be edified it becomes us not to stagger at the promise through unbelief, for a doubted Gospel

---

66. Objectors and disputers.

cannot make us wise, but truth of which we are assured will be our establishment.

Psalm 19:8 *The statutes of the LORD are right, rejoicing the heart: the commandment of the LORD is pure, enlightening the eyes.*

EXPOSITION: **Verse 8.** *The statutes of the Lord are right.* His precepts and decrees are founded in righteousness, and are such as are right or fitted to the right reason of man. As a physician gives the right medicine, and a counselor the right advice, so does the Book of God.

Rejoicing the heart. Mark the progress; he who was converted was next made wise and is now made happy; that truth which makes the heart right then gives joy to the right heart. Free grace brings heart joy. Earthborn mirth dwells on the lip, and flushes the bodily powers; but heavenly delights satisfy the inner nature, and fill the mental faculties to the brim. There is no cordial of comfort like that which is poured from the bottle of Scripture. "Retire and read your Bible to be happy."

The commandment of the Lord is pure. No mixture of error defiles it, no stain of sin pollutes it; it is the unadulterated milk, the undiluted wine.

Enlightening the eyes, purging away by its own purity the earthly grossness which mars the intellectual discernment: whether the eye is dim with sorrow or with sin, the Scripture is a skilful oculist, and makes the eye clear and bright. Look at the sun and it puts out your eyes, look at the more than sunlight of Revelation and it enlightens them. The purity of snow causes snow blindness to the Alpine traveler, but the purity of God's truth has the contrary effect, and cures the natural blindness of the soul. It is well again to observe the gradation [stages]; the convert becomes a disciple and next a rejoicing soul, he now obtains a discerning eye and as a spiritual man discerns all things, though he himself is discerned of no man.

Psalm 19:9 *The fear of the LORD is clean, enduring for ever: the judgments of the LORD are true and righteous altogether.*

EXPOSITION: **Verse 9.** *The fear of the Lord is clean.* The doctrine of truth is here described by its spiritual effect, viz., inward piety, or the fear of the Lord; this is clean in itself, and cleanses out the love of sin, sanctifying the heart in which it reigns. Mr. Godly-fear is never satisfied until every street, lane, and alley, yes, and every house and every corner of the town of Man soul[67] is clean and rid of the diabolic ones who lurk therein.

Enduring for ever. Filth brings decay, but cleanness is the great foe of corruption. The grace of God in the heart being a pure principle is also an abiding and incorruptible principle, which may be crushed for a time, but cannot be utterly destroyed. Both in the Word and in the heart, when the Lord writes, He says, *What I have written, I have written* [John 19:22]. He will make no erasures himself; much less suffer others to do so. The revealed will of God is never changed; even Jesus came not to destroy but to fulfill, and even the ceremonial law was only changed as to its shadow, the substance intended by it is eternal. When the governments of nations are shaken with revolution, and ancient constitutions are being repealed, it is comforting to know that the throne of God is unshaken, and His law unaltered.

The judgments of the Lord are true and righteous—jointly and severally the words of the Lord are true; that which is good in detail is excellent in the mass; no exception may

---

67. Mansoul, the town in John Bunyan's classic book "The Holy War."

be taken to a single clause separately, or to the Book as a whole. God's judgments, all of them together, or each of them apart, are manifestly just, and need no laborious excuses to justify them. The judicial decisions of Jehovah, as revealed in the law, or illustrated in the history of His providence, are truth itself, and commend themselves to every truthful mind. Not only is their power invincible, but their justice is unimpeachable.

Psalm 19:10 *More to be desired are they than gold, yea, than much fine gold: sweeter also than honey and the honeycomb.*

EXPOSITION: **Verse 10.** *More to be desired are they than fine gold, yea, than much fine gold.* Bible truth is enriching to the soul in the highest degree; the metaphor is one which gathers force as it is brought out—gold, fine gold, much fine gold—it is good, better, best, and therefore it is not only to be desired with a miser's avidity, but with more than that. As spiritual treasure is more noble than mere material wealth, so should it be desired and sought after with greater eagerness. Men speak of solid gold, but what is as solid as solid truth? For love of gold, pleasure is forsworn, ease renounced, and life endangered; shall we not be ready to do as much for love of truth? *Sweeter also than honey and the honeycomb.* Joseph Trapp says, "Old people are all for profit, the young for pleasure; here's gold for the one, yea, the finest gold in great quantity; here's honey for the other, yea, live honey dropping from the comb."

The pleasures arising from a right understanding of the divine testimonies are of the most delightful order; earthly enjoyments are utterly contemptible, if compared with them. The sweetest joys, yes, the sweetest of the sweetest falls to the portion of him who has God's truth to be his heritage.

Psalm 19:11 *Moreover by them is thy servant warned: and in keeping of them there is great reward.*

EXPOSITION: **Verse 11.** *Moreover by them is thy servant warned.* We are warned by the Word both of our duty, our danger, and our remedy. On the sea of life there would be many more wrecks, if it were not for the divine storm signals, which give to the watchful a timely warning. The Bible should be our Mentor, our Monitor, our Memento Mori,[68] our Reminder, and the Keeper of our Conscience. Alas, that so few men will take the warning so graciously given; none but servants of God will do so, for they alone regard their Master's will. Servants of God not only find His service delightful in itself, but they receive good recompense.

In keeping of them there is great reward. There is a wage, and a great one; though we earn no wages of debt, we win great wages of grace. Saints may be losers for a time, but they shall be glorious gainers in the long run, and even now a quiet conscience is in itself no slender reward for obedience. He who wears the herb called heart's ease in his bosom is truly blessed. However, the main reward is yet to come, and the word here used hints as much, for it signifies the heel, as if the reward would come to us at the end of life when the work was done—not while the labor was in hand, but when it was gone and we could see the heel of it. Oh the glory yet to be revealed! It is enough to make a man faint for joy at the prospect of it. *Our light affliction, which is but for a moment, is not worthy to be compared with the glory which shall be revealed in us* [2 Corinthians 4:17]. Then shall we know the value of the Scriptures when we swim in that sea of unutterable delight to which their streams will bear us, if we commit ourselves to them.

---

68. A reminder of our mortality.

Psalm 19:12 *Who can understand his errors? cleanse thou me from secret faults.*

EXPOSITION: Verse 12. *Who can understand his errors?* A question which is its own answer. It rather requires a note of exclamation than of interrogation. By the law is the knowledge of sin, and in the presence of divine truth, the psalmist marvels at the number and heinousness of his sins. He best knows himself, who best knows the Word, but even such a one will be in a maze of wonder as to what he does not know, rather than on the mount of congratulation as to what he does know. We have heard of a comedy of errors, but to a good man this is more like a tragedy. Many books have a few lines of errata at the end, but our errata might well be as large as the volume if we could but have sense enough to see them. Augustine of Hippo[69] wrote in his older days a series of Retractions; ours might make a library if we had enough grace to be convinced of our mistakes and to confess them.

Cleanse thou me from secret faults. You can show in me faults entirely hidden from myself. It would be hopeless to expect to see all my spots; therefore, O Lord, wash away in the atoning blood even those sins which my conscience has been unable to detect. Secret sins, like private conspirators, must be hunted out, or they may do deadly mischief; it is well to be much in prayer concerning them. In the Lateran Council of the Church of Rome, a decree was passed that every true believer must confess his sins, all of them, once a year to the priest, and they affixed to it this declaration, that there is no hope of pardon but in complying with that

---

69. Saint Augustine (354–430), early Christian theologian and philosopher whose writings were very influential in the development of Western Christianity and philosophy. (See *Confessions by Augustine* published as a Pure Gold Classic by Bridge-Logos, Inc.)

decree. What can equal the absurdity of such a decree as that? Do they suppose that they can tell their sins as easily as they can count their fingers?

Why, if we could receive pardon for all our sins by telling every sin we have committed in one hour, there is not one of us who would be able to enter Heaven. Because in addition to the sins that are known to us and that we may be able to confess, there are a vast mass of sins, which are as truly sins as those which we lament, but which are secret, and are not revealed to our eyes. If we had eyes like those of God, we would think very differently of ourselves. The transgressions which we see and confess are like the farmer's small samples which he brings to market, when he has left his granary full at home. We have but a very few sins which we can observe and detect, compared with those which are hidden from ourselves and unseen by our fellow creatures.

Psalm 19:13 *Keep back thy servant also from presumptuous sins; let them not have dominion over me: then shall I be upright, and I shall be innocent from the great transgression.*

EXPOSITION: **Verse 13.** *Keep back thy servant also from presumptuous sins; let them not have dominion over me.* This earnest and humble prayer teaches us that saints may fall into the worst of sins unless restrained by grace, and therefore they must watch and pray lest they enter into temptation. There is a natural proneness to sin in the best of men, and they must be held back as a horse is held back by the bit or they will run into it.

Presumptuous sins are peculiarly dangerous. All sins are great sins, but yet some sins are greater than others. Every sin has in it the very venom of rebellion, and is full of the essential marrow of traitorous rejection of God; but there are some sins which have in them a greater development of the essential mischief of rebellion, and which wear upon their faces more of the brazen pride which defies the Most High. It is wrong to suppose that because all sins will condemn us, that therefore one sin is not greater than another.

The fact is that while all transgression is a greatly grievous and sinful thing, yet there are some transgressions which have a deeper shade of blackness, and a more double scarlet dyed hue of criminality than others. The presumptuous sins of our text are the chief and worst of all sins; they rank head and foremost in the list of iniquities. It is remarkable that though atonement was provided under the Jewish law for every kind of sin, there was this one exception: *But the soul that sinneth presumptuously shall have no atonement; it shall be cut off from the midst of the people* [Numbers 15:30].

And now under the Christian dispensation, although in the sacrifice of our blessed Lord there is a great and precious atonement for presumptuous sins, whereby sinners who have erred in this manner are made clean, yet without doubt, presumptuous sinners, dying without pardon, must expect to receive a double portion of the wrath of God, and a more terrible portion of eternal punishment in the pit that is dug for the wicked. For this reason David is anxious that he may never come under the reigning power of these giant evils. *Then shall I be upright, and I shall be innocent from the great transgression.* He shudders at the thought of the unpardonable sin. Secret sin is a stepping stone to presumptuous sin, and that is the vestibule of "the sin which is unto death." He who is not willful in his sin, will be in a fair way to be innocent so far as poor sinful man can be; but he who tempts the devil to tempt him is in a path which will lead him from bad to worse, and from the worse to the worst.

Psalm 19:14 *Let the words of my mouth, and the meditation of my heart, be acceptable in thy sight, O LORD, my strength, and my redeemer.*

EXPOSITION: **Verse 14.** *Let the words of my mouth, and the meditation of my heart, be acceptable in thy sight, O Lord, my strength, and my redeemer.* A sweet prayer, and so spiritual that it is almost as commonly used in Christian worship as the apostolic benediction. Words of the mouth are mockery if the heart does not meditate; the shell is nothing without the kernel; but both together are useless unless accepted; and even if accepted by man, it is all vanity if not acceptable in the sight of God. When praying we must view Jehovah as our strength enabler, and our saving Redeemer, or we shall not pray rightly, and it is good to feel our personal interest so as to use the word *my* or *our* prayers will be hindered. Our near Kinsman's name, our *Goel* or Redeemer, makes a blessed ending to the psalm; it began with the heavens, but it ends with Him whose glory fills Heaven and Earth. Blessed Kinsman, help us now to meditate acceptably upon your most sweet love and tenderness.

PSALM 20
PSALM 20:1–PSALM 20:9

Psalm 20:1 *The Lord hear thee in the day of trouble; the name of the God of Jacob defend thee.*

EXPOSITION: **Verse 1.** *The Lord hear thee in the day of trouble.* All loyal subjects pray for their king, and most certainly citizens of Zion have good cause to pray for the Prince of Peace. In times of conflict loving subjects redouble their pleas, and surely in the sorrows of our Lord His church could not but be in earnest. All the Savior's days were days of trouble, and He also made them days of prayer; the Church joins her intercession with her Lord's, and pleads that He may be heard in His cries and tears. The agony in the garden was especially a gloomy hour, but He was *heard in that he feared* [Hebrews 5:7]. He knew that His Father heard Him always, yet in that troublous hour no reply came until He had fallen on His face three times in the garden; then sufficient strength was given in answer to prayer, and He rose a victor from the conflict.

On the Cross also His prayer was not unheard, for in Psalm 22 He tells us, *thou hast heard me from the horns of the unicorns* [Psalm 22:21].[70] The Church in this verse implies that her Lord would be himself much given to prayer; in this He is our example, teaching us that if we are to receive any advantage from the prayers of others, we must first pray for ourselves. What a mercy that we may pray in the day

---

70. In other words, "thou hast rescued me from the horns of the wild beasts."

of trouble, and what a still more blessed privilege that no trouble can prevent the Lord from hearing us! Troubles roar like thunder, but the believer's voice will be heard above the storm. O Jesus, when you plead for us in our hour of trouble, the Lord Jehovah will hear you. This is a most refreshing confidence, and it may be indulged in without fear.

The name of the God of Jacob defend thee or, as some read it, "set thee in a high place." By the name is meant the revealed character and Word of God; we are not to worship "the unknown God" [See Acts 17:23.], but we should seek to know the covenant God of Jacob, who has been pleased to reveal His name and attributes to His people. There may be much in a royal name, or a learned name, or a venerable name, but it will be a theme for heavenly scholarship to discover all that is contained in the divine name. The glorious power of God defended and preserved the Lord Jesus through the battle of His life and death, and exalted Him above all His enemies. His warfare is now accomplished in His own proper person, but in His mystical body, the Church, He is still beset with dangers, and only the eternal arm of our God in covenant can defend the soldiers of the Cross, and set them on high out of the reach of their foes. The day of trouble is not over, the pleading Savior is not silent, and the name of the God of Israel is still the defense of the faithful.

The name, God of Jacob, is suggestive; Jacob had his day of trouble, he wrestled, was heard, was defended, and in due time was set on high, and his God is our God still, the same God to all his wrestling Jacobs. The whole verse is a very fitting benediction to be pronounced by a gracious heart over a child, a friend, or a minister, in prospect of trial; it includes both temporal and spiritual protection, and directs the mind to the great source of all good. How delightful to believe that our heavenly Father has pronounced it upon our favored heads!

Psalm 20:2 *Send thee help from the sanctuary, and strengthen thee out of Zion.*

EXPOSITION: **Verse 2.** *Send thee help from the sanctuary.* Out of heaven's sanctuary came the angel to strengthen our Lord, and from the precious remembrance of God's doings in His sanctuary our Lord refreshed himself when on the tree. There is no help like that which is of God's sending, and no deliverance like that which comes out of His sanctuary. The sanctuary to us is the person of our blessed Lord, who was typified by the temple, and is the true sanctuary which God has pitched, and not man: let us fly to the Cross for shelter in all times of need and help will be sent to us. Men of the world despise sanctuary help, but our hearts have learned to prize it beyond all material aid. They seek help out of the armory, or the treasury, or the buttery,[71] but we turn to the sanctuary.

And strengthen thee out of Zion. Out of the assemblies of the pleading saints who had for ages prayed for their Lord, help might well result to the despised sufferer, for praying breath is never spent in vain. To the Lord's mystical body[72] the richest comes in answer to the pleadings of His saints assembled for holy worship as His Zion. Certain advertisers recommend a strengthening plaster, but nothing can give such strength to the loins of a saint as waiting upon God in the assemblies of His people. This verse is a benediction befitting a Sabbath morning, and may be the salutation either of a pastor to his people, or of a church to its minister. God in the sanctuary of His dear Son's person, and in the city of His chosen Church is the proper object of His people's prayers, and under such a character may they confidently look to Him for His promised aid.

---

71. A small storage room for wine and food.
72. The Church.

Psalm 20:3 *Remember all thy offerings, and accept thy burnt sacrifice; Selah.*

EXPOSITION: **Verse 3.** *Remember all thy offerings, and accept thy burnt sacrifice. Selah.* Before war kings offered sacrifice, upon the acceptance of which they depended for success; our blessed Lord presented himself as a victim, and was a sweet savor unto the Most High, and then He met and routed the embattled legions of hell. His burnt sacrifice still perfumes the courts of Heaven, and through Him the offerings of His people are received as His sacrifices and oblations. We ought to have an eye to the sacrifice of Jesus in our spiritual conflicts, and never venture to war until the Lord has first given us a token for good at the altar of the Cross, where faith beholds her bleeding Lord. Selah. It is well to pause at the Cross before we march onward to battle, and with the psalmist cry "Selah." We are in too much of a hurry to make haste. A little pausing might greatly help our speed. Stay, good man, there is a haste which hinders; rest awhile, meditate on the burnt sacrifice, and put your heart right for the stern work which lies before you.

Psalm 20:4 *Grant thee according to thine own heart, and fulfil all thy counsel.*

EXPOSITION: **Verse 4.** *Grant thee according to thine own heart, and fulfil all thy counsel.* Christ's desire and counsel were both set upon the salvation of His people; the Church of old desired for Him good speed in His design, and the Church in these latter days, with all her heart desires the complete fulfillment of His purpose. In Christ Jesus sanctified souls may appropriate this verse as a promise; they shall have their desire, and their plans to glorify their Master shall succeed. We may have our own will, when our will is God's will. This was always the case with our Lord, and yet He said, *Not as I will, but as thou wilt* [Matthew 26:39]. You ask, "What is the need for submission in our case?" If it was necessary to Him, how much more for us?

Psalm 20:5 *We will rejoice in thy salvation, and in the name of our God we will set up our banners: the* LORD *fulfil all thy petitions.*

EXPOSITION: Verse 5. *We will rejoice in thy salvation.* In Jesus there is salvation; it is His own, and hence it is called thy salvation; but it is ours to receive and ours to rejoice in. We should fixedly resolve that come what may, we will rejoice in the saving arm of the Lord Jesus. The people in this psalm felt sure of victory before their king went to battle, and therefore began to rejoice beforehand; how much more ought we to do this who have seen the victory completely won! Unbelief begins weeping for the funeral before the man is dead; why should not faith commence piping before the dance of victory begins? Buds are beautiful, and promises not yet fulfilled are worthy to be admired. If joy were more general among the Lord's people, God would be more glorified among men; the happiness of the subjects is the honor of the sovereign.

And in the name of our God we will set up our banners. We lift the standard of defiance in the face of the foe, and wave the flag of victory over the fallen adversary. Some proclaim war in the name of one king, and some of another, but the faithful go to war in Jesus' name, the name of the incarnate God, Immanuel, God with us. The times are evil at present, but so long as Jesus lives and reigns in His Church we need not furl our banners in fear, but advance them with sacred courage:

Jesus' tremendous name
puts all our foes to flight;
Jesus, the meek, the angry Lamb,
a Lion is in the fight.[73]

The Church cannot forget that Jesus is her advocate before the throne, and therefore she sums up the desires already expressed in the short sentence: *The Lord fulfil all thy petitions.* Be it never forgotten that among those petitions is that choice one, *Father, I will that they also whom thou hast given me be with me where I am* [John 17:24].

Psalm 20:6 *Now know I that the LORD saveth his anointed; he will hear him from his holy heaven with the saving strength of his right hand.*

EXPOSITION: **Verse 6.** *Now know I that the Lord saveth his anointed.* We live and learn, and what we learn we are not ashamed to acknowledge. He who thinks he knows everything will miss the joy of finding out new truth; he will never be able to cry, "now I know," for he is so wise in his own conceit that he knows all that can be revealed and more. Souls conscious of ignorance shall be taught of the Lord, and rejoice as they learn. Earnest prayer frequently leads to assured confidence. The Church pleaded that the Lord Jesus might win the victory in His great struggle, and now by faith she sees Him saved by the omnipotent arm. She evidently finds a sweet relish in the fragrant title of "anointed;" she thinks of Him as ordained before all worlds to His great work, and then endowed with the needful qualifications by being anointed of the Spirit of the Lord. This is evermore

---

73. Hymn #401 in *A collection of hymns for the use of the people called Methodist,* by John Wesley (1804 edition).

the choicest solace of the believer, that Jehovah himself has anointed Jesus to be a Prince and a Savior, and that our shield is thus the Lord's own anointed.

He will hear him from his holy heaven with the saving strength of his right hand. It is here asserted confidently that God's holiness and power would both come to the rescue of the Savior in His conflict, and surely these two glorious attributes found congenial work in answering the sufferer's cries. Since Jesus was heard, we shall be; God is in Heaven, but our prayers can scale those glorious heights; those heavens are holy, but Jesus purifies our prayers, and so they gain admittance; our need is great, but the divine arm is strong, and all its strength is "saving strength;" that strength, moreover, is in the hand which is most used and which is used most readily—the right hand. What encouragements are these for pleading saints!

Psalm 20:7 *Some trust in chariots, and some in horses: but we will remember the name of the* LORD *our God.*

EXPOSITION: **Verse 7.** Contrasts frequently bring out the truth vividly, and here the Church sets forth the creature confidences of carnal men in contrast with her reliance upon the Prince Immanuel and the invisible Jehovah.

Some trust in chariots, and some in horses. Chariots and horses make an imposing show, and with their rattling, and dust, and fine caparisons, make so great a figure that vain man is much taken with them; yet the discerning eye of faith sees more in an invisible God than in all these. The most dreaded war engine of David's day was the war chariot, armed with scythes, which mowed down men like grass: this was the boast and glory of the neighboring nations; but the saints considered the name of Jehovah to be a far better defense.

As the Israelites might not keep horses, it was natural for them to regard the enemy's cavalry with more than usual dread. It is, therefore, all the greater evidence of faith that the bold songster can here disdain even the horse of Egypt in comparison with the Lord of hosts. Alas, how many in our day who profess to be the Lord's are as abjectly dependent upon their fellow men or upon an arm of flesh in some shape or other, as if they had never known the name of Jehovah at all. Jesus, may you alone be our rock and refuge, and never may we mar the simplicity of our faith.

We will remember the name of the Lord our God. "Our God" in covenant, who has chosen us and whom we have chosen; this God is our God. The name of our God is *Jehovah,* and this should never be forgotten; the self-existent, independent, immutable, ever-present, all-filling I AM. Let us adore that matchless name, and never dishonor it by distrust or creature confidence. Reader, you must know it before you can remember it. May the blessed Spirit reveal it graciously to your soul!

Psalm 20:8 *They are brought down and fallen: but we are risen, and stand upright.*

EXPOSITION: **Verse 8.** How different the end of those whose trusts are different! The enemies of God are uppermost at first, but they are before long brought down by force, or else fall of their own accord. Their foundation is rotten, and therefore when the time comes it gives way under them; their chariots are burned in the fire, and their horses die of pestilence, and where is their boasted strength? As for those who rest on Jehovah, they are often cast down at the first onset, but an Almighty arm uplifts them, and they joyfully stand upright. The victory of Jesus is the inheritance of His people. The world, death, Satan, and sin, shall all be trampled beneath the feet of the champions of faith; while those who rely upon an arm of flesh shall be ashamed and confounded forever.

Psalm 20:9 *Save,* LORD: *let the king hear us when we call.*

EXPOSITION: Verse 9. The psalm is here recapitulated. That Jesus might himself be delivered, and might then, as our King, hear us, is the twofold desire of the psalm. The first request is granted, and the second is sure to all the seed; and therefore we may close the psalm with the hearty shout, "God save the King."

"God save King Jesus, and may He soon come to reign!"

PSALM 21
PSALM 21:1–PSALM 21:13

Psalm 21:1 *The king shall joy in thy strength, O Lord; and in thy salvation how greatly shall he rejoice!*

EXPOSITION: **Verse 1.** *The king shall joy in thy strength, O Lord.* Jesus is a Royal Personage. The question, *Art thou a King then?* received a full answer from the Savior's lips: *Thou sayest that I am a King. To this end was I born, and for this purpose came I into the world, that I might bear witness unto the truth* [John 18:37].

He is not merely a King, but *the* King; King over minds and hearts, reigning with a dominion of love, before which all other rule is but mere brute force. He was proclaimed King even on the Cross, for there, indeed, to the eye of faith; He reigned as on a throne, blessing with more than imperial munificence the needy sons of Earth. Jesus has wrought out the salvation of His people, but as a man He found His strength in Jehovah His God, to whom He addressed himself in prayer upon the lonely mountain's side, and in the garden's solitary gloom.

That strength so abundantly given is here gratefully acknowledged, and made the subject of joy. The Man of Sorrows is now anointed with the oil of gladness above His fellows. Returned in triumph from the overthrow of all His foes, He offers His own rapturous *Te Deum*[74] in the temple above, and joys in the power of the Lord. Herein let every subject of King Jesus imitate the King; let us lean upon

---

74. A hymn of praise to God.

Jehovah's strength, let us joy in it by unstaggering faith, let us exult in it in our thankful songs. Jesus not only has thus rejoiced, but He shall do so as He sees the power of divine grace bringing out from their sinful hiding places the purchase of His soul's travail; we also shall rejoice more and more as we learn by experience more and more fully the strength of the arm of our covenant God. Our weakness unstrings our harps, but His strength tunes them anew. If we cannot sing a note in honor of our own strength, we can at any rate rejoice in our omnipotent God.

And in thy salvation how greatly shall he rejoice! Everything is ascribed to God; the source is your strength and the stream is your salvation. Jehovah planned and ordained it, works it and crowns it, and therefore it is His salvation. The joy here spoken of is described by a note of exclamation and a word of wonder: "how greatly!" The rejoicing of our risen Lord must be unutterable like His agony. If the mountains of His joy rise in proportion to the depth of the valleys of His grief, then His sacred bliss is high as the seventh Heaven.

For the joy which was set before Him as He endured the Cross, despising the shame, and now that joy daily grows, for He rests in His love and rejoices over His redeemed with singing, [See Zephaniah 3:17.] as in due order they are brought to find their salvation in His blood. Let us with our Lord rejoice in salvation, as coming from God, as coming to us, as extending itself to others, and as soon to encompass all lands. We need not be afraid of too much rejoicing in this respect; this solid foundation will well sustain the loftiest edifice of joy. The shouting of the early Methodists in the excitement of the joy were far more pardonable than our own lukewarmness. Our joy should have some sort of inexpressibleness in it.

Psalm 21:2 *Thou hast given him his heart's desire, and hast not withholden the request of his lips. Selah.*

EXPOSITION: Verse 2. *Thou hast given him his heart's desire.* That desire He ardently pursued when He was on Earth, both by His prayer, His actions, and His suffering; He manifested that His heart longed to redeem His people, and now in Heaven He has His desire granted Him, for He sees His beloved coming to be with Him where He is. The desires of the Lord Jesus were from His heart, and the Lord heard them; if our hearts are right with God, He will in our case also *fulfil the desires of them that fear him.* [See Psalm 145:19.]

And hast not withholden the request of his lips. What is in the well of the heart is sure to come up in the bucket of the lips, and those are the only true prayers where the heart's desire is first, and the lip's request follows after. Jesus prayed vocally as well as mentally; speech is a great assistance to thought. Some of us feel that even when alone we find it easier to collect our thoughts when we can pray aloud. The requests of the Savior were not withheld. He was and still is a prevailing Pleader. Our Advocate on high returns not empty from the throne of grace. He asked for His elect in the eternal council chamber, He asked for blessings for them here, He asked for glory for them hereafter, and His requests have speeded. He is ready to ask for us at the mercy seat. Have we not at this hour some desire to send up to His Father by Him? Let us not be slack to use our willing, loving, all prevailing Intercessor.

Selah. Here a pause is very properly inserted that we may admire the blessed success of the king's prayers, and that we may prepare our own requests which may be presented through Him. If we had a few more quiet rests, a few more times of Selah in our public worship, it might be profitable.

271

Psalm 21:3 *For thou preventest him with the blessings of goodness: thou settest a crown of pure gold on his head.*

EXPOSITION: **Verse 3.** *For thou preventest him with the blessings of goodness.* The word prevent formerly signified to precede or go before, and assuredly Jehovah preceded His Son with blessings. Before He died saints were saved by the anticipated merit of His death, before He came believers saw His day and were glad, and He himself had His delights with the sons of men. The Father is so willing to give blessings through His Son that instead of His being constrained to bestow His grace, He outstrips the Mediatorial march of mercy. *I say not that I will pray the Father for you, for the Father himself loveth you* [See John 16:26.]. Before Jesus calls the Father answers, and while He is yet speaking He hears. Mercies may be bought with blood, but they are also freely given. The love of Jehovah is not caused by the Redeemer's sacrifice, but that love, with its blessings of goodness, preceded the great atonement, and provided it for our salvation.

Reader, it will be a happy thing for you, if, like your Lord, you can see both providence and grace preceding you, forestalling your needs, and preparing your path. Mercy, in the case of many of us, ran before our desires and prayers, and it ever outruns our endeavors and expectancies, and even our hopes are left to lag behind. Prevenient grace deserves a song; we may make one out of this sentence; let us try. All our mercies are to be viewed as "blessings;" gifts of a blessed God, meant to make us blessed; they are "blessings of goodness," not of merit, but of free favor; and they come to us in a preventing way, a way of prudent foresight, such as only preventing love could have arranged. In this light the verse is itself a sonnet!

Thou settest a crown of pure gold on his head. Jesus wore the thorn-crown, but now wears the glory-crown. It is a "crown," indicating royal nature, imperial power, deserved honor, glorious conquest, and divine government. The crown is of the richest, rarest, most resplendent, and most lasting order—"gold," and that gold of the most refined and valuable sort, "pure gold," to indicate the excellence of His dominion. This crown is set upon His head most firmly, and whereas other monarchs find their diadems fitting loosely, His is fixed so that no power can move it, for Jehovah himself has set it upon His brow. Napoleon crowned himself, but Jehovah crowned the Lord Jesus; the empire of the one melted in an hour, but the other has an abiding dominion. Some versions read, "a crown of precious stones;" this may remind us of those beloved ones who shall be as jewels in His crown, of whom He has said, *They shall be mine in the day when I make up my jewels* [See Malachi 3:17.]. May we be set in the golden circle crown of the Redeemer's glory, and adorn His head forever!

Psalm 21:4 *He asked life of thee, and thou gavest it him, even length of days for ever and ever.*

EXPOSITION: **Verse 4.** *He asked life of thee, and thou gavest it him, even length of days for ever and ever.* The first words may suit King David, but the length of days forever and ever can only refer to the King Messiah. Jesus, as man, prayed for resurrection and He received it, and now possesses it in immortality. He died once, but being raised from the dead He dies no more. *Because I live, ye shall live also* [See John 14:19.] is the delightful intimation which the Savior gives us, that we are partakers of His eternal life. We would never have found this jewel, if He had not rolled away the stone which covered it.

Psalm 21:5 *His glory is great in thy salvation: honour and majesty hast thou laid upon him.*

EXPOSITION: **Verse 5.** *His glory is great in thy salvation.* Immanuel bears the palm; He once bore the Cross. The Father has glorified the Son, so that there is no glory like unto that which surrounds Him. See His person as it is described by John in the Revelation; see His dominion as it stretches from sea to sea; see His splendor as He is revealed in flaming fire. Lord, who is like unto thee? Solomon in all his glory could not be compared with you, the once despised Man of Nazareth! Note this reader: salvation is ascribed to God; and thus the Son, as our Savior, magnifies His Father; but the Son's glory is also greatly seen, for the Father glorifies His Son.

Honor and majesty thou hast laid upon him. Parkhurst[75] reads, "Splendor and beauty." These are put upon Jesus as chains of gold, and stars and tokens of honor are placed upon princes and great men. As the wood of the tabernacle was overlaid with pure gold, so is Jesus covered with glory and honor. If there be a far more exceeding and eternal weight of glory for His humble followers, what must there be for our Lord himself? The whole weight of sin was laid upon Him; it is right that the full measure of the glory of bearing it away should be laid upon the same beloved person. A glory commensurate with His shame he must and will receive, for well has He earned it. It is not possible for us to honor Jesus too much; what our God delights to do, we may certainly do to our utmost. Oh for new crowns for the lofty brow which once was marred with thorns!

---

75. Charles H. Parkhurst (1842–1933), American clergyman and social reformer.

Let him be crowned with majesty
Who bowed his head to death,
And be his honors sounded high
By all things that have breath.[76]

Psalm 21:6 *For thou hast made him most blessed for ever: thou hast made him exceeding glad with thy countenance.*

EXPOSITION: Verse 6. *For thou hast made him most blessed for ever.* He is most blessed in himself, for He is God over all, blessed forever; but this relates to Him as our Mediator, in which capacity blessedness is given to Him as a reward. The margin reads, "thou hast set him to be blessings; he is an overflowing wellspring of blessings to others, a sun filling the universe with light." According as the Lord swore unto Abraham, the promised seed is an everlasting source of blessings to all the nations of the Earth. He is set for this, ordained, appointed, made incarnate with this very design, that He may bless the sons of men. Oh, if only sinners had sense enough to use the Savior for that end to which He is ordained, viz., to be a Savior to lost and guilty souls.

Thou hast made him exceeding glad with thy countenance. He who is a blessing to others cannot but be glad himself; the unbounded good doing of Jesus ensures Him unlimited joy. The loving favor of His Father, the countenance of God, gives Jesus exceeding joy. This is the purest stream to drink of, and Jesus chooses no other. His joy is full. Its source is divine. Its continuance is eternal. Its degree exceeding all bounds.

The countenance of God makes the Prince of Heaven glad; how ought we to seek it, and how careful should we

---

76. Hymn: "O Lord, Our Lord, How Wondrous Great," written by Isaac Watts in 1719.

be lest we should provoke Him by our sins to hide His face from us! Our anticipations may cheerfully fly forward to the hour when the joy of our Lord shall be shed abroad on all the saints, and the countenance of Jehovah shall shine upon all the blood bought. So shall we *enter into the joy of our Lord* [See Matthew 25:23.].

So far all has been—"the shout of them that triumph, the song of them that feast."[77] Let us shout and sing with them, for Jesus is our King, and in His triumphs we share a part.

Psalm 21:7 *For the king trusteth in the* LORD, *and through the mercy of the most High he shall not be moved.*

EXPOSITION: **Verse 7.** *For the king trusteth in the Lord.* Our Lord, like a true King and leader, was a master in the use of the weapons, and could handle well the shield of faith, for He has set us a brilliant example of unwavering confidence in God. He felt himself safe in His Father's care until His hour was come, He knew that He was always heard in Heaven; He committed His cause to Him that judges right, and in His last moments He committed His spirit into the same hands. The joy expressed in the former verses was the joy of faith, and the victory achieved was due to the same precious grace. A holy confidence in Jehovah is the true mother of victories. This psalm of triumph was composed long before our Lord's conflict began, but faith overleaps the boundaries of time, and chants her "Io triumphe,"[78] while yet she sings her battle song.

Through the mercy of the Most High he shall not be

---

77. Words taken from verse 3 of "Jerusalem the Golden" written in 1146 by Bernard of Morlaix and translated from Latin to English by John M. Neale in 1858.

78. Latin for "hail for the triumph!"

moved. Eternal mercy secures the mediatorial throne of Jesus. He, who is Most High in every sense, engages all His infinite perfections to maintain the throne of grace upon which our King in Zion reigns. He was not moved from His purpose, nor in His sufferings, nor by His enemies, nor shall He be moved from the completion of His designs. *He is the same yesterday, today, and for ever* [See Hebrews 13:8.]. Other empires are dissolved by the lapse of years, but eternal mercy maintains His growing dominion evermore; other kings fail because they rest upon an arm of flesh, but our monarch reigns on in splendor because He trusts in Jehovah.

It is a great display of divine mercy to men that the throne of King Jesus is still among them: nothing but divine mercy could sustain it, for human malice would overturn it tomorrow if it could. We ought to trust in God for the promotion of the Redeemer's kingdom, for in Jehovah the King himself trusts: all unbelieving methods of action, and especially all reliance upon mere human ability, should be forever discarded from a kingdom where the monarch sets the examples of walking by faith in God.

Psalm 21:8 *Thine hand shall find out all thine enemies: thy right hand shall find out those that hate thee.*

EXPOSITION: Verse 8. *Thine hand shall find out all thine enemies: thy right hand shall find out those that hate thee.* The destruction of the wicked is a fitting subject for joy to the friends of righteousness; hence here, and in most scriptural songs, it is noted with calm thanksgiving. *Thou hast put down the mighty from their seats,* is a note of the same song which sings, *and hast exalted them of low degree* [Luke 1:50–55]. We pity the lost for they are men, but we cannot pity them as enemies of Christ. None can escape from the wrath of the victorious King, nor is it desirable that they should. Without looking for His flying foes He will find them with His hand, for His presence is about and around them.

In vain shall any hope for escape, He will find out all, and be able to punish all, and that, too, with the ease and rapidity which belong to the warrior's right hand. The finding-out relates, we think, not only to the discovery of the hiding places of the haters of God, but to the touching of them in their most tender parts, so as to cause the severest suffering. When He appears to judge the world hard hearts will be subdued into terror, and proud spirits humbled into shame. He who has the key of human nature can touch all its springs at His will, and find out the means of bringing the utmost confusion and terror upon those who aforetime boastfully expressed their hatred of Him.

Psalm 21:9 *Thou shalt make them as a fiery oven in the time of thine anger: the* LORD *shall swallow them up in his wrath, and the fire shall devour them.*

EXPOSITION: **Verse 9.** *Thou shalt make them as a fiery oven in the time of thine anger.* They themselves shall be an oven to themselves, and so their own tormentors. Those who burned with anger against you shall be burned by your anger. The fire of sin will be followed by the fire of wrath. Even as the smoke of Sodom and Gomorrah went up to Heaven, so shall the enemies of the Lord Jesus be utterly and terribly consumed.

Some read it, "Thou shalt put them as it were into a furnace of fire." Like faggots cast into an oven they shall burn furiously beneath the anger of the Lord; they shall be cast into a furnace of fire, there shall be weeping and gnashing of teeth. These are terrible words, and those teachers do not well who endeavor by their sophistical[79] reasonings to weaken their force. Reader, never tolerate slight thoughts of hell, or you will soon have low thoughts of sin. The hell of sinners must be fearful beyond all conception, or such language as the present would not be used. Who wants the Son of God to be his enemy when such an overthrow awaits His foes? The expression, *the time of thine anger,* reminds us that as now is the time of His grace, so there will be a set time for His wrath. The judge goes upon assize[80] at an appointed time. There is a day of vengeance of our God; let those who despise the day of grace remember this day of wrath.

The Lord shall swallow them up in his wrath, and the fire shall devour them. Jehovah will himself visit with His anger the enemies of His Son. The Lord Jesus will judge by commission from God, whose solemn assent and cooperation shall be with Him in His sentences upon impenitent sinners. An utter destruction of soul and body, so that both shall be swallowed up with misery, and be devoured with anguish, is here intended. Oh, the wrath to come! The wrath to come! Who can endure it? Lord, save us from it, for Jesus' sake.

Psalm 21:10 *Their fruit shalt thou destroy from the earth, and their seed from among the children of men.*

EXPOSITION: Verse 10. *Their fruit shalt thou destroy from the earth.* Their life's work shall be a failure, and the result of their toil shall be disappointment. That in which they prided themselves shall be forgotten; their very names shall be wiped out as abominable, and their seed from among the children of men. Their posterity following in their footsteps shall meet with a similar overthrow, until at last the race shall come to an end. Doubtless the blessing of God is often

---

79. misleading
80. Judicial writ.

handed down by the righteous to their sons, as almost an heirloom in the family, while the dying sinner bequeaths a curse to his descendants. If men will hate the Son of God, they must not wonder if their own sons meet with no favor.

Psalm 21:11 *For they intended evil against thee: they imagined a mischievous device, which they are not able to perform.*

EXPOSITION: **Verse 11.** *For they intended evil against thee.* God takes notice of intentions. He who would but could not is as guilty as he who did. Christ's Church and cause are not only attacked by those who do not understand it, but there are many who have the light and yet hate it. Intentional evil has a virus in it which is not found in sins of ignorance; now as ungodly men with malice prepared in advance, attack the Gospel of Christ, their crime is great, and their punishment will be proportionate. The words "against thee" show us that he who intends evil against the poorest believer means evil to the King himself: let persecutors beware.

They imagined a mischievous device, which they are not able to perform. Want of power is the clog on the foot of the haters of the Lord Jesus. They have the wickedness to imagine, and the cunning to devise, and the malice to plot mischief, but blessed be God, they fail in ability. Yet they shall be judged as to their hearts, and the will shall be taken for the deed in the great day of account. When we read the boastful threatening of the enemies of the Gospel at the present day, we may close our reading by cheerfully repeating, *which they are not able to perform.* The serpent may hiss, but his head is broken; the lion may roar, but he cannot devour: the tempest may thunder, but cannot strike. Old Giant Pope bites his nails at the pilgrims, but he cannot pick their bones as was done in times past. Growling forth a hideous *non possumus*,[81] the devil and all his allies retire in dismay from the walls of Zion, for the Lord is there.

Psalm 21:12 *Therefore shalt thou make them turn their back, when thou shalt make ready thine arrows upon thy strings against the face of them.*

EXPOSITION: Verse 12. *Therefore shalt thou make them turn their back, when thou shalt make ready thine arrows upon thy strings against the face of them.* For a time the foes of God may make bold advances, and threaten to overthrow everything, but a few ticks of the clock will alter the face of their affairs. At first they advance impudently enough, but Jehovah meets them to their teeth, and a taste of the sharp judgment of God speedily makes them flee in dismay. The original has in it the thought of the wicked being set as a butt for God to shoot at, a target for His wrath to aim at. What a dreadful situation! As an illustration upon a large scale, remember Jerusalem during the siege; and for an example in an individual, read the story of the deathbed of Francis Spira.[82] God takes sure aim; who would be His target? His arrows are sharp and transfix the heart; who would wish to be wounded by them? Ah, you enemies of God, your boastings will soon be over when once the shafts begin to fly!

Psalm 21:13 *Be thou exalted, LORD, in thine own strength: so will we sing and praise thy power.*

EXPOSITION: Verse 13. *Be thou exalted, Lord, in thine own strength.* A sweet concluding verse. Our hearts

---

81. Inability
82. In a book by Nathaniel Bacon called *The Fearful Estate of Francis Spira* (1638).

shall join in it. It is always right to praise the Lord when we call to remembrance His goodness to His Son, and the overthrow of His foes. The exaltation of the name of God should be the business of every Christian; but since such poor things as we fail to honor Him as He deserves, we may, however, invoke His own power to aid us. Be high, O God, but maintain your loftiness by your own almightiness, for no other power can worthily do it.

So will we sing and praise thy power. For a time the saints may mourn, but the glorious appearance of their divine Helper awakens their joy. Joy should always flow in the channel of praise. All the attributes of God are fitting subjects to be celebrated by the music of our hearts and voices, and when we observe a display of His power, we must extol it. He wrought our deliverance alone, and He alone shall have the praise.

PSALM 22
PSALM 22:1–PSALM 22:31

Psalm 22:1 *My God, my God, why hast thou forsaken me? why art thou so far from helping me, and from the words of my roaring?*

EXPOSITION: **Verse 1.** *My God, my God, why hast thou forsaken me?* This was the startling cry of Golgotha: *Eloi, Eloi, lama sabachthani.* The Jews mocked, but the angels adored when Jesus cried this exceeding bitter cry. Nailed to the tree we behold our great Redeemer in extremities, and so what see we? Having ears to hear let us hear, and having eyes to see let us see! Let us gaze with holy wonder, and mark the flashes of light amid the awful darkness of that midday midnight. First, our Lord's faith beams forth and deserves our reverent imitation; He keeps His hold upon His God with both hands and cries twice, *My God, my God!*

The spirit of adoption was strong within the suffering Son of Man, and He felt no doubt about His trust in His God. Oh that we could imitate this cleaving to an afflicting God! Nor does the sufferer distrust the power of God to sustain Him, for the title used—"El"—signifies strength, and is the name of the Mighty God. He knows the Lord to be the all-sufficient support and comfort of His spirit, and therefore appeals to Him in the agony of grief, but not in the misery of doubt. He questions why He was left and He raises that question and repeats it, but neither the power nor the faithfulness of God does He mistrust. What a question this is before us!

Why hast thou forsaken me? We must lay the emphasis on every word of this saddest of all utterances. *Why?* what is the great cause of such a strange fact as for God to leave His own Son at such a time and in such a plight? There was no cause in Him, why then was He deserted?

Hast: it is done, and the Savior is feeling its dread effect as He asks the question; it is surely true, but how mysterious! It was no threatening of forsaking which made the great Surety cry aloud, He endured that forsaking in very deed. *Thou:* I can understand why traitorous Judas and timid Peter should be gone, but you, my God, my faithful friend, how can you leave me? This is worst of all, yes, worse than all put together. Hell itself has for its fiercest flame the separation of the soul from God. *Forsaken:* if you had chastened I might bear it, for your face would shine; but to forsake me utterly, why is this? *Me:* thine innocent, obedient, suffering Son, do you leave me to perish? A sight of self seen by penitence and of Jesus on the Cross seen by faith will best expound this question. Jesus is forsaken because our sins had come between us and our God.

Why art thou so far from helping me, and from the words of my roaring? The Man of Sorrows had prayed until His speech failed Him, and He could only utter moaning and groaning as men do in severe sicknesses, like the roaring of a wounded animal. To what extremity of grief was our Master driven? What strong crying and tears were those which made Him too hoarse for speech! What must have been His anguish to find His own beloved and trusted Father standing afar off, and neither granting help nor apparently hearing prayer! This was good cause to make Him "roar." Yet there was reason for all this which those who rest in Jesus as their Substitute well know.

Psalm 22:2 *O my God, I cry in the day time, but thou hearest not; and in the night season, and am not silent.*

EXPOSITION: **Verse 2.** *O my God, I cry in the daytime, but thou hearest not.* For our prayers to appear to be unheard is no new trial, Jesus felt it before us, and it is observable that He still held fast His believing hold on God, and cried still, "My God." On the other hand His faith did not render him less importunate, for amid the hurry and horror of that dismal day He ceased not His cry, even as in Gethsemane He had agonized all through the gloomy night. Our Lord continued to pray even though no comfortable answer came, and in this He set us an example of obedience to His own words, *men ought always to pray, and not to faint* [Luke 18:1]. No daylight is too glaring, and no midnight too dark to pray in; and no delay or apparent denial, however grievous, should tempt us to forbear from importunate pleading.

Psalm 22:3 *But thou art holy, O thou that inhabitest the praises of Israel.*

EXPOSITION: **Verse 3.** *But thou art holy, O thou that inhabitest the praises of Israel.* However difficult things may look, there is no ill will in thee, O God! We are very apt to think and speak harshly of God when we are under His afflicting hand, but not so the obedient Son. He knows too well His Father's goodness to let outward circumstances libel His character. There is no unrighteousness with the God of Jacob, He deserves no censure; let Him do what He wills to do, He is to be praised, and to reign enthroned amid the songs of His chosen people.

If prayer is unanswered it is not because God is unfaithful,

285

but for some other good and weighty reason. If we cannot perceive any ground for the delay, we must leave the riddle unsolved, but we must not fly in God's face in order to invent an answer. While the holiness of God is in the highest degree acknowledged and adored, the afflicted speaker in this verse seems to marvel how the holy God could forsake Him, and be silent to His cries. The argument is you are holy. Why is it that you disregard your holy One in His hour of sharpest anguish!? We may not question the holiness of God, but we may argue from it, and use it as a plea in our petitions.

Psalm 22:4 *Our fathers trusted in thee: they trusted, and thou didst deliver them.*

EXPOSITION: Verse 4. *Our fathers trusted in thee: they trusted, and thou didst deliver them.* This is the rule of life with all the chosen family. Three times over is it mentioned, they trusted, and trusted, and trusted, and never stopped trusting, for it was their very life; and they fared well, for you delivered them out of all their straits, difficulties, and miseries faith brought them by calling their God to the rescue. But in the case of our Lord it appeared as if faith would bring no assistance from Heaven, He alone of all the trusting ones was to remain without deliverance.

The experience of other saints may be a great consolation to us when in deep waters if faith can be sure that their deliverance will be ours; but when we feel ourselves sinking, it is poor comfort to know that others are swimming. Our Lord here pleads the past dealings of God with His people as a reason why He should not be left alone; here again He is an example to us in the skilful use of the weapon of all prayer. The use of the plural pronoun "our" shows how one with His people Jesus was—even on the Cross. We say,

"Our Father which art in heaven," and He calls those "our fathers" through whom we came into the world, although He was without a father as to the flesh.

Psalm 22:5 *They cried unto thee, and were delivered: they trusted in thee, and were not confounded.*

EXPOSITION: Verse 5. *They cried unto thee, and were delivered: they trusted in thee, and were not confounded.* As if He had said, "How is it that I am now left without aid in my overwhelming griefs, while all others have been helped?" We may remind the Lord of His former loving-kindnesses to His people, and beseech Him to be still the same. This is true wrestling; let us learn the art. Observe, that ancient saints cried and trusted, and that in trouble we must do the same; and the invariable result was that they were not ashamed of their hope, for deliverance came in due time; this same happy portion shall be ours. The prayer of faith can do the deed when nothing else can. Let us seek to know and understand more when we see Jesus using the same pleas as ourselves, and immersed in griefs far deeper than our own.

Psalm 22:6 *But I am a worm, and no man; a reproach of men, and despised of the people.*

EXPOSITION: Verse 6. *But I am a worm, and no man.* This verse is a miracle in language. How could the Lord of glory be brought to such abasement as to be not only lower than the angels, but even lower than men? What a contrast between "I AM" and "I am a worm"! Yet such a double nature was found in the person of our Lord Jesus when bleeding upon the tree. He felt himself to be comparable to a helpless, powerless, downtrodden worm, passive while

287

crushed, and unnoticed and despised by those who trod upon Him. He selects the weakest of creatures, which is all flesh; and becomes, when trodden upon, writhing, quivering flesh, utterly devoid of any might except strength to suffer.

This was a true likeness of himself when His body and soul had become a mass of misery—the very essence of agony—in the dying pangs of crucifixion. Man by nature is but a worm; but our Lord puts himself even beneath man, on account of the scorn that was heaped upon Him and the weakness which He felt, and therefore He adds, "and no man." The privileges and blessings which belonged to the fathers He could not obtain while deserted by God, and common acts of humanity were not allowed Him, for He was rejected of men; He was outlawed from the society of Earth, and shut out from the smile of Heaven. How utterly did the Savior empty himself of all glory, and become of no reputation for our sakes!

A reproach of men—their scapegoat and object of jest; a byword and a proverb unto them: the sport of the rabble, and the scorn of the rulers. Oh the caustic power of reproach, to those who endure it with patience, yet smart under it most painfully!

And despised of the people. The *vox populi*[83] was against Him. The very people who would once have crowned Him then condemned Him, and they who were benefited by His cures sneered at Him in His woes. Sin is worthy of all reproach and contempt, and for this reason Jesus, the Sin Bearer, was given up to be unworthily and shamefully treated.

Psalm 22:7 *All they that see me laugh me to scorn: they shoot out the lip, they shake the head, saying,*

---

83. Voice of the people.

EXPOSITION: **Verse 7.** *All they that see me laugh me to scorn.* Read the evangelistic narrative of the ridicule endured by the Crucified One, and then consider, in the light of this expression, how it grieved Him. The iron entered into His soul. Mockery has for its distinctive description "cruel mocking," and those endured by our Lord were of the most cruel kind. The scornful ridicule of our Lord was universal; all sorts of men were unanimous in the derisive laughter, and vied with each other in insulting Him. Priests and people, Jews and Gentiles, soldiers and civilians, all united in the general scoff, at the time when He was prostrate in weakness and ready to die. Which shall we wonder at the most, the cruelty of man or the love of the bleeding Savior? How can we ever complain of ridicule after this?

They shoot out the lip, they shake the head. These were gestures of contempt. Pouting, grinning, shaking of the head, thrusting out of the tongue, and other modes of derision were endured by our patient Lord; men made faces at Him before whom angels veil their faces and adore. The basest signs of disgrace which disdain could devise were maliciously cast at Him. They punned[84] upon His prayers; they made it a matter for laughter of His sufferings, and set Him utterly at nought. In the poem "The Sacrifice" George Herbert[85] sings of our Lord as saying—

> Shame tears my soul, my body many a wound;
> Sharp nails pierce this, but sharper that confound;
> Reproaches which are free, while I am bound.
> Was ever grief like mine?

---

84. joked
85. George Herbert (1593–1633), poet, Anglican priest

Psalm 22:8 *He trusted on the* LORD *that he would deliver him: let him deliver him, seeing he delighted in him.*

EXPOSITION: **Verse 8.** Saying, *He trusted on the Lord that he would deliver him: let him deliver him, seeing he delighted in him.* Here the taunt is cruelly aimed at the sufferer's faith in God, which is the tenderest point in a good man's soul, the very apple of his eye. They must have learned the diabolical art from Satan himself, for they made rare proficiency in it. According to Matthew 27:39–44, there were five forms of taunt hurled at the Lord Jesus; this special piece of mockery is probably mentioned in this psalm because it is the most bitter of the whole; it has a biting, sarcastic irony in it, which gives it a peculiar venom; it must have stung the Man of Sorrows to the quick.

When we are tormented in the same manner, let us remember Him who endured such contradiction of sinners against himself, and we shall be comforted. On reading these verses, it makes one ready to ask as Joseph Trapp has, "Is this a prophecy or a history? for the description is so accurate." We must not lose sight of the truth which was unwittingly uttered by the Jewish scoffers. They themselves are witnesses that Jesus of Nazareth trusted in God: why then was He permitted to perish? Before He went to the Cross, Jehovah had delivered those who rolled their burdens upon Him: why was this man deserted? Oh that they had understood the answer!

Note further, that their ironical jest, seeing God delighted in Him, was true. The Lord did delight in His dear Son, and when He was found in fashion as a man, and became obedient unto death, God was still well pleased with Him. Strange mixture! Jehovah delights in Him, and yet bruises Him; is well pleased, and yet slays Him.

Psalm 22:9 *But thou art he that took me out of the womb: thou didst make me hope when I was upon my mother's breasts.*

EXPOSITION: **Verse 9.** *But thou art he that took me out of the womb.* Kindly providence attends with the surgery of tenderness at every human birth; but the Son of Man, who was marvelously begotten of the Holy Ghost, was in an especial manner watched over by the Lord when brought forth by Mary. The destitute state of Joseph and Mary, far away from friends and home, led them to see the cherishing hand of God in the safe delivery of the mother, and the happy birth of the child; that Child now fighting the great battle of His life, uses the mercy of His nativity as an argument with God. Faith finds weapons everywhere. He who wills to believe shall never lack reasons for believing.

Thou didst make me hope when I was upon my mother's breasts. Was our Lord so early a believer? Was He one of those babes and sucklings out of whose mouths strength is ordained? [See Psalm 8:2.] So it would seem; and if so, what a plea for help! Early piety gives peculiar comfort in our after trials, for surely He who loved us when we were children is too faithful to cast us off in our riper years. Some give the text the sense of "gave me cause to trust, by keeping me safely," and assuredly there was a special providence which preserved our Lord's infant days from the fury of Herod, the dangers of travelling, and the ills of poverty.

Psalm 22:10 *I was cast upon thee from the womb: thou art my God from my mother's belly.*

EXPOSITION: **Verse 10.** *I was cast upon thee from the womb.* Into the Almighty arms He was first received, as into those of a loving parent. This is a sweet thought.

God begins His care over us from the earliest hour. We are dandled upon the knee of mercy, and cherished in the lap of goodness; our cradle is canopied by divine love, and our first tottering steps are guided by His care. *Thou art my God from my mother's belly.* The psalm begins with *My God, my God,* and here, not only is the claim repeated, but its early date is urged. Oh noble perseverance of faith, thus to continue pleading with holy ingenuity of argument! Our birth was our weakest and most perilous period of existence; if we were then secured by Omnipotent tenderness, surely we have no cause to suspect that divine goodness will fail us now. He, who was our God when we left our mother, will be with us until we return to mother Earth, and will keep us from perishing in the belly of hell.

Psalm 22:11 *Be not far from me; for trouble is near; for there is none to help.*

EXPOSITION: Verse 11. The crucified Son of David continues to pour out His complaint and prayer. We need much grace that while reading we may have fellowship with His sufferings. May the blessed Spirit conduct us into a most clear and affecting sight of our Redeemer's woes.

Be not far from me. This is the petition for which He has been using such varied and powerful pleas. His great woe was that God had forsaken Him; His great prayer is that He would be near Him. A lively sense of the divine presence is a mighty stay to the heart in times of distress.

For trouble is near; for there is none to help. There are two "for's," as though faith gave a double knock at mercy's gate; that is a powerful prayer which is full of holy reasons and thoughtful arguments. The nearness of trouble is a weighty motive for divine help; this moves our heavenly Father's heart, and brings down His helping hand. It is His glory to be our very present help in trouble. Our Substitute had trouble in His inmost heart, for He said, "be not far from me." The absence of all other helpers is another telling plea. In our Lord's case none either could or would help Him, it was needful that He should tread the winepress alone; yet was it a sore aggravation to find that all His disciples had forsaken Him, and lover and friend were put far from Him. There is an awfulness about absolute friendlessness which is crushing to the human mind, for man was not made to be alone, and is like a dismembered limb when he has to endure heart loneliness.

Psalm 22:12 *Many bulls have compassed me: strong bulls of Bashan have beset me round.*

EXPOSITION: Verse 12. *Many bulls have compassed me: strong bulls of Bashan have beset me round.* The mighty ones in the crowd are here marked by the tearful eye of their victim. The priests, elders, scribes, Pharisees, rulers, and captains bellowed round the Cross like wild cattle, fed in the fat and solitary pastures of Bashan, full of strength and fury; they stamped and foamed around the innocent One, and longed to gore Him to death with their cruelties. Conceive of the Lord Jesus as a helpless, unarmed, naked man, cast into the midst of a herd of infuriated wild bulls. They were brutal as bulls, many, and strong, and the Rejected One was all alone, and bound naked to the tree. His position throws great force into the earnest entreaty, *Be not far from me.*

Psalm 22:13 *They gaped upon me with their mouths, as a ravening and a roaring lion.*

EXPOSITION: Verse 13. *They gaped upon me with their mouths, as a ravening and a roaring lion.* Like hungry cannibals they opened their blasphemous mouths as if they were about to swallow the man whom they abhorred. They could not vomit forth their anger fast enough through the ordinary aperture of their mouths, and therefore set the doors of their lips wide open like those who gape. Like roaring lions they howled out their fury, and longed to tear the Savior in pieces, as wild beasts raven over their prey. Our Lord's faith must have passed through a most severe conflict while He found himself abandoned to the tender mercies of the wicked, but He came off victorious by prayer; the very dangers to which He was exposed being used to add prevalence to His entreaties.

Psalm 22:14 *I am poured out like water, and all my bones are out of joint: my heart is like wax; it is melted in the midst of my bowels.*

EXPOSITION: Verse 14. Turning from his enemies, our Lord describes his own personal condition in language which should bring the tears into every loving eye. *I am poured out like water.* He was utterly spent, like water poured upon the earth; His heart failed Him, and had no more firmness in it than running water, and His whole being was made a sacrifice, like a libation poured out before the Lord. He had long been a fountain of tears; in Gethsemane His heart welled over in sweat, and on the Cross He gushed forth with blood; He poured out His strength and spirit, so that He was reduced to the most feeble and exhausted state.

All my bones are out of joint, as if distended upon a rack. Is it not most probable that the fastenings of the hands and feet, and the jarring occasioned by fixing the Cross in the earth, may have dislocated the bones of the Crucified One? If this is not intended, we must refer the expression to that extreme weakness which would occasion relaxation of the muscles and a general sense of parting asunder throughout the whole system.

My heart is like wax; it is melted in the midst of my bowels. Excessive debility and intense pain made His inmost life to feel like wax melted in the heat. The Greek liturgy uses the expression, "thine unknown sufferings," and well it may. The fire of Almighty wrath would have consumed our souls forever in hell; it was no light work to bear as a substitute the heat of an anger so justly terrible. Dr. Gill[86] wisely observes, "If the heart of Christ, the Lion of the tribe of Judah, melted at it, what heart can endure, or hands be strong, when God deals with them in His wrath?"

Psalm 22:15 *My strength is dried up like a potsherd; and my tongue cleaveth to my jaws; and thou hast brought me into the dust of death.*

EXPOSITION: Verse 15. *My strength is dried up like a potsherd.* Most complete debility is here portrayed; Jesus likens himself to a broken piece of earthenware, or an earthen pot, baked in the fire till the last particle of moisture is driven out of the clay. No doubt a high degree of feverish burning afflicted the body of our Lord. All His strength was dried up in the tremendous flames of avenging justice, even as the paschal lamb was roasted in the fire.

My tongue cleaveth to my jaws. Thirst and fever fastened His tongue to His jaws. Dryness and a horrible clamminess tormented His mouth, so that He could scarcely speak.

Thou hast brought me into the dust of death, so tormented in every single part as to feel dissolved into separate atoms, and each atom full of misery; the full price of our redemption was paid, and no part of the Surety's body or soul escaped its share of agony. The words may set forth Jesus as having wrestled with Death until He rolled into the dust with His

---

86. Dr. John Gill, theologian in the 1700s.

antagonist. Behold the humiliation of the Son of God! The Lord of Glory stoops to the dust of death. Amid the moldering relics of mortality Jesus condescends to lodge! Bishop Mant[87] wrote a version of the two preceding verses that are forcible and accurate:

> Poured forth like water is my frame;
> My bones asunder start;
> As wax that feels the searching flame,
> Within me melts my heart.
> My withered sinews shrink unstrung
> Like potsherd dried and dead:
> Cleaves to my jaws my burning tongue
> The dust of death my bed.

Psalm 22:16 *For dogs have compassed me: the assembly of the wicked have inclosed me: they pierced my hands and my feet.*

EXPOSITION: **Verse 16.** We are to understand every item of this sad description as being urged by the Lord Jesus as a plea for divine help; and this will give us a high idea of His perseverance in prayer.

For dogs have compassed me. Here He marks the more ignoble crowd, who, while less strong than their brutal leaders, were not less ferocious, for there they were howling and barking like unclean and hungry dogs. Hunters frequently surround their game with a circle, and gradually encompass them with an ever narrowing ring of dogs and men. Such a picture is before us. In the center stands, not a panting stag, but a bleeding, fainting man, and around Him are the enraged and unpitying wretches who have hounded Him to His doom. Here we have the "hind of the morning" of whom

---

87. Bishop Richard Mant, Bishop of Down in the 1700s.

the psalm so plaintively sings, hunted by bloodhounds, all thirsting to devour Him.

The assembly of the wicked have inclosed me: thus the Jewish people that had not accepted Christ as their Savior and called themselves an assembly of the righteous is marked upon the forehead as an assembly of the wicked, and justly so. This is not the only occasion when professed churches of God have become synagogues of Satan, and have persecuted the Holy One and the Just.

They pierced my hands and my feet. This can by no means refer to David, or to any one but Jesus of Nazareth, the once crucified but now exalted Son of God. . . pause, dear reader, and view the wounds of your Redeemer.

Psalm 22:17 *I may tell all my bones: they look and stare upon me.*

EXPOSITION: **Verse 17.** So emaciated was Jesus by His fasting and sufferings that He says, *"I may tell all my bones."* He could count and recount them. Bishop George Horne, [English churchman, writer, and university administrator] thinks the posture of the body on the Cross would so distend the flesh and skin as to make the bones visible, so that they might be numbered. The zeal of His Father's house had eaten him up; like a good soldier he had endured hardness. Oh that we cared less for the body's enjoyment and ease and more for our Father's business! It would be better to count the bones of an emaciated body than to bring leanness into our souls.

They look and stare upon me. Unholy eyes gazed insultingly upon the Savior's nakedness, and shocked the sacred delicacy of His holy soul. The sight of the agonizing body ought to have ensured sympathy from the throng, but it only increased their savage mirth, as they gloated their cruel eyes upon

His miseries. Let us blush for human nature, and mourn in sympathy with our Redeemer's shame. The first Adam made us all naked, and therefore the second Adam became naked that He might clothe our naked souls.

Psalm 22:18 *They part my garments among them, and cast lots upon my vesture.*

EXPOSITION: **Verse 18.** *They part my garments among them, and cast lots upon my vesture.* The garments of the executed were the perquisites of the executioners in most cases, but it was not often that they cast lots at the division of the spoil; this incident shows how clearly David in vision saw the day of Christ, and how surely the Man of Nazareth is He of whom the prophets spake: *"these things, therefore, the soldiers did."* [See John 19:24.] He who gave His blood to cleanse us gave His garments to clothe us. Christopher Ness, English preacher and author says. "This precious Lamb of God gave up his golden fleece for us." How every incident of Jesus' griefs is stored up in the treasury of inspiration, and embalmed in the amber of sacred song; therefore, we must learn to be very mindful of all that concerns our Beloved, and to think much more of everything which has a connection with Him. It may be noted that the habit of gambling is of all others the most hardening, for men could practice it even at the foot of the Cross while sprinkled with the blood of the Crucified. No Christian will endure the rattle of the dice when he thinks of this.

Psalm 22:19 *But be not thou far from me, O LORD: O my strength, haste thee to help me.*

EXPOSITION: **Verse 19.** *But be thou not far from me, O Lord.* Invincible faith returns to the charge, and uses the same means, viz., importunate prayer. He repeats the petition so piteously offered before. He wants nothing but His God, even in His lowest state. He does not ask for the most comfortable or nearest presence of God, He will be content if He is not far from Him; humble requests speed at the throne.

O my strength, haste thee to help me. Hard cases need timely aid: when necessity justifies it we may be urgent with God as to time, and cry, "make haste;" but we must not do this out of willfulness. Note how in the last degree of personal weakness He calls the Lord my strength; after this fashion the believer can sing, "*When I am weak, then am I strong.*" [See 2 Corinthians 12:10.]

Psalm 22:20 *Deliver my soul from the sword; my darling from the power of the dog.*

EXPOSITION: Verse 20. *Deliver my soul from the sword.* By the sword is probably meant entire destruction, which as a man He dreaded; or perhaps He sought deliverance from the enemies around Him, who were like a sharp and deadly sword to Him. The Lord had said, "Awake, O sword," and now from the terror of that sword the Shepherd would fain be delivered as soon as justice should see fit.

My darling from the power of the dog. Meaning His soul, His life, which is most dear to every man. The original is, "my only one," and therefore is our soul dear, because it is our only soul. Would that all men made their souls their darlings, but many treat them as if they were not worth so much as the mire of the streets.

The dog may mean Satan, that infernal Cerberus, that cursed and cursing cur; or else the whole company of Christ's foes, who though many in number were as unanimous as if there were but one, and with one consent sought to rend Him in pieces. If Jesus cried for help against the dog of hell, much more may we. Cave canem,[88] for his power is great, and only God can deliver us from him. When he fawns upon us, we must not put ourselves in his power; and when he howls at us, we may remember that God holds him with a chain.

Psalm 22:21 *Save me from the lion's mouth: for thou hast heard me from the horns of the unicorns.*

EXPOSITION: Verse 21. *Save me from the lion's mouth: for thou hast heard me from the horns of the unicorns.* Having experienced deliverance in the past from great enemies, who were strong as the unicorns, the Redeemer utters His last cry for rescue from death, which is fierce and mighty as the lion. This prayer was heard, and the gloom of the Cross departed. Thus faith, though sorely beaten, and even cast beneath the feet of her enemy, ultimately wins the victory. It was so in our Head, it shall be so in all the members. We have overcome the unicorn, we shall conquer the lion, and from both lion and unicorn we shall take the crown.

--- **EXPOSITION:** ---

Verses 22–23. The transition is very marked; from a horrible tempest all is changed into calm. The darkness of Calvary at length passed away from the face of nature, and from the soul of the Redeemer, and beholding the light of His triumph and its future results the Savior smiled. We have followed Him through the gloom, let us attend Him in the returning light. It will be well still to regard the words as a part of our Lord's soliloquy upon the Cross, uttered in His mind during the last few moments before His death.

Psalm 22:22 *I will declare thy name unto my brethren: in the midst of the congregation will I praise thee.*

---

88. Beware of the dog.

EXPOSITION: **Verse 22.** *I will declare thy name unto my brethren.* The delights of Jesus are always with His Church, and hence His thoughts, after much distraction, return at the first moment of relief to their usual channel; He forms fresh designs for the benefit of His beloved ones. He is not ashamed to call them brethren, saying, *I will declare thy name unto my brethren, in the midst of the church will I sing praise unto thee.* Among His first resurrection words were these, *Go to my brethren* [John 20:17]. In the verse before us, Jesus anticipates happiness in having communication with His people; He purposes to be their teacher and minister, and fixes His mind upon the subject of His discourse.

The name, i.e., the character and conduct of God, are by Jesus Christ's gospel proclaimed to all the holy brotherhood; they behold the fullness of the Godhead dwelling bodily in Him, and rejoice greatly to see all the infinite perfections manifested in one who is bone of their bone and flesh of their flesh. What a precious subject is the name of our God! It is the only one worthy of the only Begotten, whose meat and drink it was to do the Father's will. We may learn from this resolution of our Lord that one of the most excellent methods of showing our thankfulness for deliverances is to tell to our brethren what the Lord has done for us. We mention our sorrows readily enough; why are we so slow in declaring our deliverances?

In the midst of the congregation will I praise thee. Not in a little household gathering merely does our Lord resolve to proclaim His Father's love, but in the great assemblies of His saints, and in the general assembly and Church of the firstborn. This the Lord Jesus is always doing by His representatives, who are the heralds of salvation, and labor to praise God. In the great universal Church Jesus is the One authoritative teacher, and all others, so far as they are worthy to be called teachers, are nothing but echoes of His voice. Jesus, in this second sentence, reveals His object in declaring the divine name, it is that God may be praised; the Church continually magnifies Jehovah for manifesting himself in the person of Jesus, and Jesus himself leads the song, and is both precentor[89] and preacher in His church. Delightful are the seasons when Jesus communes with our hearts concerning divine truth; joyful praise is the sure result.

Psalm 22:23 *Ye that fear the LORD, praise him; all ye the seed of Jacob, glorify him; and fear him, all ye the seed of Israel.*

EXPOSITION: **Verse 23.** *Ye that fear the Lord praise him.* The reader must imagine the Savior as addressing the congregation of the saints. He exhorts the faithful to unite with Him in thanksgiving. The description of "fearing the Lord" is very frequent and very instructive; it is the *beginning of wisdom*, and is an essential sign of grace [See Psalm 111:10.]. *I am a Hebrew and I fear God* was Jonah's confession of faith. [See Jonah 1:9.] Humble awe of God is so necessary a preparation for praising Him that none are fit to sing to His honor but such as reverence His Word; but this fear is consistent with the highest joy, and is not to be confounded with legal bondage, which is a fear which perfect love casts out. Holy fear should always keep the key of the singing pew. Where Jesus leads the tune none but holy lips may dare to sing.

All ye the seed of Jacob glorify him. The genius of the Gospel is praise. Jew and Gentile saved by sovereign grace should be eager in the blessed work of magnifying the God of our salvation. All saints should unite in the song; no tongue may be silent, no heart may be cold. Christ calls us to glorify God, and can we refuse? *And fear him, all ye the seed of*

---

89. cantor or choirmaster

Israel. The spiritual Israel all do this and we hope the day will come when Israel after the flesh will be brought to the same mind. The more we praise God the more reverently shall we fear Him, and the deeper our reverence the sweeter our songs. So much does Jesus value praise that we have it here under His dying hand and seal that all the saints must glorify the Lord.

Psalm 22:24 *For he hath not despised nor abhorred the affliction of the afflicted; neither hath he hid his face from him; but when he cried unto him, he heard.*

EXPOSITION: Verse 24. *For he hath not despised nor abhorred the affliction of the afflicted.* Here is good matter and motive for praise. The experience of our covenant Head and Representative should encourage all of us to bless the God of grace. Never was man so afflicted as our Savior in body and soul from friends and foes, by Heaven and hell, in life and death; He was the foremost in the ranks of the afflicted, but all those afflictions were sent in love, and not because His Father despised and abhorred Him. It is true that justice demanded that Christ should bear the burden which as a substitute He undertook to carry, but Jehovah always loved Him, and in love laid that load upon Him with a view to His ultimate glory and to the accomplishment of the dearest wish of His heart. Under all His woes our Lord was honorable in the Father's sight, the matchless jewel of Jehovah's heart.

Neither hath he hid his face from him. That is to say, the hiding was but temporary, and was soon removed; it was not final and eternal. *But when he cried unto him, he heard.* Jesus was heard in that He feared. He cried *in extremis*[90]

---

90. At the point of death.

and *de profundis*,[91] and was speedily answered; He therefore bids His people join Him in singing a *Gloria in excelsis*.[92] "Glory to God in the highest." Every child of God should seek refreshment for his faith in this testimony of the Man of Sorrows. What Jesus here witnesses is as true today as when it was first written. It shall never be said that any man's affliction or poverty prevented his being an accepted suppliant at Jehovah's throne of grace. The meanest applicant is welcome at mercy's door—"None that approach His throne shall find a God unfaithful or unkind."

Psalm 22:25 *My praise shall be of thee in the great congregation: I will pay my vows before them that fear him.*

EXPOSITION: **Verse 25.** *My praise shall be of thee in the great congregation.* The one subject of our Master's song is the Lord alone. The Lord and the Lord only is the theme which the believer handles when he gives himself to imitate Jesus in praise. The word in the original is "from thee"—true praise is of celestial origin. The rarest harmonies of music are nothing unless they are sincerely consecrated to God by hearts sanctified by the Spirit. The choirmaster says, "Let us sing to the praise and glory of God;" but the choir often sings to the praise and glory of themselves. Oh when shall our service of song be a pure offering? Observe in this verse how Jesus loves the public praises of the saints, and thinks with pleasure of the great congregation. It would be wicked on our part to despise the twos and threes; but, on the other hand, let not the little companies snarl at the greater assemblies as though they were necessarily less pure and less approved, for Jesus loves the praise of the great congregation.

---

91. From the depths.
92. Glory in the highest degree.

I will pay my vows before them that fear him. Jesus dedicates himself anew to the carrying out of the divine purpose in fulfillment of His vows made in anguish. Did our Lord when He ascended to the skies proclaim amid the redeemed in glory the goodness of Jehovah? And was that the vow meant here? Undoubtedly the publication of the Gospel is the constant fulfillment of covenant engagements made by our Surety in the councils of eternity. Messiah vowed to build up a spiritual temple for the Lord, and He will surely keep His Word.

Psalm 22:26 *The meek shall eat and be satisfied: they shall praise the LORD that seek him: your heart shall live for ever.*

EXPOSITION: Verse 26. *The meek shall eat and be satisfied.* Note how the dying Lover of our souls solaces himself with the result of His death. The spiritually poor find a feast in Jesus, they feed upon Him to the satisfaction of their hearts, they were famished until He gave himself for them, but now they are filled with royal dainties. The thought of the joy of His people gave comfort to our expiring Lord. Note the characters who partake of the benefit of His passion; "the meek," the humble and lowly. Lord, make us so. Note also the certainty that gospel provisions shall not be wasted, "they shall eat;" and the sure result of such eating, "and be satisfied."

They shall praise the Lord that seek him. For a while they may keep a fast, but their thanksgiving days must and shall come. *Your heart shall live for ever.* Your spirits shall not fail through trial, you shall not die of grief, and immortal joys shall be your portion. Thus Jesus speaks even from the Cross to the troubled seeker. If His dying words are so assuring, what consolation may we not find in the truth that *He ever lives to make intercession for us*! [See Hebrews 7:25.] They who eat at Jesus' table receive the fulfillment of the promise, *Whosoever eateth of this bread shall live for ever* [See John 6:58.].

Psalm 22:27 *All the ends of the world shall remember and turn unto the* LORD: *and all the kindreds of the nations shall worship before thee.*

EXPOSITION: Verse 27. In reading this verse one is struck with the Messiah's missionary spirit. It is evidently His grand consolation that Jehovah will be known throughout all places of His dominion.

All the ends of the world shall remember and turn unto the Lord. Out from the inner circle of the present Church the blessing is to spread in growing power until the remotest parts of the Earth shall be ashamed of their idols, mindful of the true God, penitent for their offences, and unanimously earnest for reconciliation with Jehovah. Then shall false worship cease, *and all the kindreds of the nations shall worship before thee,* the only living and true God. This hope which was the reward of Jesus is a stimulus to those who fight His battles. It is well to mark the order of conversion as here set forth; they shall *remember*—this is reflection, like the prodigal who came unto himself; *and turn unto the Lord*—this is repentance, like Manasseh who left his idols, and *worship*—this is holy service, as Paul adored the Christ whom once he abhorred.

Psalm 22:28 *For the kingdom is the* LORD's: *and he is the governor among the nations.*

EXPOSITION: Verse 28. *For the kingdom is the Lord's.* As an obedient Son the dying Redeemer rejoiced to know that His Father's interests would prosper through His pains. "The Lord reigns" was his song as it is ours. He who by His own power reigns supreme in the domains of creation and providence, has set up a kingdom of grace, and by the conquering power of the Cross that kingdom will grow until all people shall own its sway and proclaim that He is the governor among the nations. Amid the tumults and disasters of the present the Lord reigns; but in the halcyon days of peace the rich fruit of His dominion will be apparent to every eye. Great Shepherd, let your glorious kingdom come.

Psalm 22:29 *All they that be fat upon earth shall eat and worship: all they that go down to the dust shall bow before him: and none can keep alive his own soul.*

EXPOSITION: **Verse 29.** *All they that be fat upon earth*—the rich and great are not shut out. Grace now finds the most of its jewels among the poor, but in the latter days the mighty of the Earth shall eat, shall taste of redeeming grace and dying love, and shall worship with all their hearts the God who deals so bountifully with us in Christ Jesus. Those who are spiritually fat with inward prosperity shall be filled with the marrow of communion, and shall worship the Lord with peculiar fervor. In the covenant of grace Jesus has provided good cheer for our high estate, and He has taken equal care to console us in our humiliation, for the next sentence is *all they that go down to the dust shall bow before him.* There is relief and comfort in bowing before God when our case is at its worst; even amid the dust of death prayer kindles the lamp of hope.

While all who come to God by Jesus Christ are thus blessed, whether they be rich or poor, none of those who despise him may hope for a blessing. *None can keep alive his own soul.* This is the stern counterpart of the gospel message of "look and live." There is no salvation out of Christ. We must hold life, and have life as Christ's gift, or we shall die eternally. This is very solid evangelical doctrine, and should be proclaimed in every corner of the Earth, that like a great hammer it may break in pieces all self-confidence.

Psalm 22:30 *A seed shall serve him; it shall be accounted to the Lord for a generation.*

EXPOSITION: Verse 30. *A seed shall serve him.* Posterity shall perpetuate the worship of the Most High. The kingdom of truth on Earth shall never fail. As one generation is called to its rest, another will arise in its stead. We need have no fear for the true apostolic succession; that is safe enough. *It shall be accounted to the Lord for a generation.* He will reckon the ages by the succession of the saints, and set His accounts according to the families of the faithful. Generations of sinners come not into the genealogy of the skies. God's family register is not for strangers, but for the children only.

Psalm 22:31 *They shall come, and shall declare his righteousness unto a people that shall be born, that he hath done this.*

EXPOSITION: Verse 31. *They shall come.* Sovereign grace shall bring out from among men the blood-bought ones. Nothing shall thwart the divine purpose. The chosen shall come to life, to faith, to pardon, to Heaven. In this the dying Savior finds a sacred satisfaction. Toiling servant of God be glad at the thought that the eternal purpose of God shall neither suffer nor be hindered.

And shall declare his righteousness unto a people that

shall be born. None of the people who shall be brought to God by the irresistible attractions of the Cross shall lack understanding nor be able to speak; they shall be able to tell forth the righteousness of the Lord, so that future generations shall know the truth. Fathers shall teach their sons, who shall hand it down to their children; the burden of the story always being that *"He has done this,"* or, that *"It is finished."* Salvation's glorious work is done; there is peace on Earth, and glory in the highest. *It is finished,* these were the expiring words of the Lord Jesus [John 19:30], as they are the last words of this psalm. May we by living faith be enabled to see our salvation finished by the death of Jesus!

PSALM 23
PSALM 23:1–23:6

Psalm 23:1 *The Lord is my shepherd; I shall not want.*

EXPOSITION: **Verse 1.** *The Lord is my shepherd.*
What condescension this is that the infinite Lord assumes towards His people the office and character of a Shepherd! It should be the subject of grateful admiration that the great God allows himself to be compared to anything which will set forth His great love and care for His own people. David had himself been a keeper of sheep, and understood both the needs of the sheep and the many cares of a shepherd. He compares himself to a creature weak,

defenseless, and foolish, and he takes God to be his Provider, Preserver, Director, and, indeed, his everything.

No man has a right to consider himself the Lord's sheep unless his nature has been renewed for the scriptural description of unconverted men does not picture them as sheep, but as wolves or goats. A sheep is an object of property, not a wild animal; its owner sets great store by it, and frequently it is bought with a great price. It is well to know, as certainly David did, that we belong to the Lord. There is a noble tone of confidence about this sentence. There is no "if" nor "but," nor even "I hope so"; but he says, *The Lord is my shepherd*. We must cultivate the spirit of assured dependence upon our heavenly Father. The sweetest word of the whole is that monosyllable, *My*. He does not say, "The Lord is the shepherd of the world at large, and leads forth the multitude as His flock," but *The Lord is my shepherd;* if He is a Shepherd to no one else, He is a Shepherd to me; He cares for me, watches over me, and preserves me. The words are in the present tense. Whatever the believer's position, he is even now under the pastoral care of Jehovah.

The next words are a sort of inference from the first statement—they are sententious and positive—*I shall not want*. I might want otherwise, but when the Lord is my Shepherd He is able to supply my needs, and He is certainly willing to do so, for His heart is full of love, and therefore *I shall not want*. I shall not lack for temporal things. Does He not feed the ravens, and cause the lilies to grow? How, then, can He leave His children to starve? I shall not want for spirituals; I know that His grace will be sufficient for me. Resting in Him, He will say to me, *As thy days so shall thy strength be* [Deuteronomy 33:25]. I may not possess all that I wish for, but *I shall not want*. Others, far wealthier and wiser than I, may want, but *I shall not*.

The young lions do lack, and suffer hunger: but they that seek the Lord shall not want any good thing [Psalm 34:10]. It is not only "I do not want," but *I shall not want*. Come what may, if famine should devastate the land, or calamities destroy the city, *I shall not want*. Old age with its feebleness shall not bring me any lack, and even death with its gloom shall not find me destitute. I have all things and abound; not because I have a good store of money in the bank, not because I have skill and wit with which to win my bread, but because *The Lord is my shepherd.* The wicked always want, but the righteous never; a sinner's heart is far from satisfaction, but a gracious spirit dwells in the palace of content.

Psalm 23:2 *He maketh me to lie down in green pastures: he leadeth me beside the still waters.*

EXPOSITION: **Verse 2.** *He maketh me to lie down in green pastures: he leadeth me beside the still waters.* The Christian life has two elements in it, the contemplative and the active, and both of these are richly provided for. First, the contemplative. *He maketh me to lie down in green pastures.* What are these "green pastures" but the Scriptures of truth—always fresh, always rich, and never exhausted? There is no fear of biting the bare ground where the grass is long enough for the flock to lie down in it. Sweet and full are the doctrines of the Gospel; fit food for souls, as tender grass is natural nutriment for sheep. When by faith we are enabled to find rest in the promises, we are like the sheep that lie down in the midst of the pasture; we find at the same moment both provender and peace, rest and refreshment, serenity and satisfaction.

But observe: *He maketh me to lie down.* It is the Lord who graciously enables us to perceive the preciousness of His truth, and to feed upon it. How grateful ought we to be for the power to appropriate the promises! There are some distracted souls who would give worlds if they could but do this. They know the blessedness of it, but they cannot say that this blessedness is theirs. They know the "green pastures," but they are not made to "lie down" in them.

313

Those believers who have for years enjoyed a "full assurance of faith" should greatly bless their gracious God.

The second part of a vigorous Christian's life consists in gracious activity. We not only think, but we act. We are not always lying down to feed, but are journeying onward toward perfection; hence we read, *he leadeth me beside the still waters.* What are these "still waters" but the influences and graces of His blessed Spirit? His Spirit attends us in various operations, like waters—in the plural—to cleanse, to refresh, to fertilize, and to cherish. They are "still waters," for the Holy Ghost loves peace, and sounds no trumpet of ostentation in His operations. He may flow into our soul, but not into our neighbor's, and therefore our neighbor may not perceive the divine presence; and though the blessed Spirit may be pouring His floods into one heart, yet he that sits next to the favored one may know nothing of it. "In secret silence of the mind, My heaven—and there my God I find."[93]

Still waters run deep. Nothing noisier than an empty drum. That silence is golden indeed in which the Holy Spirit meets with the souls of His saints. Not to raging waves of strife, but to peaceful streams of holy love does the Spirit of God conduct the chosen sheep. He is a dove, not an eagle; the dew, not the hurricane. Our Lord leads us beside these "still waters"; we could not go there of ourselves, we need His guidance, therefore it is said, "he leadeth me." He does not drive us. Moses drives us by the law, but Jesus leads us by His example, and the gentle drawing of His love.

Psalm 23:3 *He restoreth my soul: he leadeth me in the paths of righteousness for his name's sake.*

---

93. Hymn #122, verse 4, from *Psalms, Hymns, Spiritual Songs,* by Isaac Watts.

EXPOSITION: **Verse 3.** *He restoreth my soul.* When the soul grows sorrowful He revives it; when it is sinful He sanctifies it; when it is weak He strengthens it. "He" does it. His ministers could not do it if He did not. His Word would not avail by itself. *He restoreth my soul.* Are any of us low in grace? Do we feel that our spirituality is at its lowest ebb? He who turns the ebb into the flood can soon restore our soul. Pray to Him, then, for the blessing—"Restore me, Shepherd of my soul!"

He leadeth me in the paths of righteousness for his name's sake. The Christian delights to be obedient, but it is the obedience of love, to which he is constrained by the example of his Master. *He leadeth me.* The Christian is not obedient to some commandments and neglectful of others; he does not pick and choose, but yields to all. Observe, that the plural is used—*the paths of righteousness.* Whatever God may give us to do we would do it, led by His love. Some Christians overlook the blessing of sanctification, and yet to a thoroughly renewed heart this is one of the sweetest gifts of the covenant. If we could be saved from wrath, and yet remain unregenerate, impenitent sinners, we would not be saved as we desire, for we mainly and chiefly pant to be saved from sin and led in the way of holiness. All this is done out of pure free grace; *for his name's sake.* It is to the honor of our great Shepherd that we should be a holy people, walking in the narrow way of righteousness. If we are so led and guided we must not fail to adore our heavenly Shepherd's care.

Psalm 23:4 *Yea, though I walk through the valley of the shadow of death, I will fear no evil: for thou art with me; thy rod and thy staff they comfort me.*

EXPOSITION: **Verse 4.** *Yea, though I walk through the valley of the shadow of death, I will fear no evil: for thou art with me; thy rod and thy staff they comfort me.* This unspeakably delightful verse has been sung on many a dying bed, and has helped to make the dark valley bright, time and time again. Every word in it has a wealth of meaning. *Yea, though I walk,* as if the believer did not quicken his pace when he came to die, but still calmly walked with God. To walk indicates the steady advance of a soul which knows its road, knows its end, resolves to follow the path, feels quite safe, and is therefore perfectly calm and composed. The dying saint is not in a flurry, he does not run as though he were alarmed, nor stand still as though he would go no further, he is not confounded nor ashamed, and therefore keeps to his old pace. Observe that it is not walking in the valley, but through the valley. We go through the dark tunnel of death and emerge into the light of immortality. We do not die; we do but sleep to wake in glory. Death is not the house but the porch, not the goal but the passage to it.

The dying article is called a valley. The storm breaks on the mountain, but the valley is the place of quietude, and thus very often the last days of the Christian are the most peaceful of his whole career; the mountain is bleak and bare, but the valley is rich with golden sheaves, and many a saint has reaped more joy and knowledge when he came to die than he ever knew while he lived. And, then, it is not "the valley of death," but *the valley of the shadow of death,* for death in its substance has been removed, and only the shadow of it remains. Someone has said that when there is a shadow there must be light somewhere, and so there is. Death stands by the side of the highway in which we have to travel, and the light of Heaven shining upon him throws a shadow across our path; let us then rejoice that there is a light beyond. Nobody is afraid of a shadow, for a shadow cannot stop a man's pathway even for a moment. The shadow of a dog cannot bite; the shadow of a sword cannot kill; the shadow of death cannot destroy us. Let us not, therefore, be afraid.

I will fear no evil. He does not say there shall not be any evil; he had got beyond even that high assurance, and knew that Jesus had put all evil away; but *I will fear no evil;* as if even his fears, those shadows of evil, were gone forever. The worst evils of life are those which do not exist except in our imagination. If we had no troubles but real troubles, we would not have a tenth part of our present sorrows. We feel a thousand deaths in fearing one, but the psalmist was cured of the disease of fearing. *I will fear no evil,* not even the Evil One himself; I will not dread the last enemy; I will look upon him as a conquered foe, an enemy to be destroyed, *For thou art with me.* This is the joy of the Christian! *Thou art with me.* The little child out at sea in the storm is not frightened like all the other passengers on board the vessel, it sleeps in its mother's bosom; it is enough for it that its mother is with it; and it should be enough for the believer to know that Christ is with him. *Thou art with me;* I have, in having you, all that I can crave: I have perfect comfort and absolute security, for *thou art with me.*

Thy rod and thy staff, by which you govern and rule your flock, the ensigns of your sovereignty and of your gracious care—*they comfort me.* I will believe that you reign still. The rod of Jesse shall still be over me as the sovereign succor[94] of my soul. Many persons profess to receive much comfort from the hope that they shall not die. Certainly there will be some who will be "alive and remain" at the coming of the Lord, but is there advantage in such an escape from death as to make it the object of Christian desire? [See 1 Thessalonians

---

94. comfort

4:17.] A preference of the wise man might be to die, for those who shall not die, but who *shall be caught up together with the Lord in the air,* will be losers rather than gainers. They will lose that actual fellowship with Christ in the tomb which dying saints will have, and we are expressly told that they shall have no preference beyond those who are asleep. Let us be of Paul's mind when he said that *To die is gain,* and think of "departing to be with Christ, which is far better." [See Philippians 1:21.] This twenty-third psalm is not worn out, and it is as sweet in a believer's ear now as it was in David's time, let novelty hunters say what they will.

Psalm 23:5 *Thou preparest a table before me in the presence of mine enemies: thou anointest my head with oil; my cup runneth over.*

EXPOSITION: Verse 5. *Thou preparest a table before me in the presence of mine enemies.* The good man has his enemies. He would not be like his Lord if he had not. If we were without enemies we might fear that we were not the friends of God, for the friendship of the world is enmity to God. Yet see the quietude of the godly man in spite of, and in the sight of, his enemies. How refreshing is his calm bravery! *Thou preparest a table before me.* When a soldier is in the presence of his enemies, if he eats at all he snatches a hasty meal, and away he hastens to the fight. But observe: *Thou preparest a table,* just as a servant does when she unfolds the damask cloth and displays the ornaments of the feast on an ordinary peaceful occasion. Nothing is hurried, there is no confusion, no disturbance, the enemy is at the door, and yet God prepares a table, and the Christian sits down and eats as if everything were in perfect peace. Oh the peace which Jehovah gives to His people, even in the midst of the most trying circumstances!

Let earth be all in arms abroad,
They dwell in perfect peace.[95]

Thou anointest my head with oil. May we live in the
daily enjoyment of this blessing, receiving a fresh anointing
for every day's duties. Every Christian is a priest, but he
cannot execute the priestly office without unction, and hence
we must go day by day to God the Holy Ghost that we
may have our heads anointed with oil. A priest without oil
misses the chief qualification for his office, and the Christian
priest lacks his chief fitness for service when he is devoid
of new grace from on high. *My cup runneth over.* He had
not only enough, a cup full, but more than enough, a cup
which overflowed. A poor man may say this as well as those
in higher circumstances. "What, all this, and Jesus Christ
too?" said a poor cottager as she broke a piece of bread
and filled a glass with cold water. Whereas a man may be
ever so wealthy, but if he is discontented his cup cannot run
over; it is cracked and leaks. Content is the philosopher's
stone which turns all it touches into gold; happy is he who
has found it. Content is more than a kingdom, it is another
word for happiness.

Psalm 23:6 *Surely goodness and mercy shall follow
me all the days of my life: and I will dwell in the
house of the LORD for ever.*

EXPOSITION: **Verse 6.** *Surely goodness and mercy
shall follow me all the days of my life.* This is a fact as
indisputable as it is encouraging, and therefore a heavenly
verily or "surely" is set as a seal upon it. This sentence
may be read, "only goodness and mercy," for there shall be

---

95. Hymn #575, verse 2, from *The Shilling Hymnbook*, by
William Stone.

unmingled mercy in our history. These twin guardian angels will always be with me at my back and my call. Just as when great princes go abroad they must not go unattended, so it is with the believer. Goodness and mercy follow him always—all the days of his life—the black days as well as the bright days, the days of fasting as well as the days of feasting, the dreary days of winter as well as the bright days of summer. Goodness supplies our needs, and mercy blots out our sins. *And I will dwell in the house of the Lord for ever.*

A servant abideth not in the house for ever, but the son abideth ever [John 8:35]. While I am here I will be a child at home with my God; the whole world shall be His house to me; and when I ascend into the upper chamber, I shall not change my company, nor even change the house; I shall only go to dwell in the upper storey of the house of the Lord forever. May God grant us grace to dwell in the serene atmosphere of this most blessed psalm!

PSALM 24

PSALM 24:1–PSALM 24:10

Psalm 24:1 *The earth is the Lord's, and the fulness thereof; the world, and they that dwell therein.*

EXPOSITION: Verse 1. How very different is this from the ignorant Jewish notion of God which prevailed in our Savior's day? The Jews said, "The holy land is God's, and the seed of Abraham are His only people;" but their great Monarch had long before instructed them—*The earth is the Lord's and the fulness thereof.* The whole round world is claimed for Jehovah, and they that dwell therein are declared to be His subjects. When we consider the bigotry of the Jewish people at the time of Christ, and how angry they were with our Lord for saying that many widows were in Israel, but unto none of them was the prophet sent, save only to the widow of Sarepta, [See Luke 4:26.] and that there were many lepers in Israel, but none of them was healed except Naaman the Syrian. When also we recollect, how angry they were at the mention of Paul's being sent to the Gentiles, we are amazed that they should have remained in such blindness, and yet have sung this psalm, which shows so clearly that God is not the God of the Jews only, but of the Gentiles also.

What a rebuke this is to those upstarts who speak of the black people and other races as though they were not cared for by the God of Heaven! If a man is but a man the Lord claims him, and who dares to brand him as a mere piece of merchandise! The meanest of men is a dweller in the world, and therefore belongs to Jehovah. Jesus Christ had made an end of the exclusiveness of nationalities. There is neither barbarian, Scythian, bond not free; but we all are one in Christ Jesus. Man lives upon the Earth, and parcels out its soil among his mimic kings and autocrats; but the Earth is not man's. He is but a tenant at will, a leaseholder upon the most precarious tenure, liable to instantaneous eviction. The great Landowner and true Proprietor holds His court above the clouds, and laughs at the title deeds of worms of the dust. The deed is not with the lord of the manor nor the freeholder, but with the Creator. The fullness of the Earth may mean its harvests, its wealth, its life, or its worship; in all these senses the Most High God is Possessor of all. The Earth is full of God; He made it full and He keeps it full, notwithstanding all the demands which living creatures make upon its stores.

The sea is full, despite all the clouds which rise from it; the air is full, notwithstanding all the lives which breathe it; the soil is full, though millions of plants derive their nourishment from it. Under man's tutored hand the world is coming to a greater fullness than ever, but it is all the Lord's; the field and the fruit, the Earth and all Earth's wonders are Jehovah's. We look also for a more sublime fullness when the true ideal of a world for God shall have been reached in millennial glories, and then most clearly the Earth will be the Lord's and the fullness thereof. These words are now upon London's Royal Exchange, they shall one day be written in letters of light across the sky. The term world indicates the habitable regions, wherein Jehovah is especially to be acknowledged as Sovereign.

He who rules the fish of the sea and the fowl of the air should not be disobeyed by man, His noblest creature. Jehovah is the Universal King; all nations are beneath His sway: true Autocrat of all the nations, emperors and czars are but His slaves. Men are not their own, nor may they

PSALM 24

call their lips, their hearts, or their substance their own; they are Jehovah's rightful servants. This claim especially applies to us who are born from Heaven. We do not belong to the world or to Satan, but by creation and redemption we are the peculiar portion of the Lord. Paul uses this verse twice, to show that no food is unclean, and that nothing is really the property of false gods. All things are God's; no ban is on the face of nature, nothing is common or unclean. The world is all God's world, and the food which is sold in the shambles is sanctified by being my Father's, and I need not hesitate to eat thereof.

Psalm 24:2 *For he hath founded it upon the seas, and established it upon the floods.*

EXPOSITION: Verse 2. In the second verse we have the reason why the world belongs to God, namely, because He has created it, which is a title beyond all dispute. *For he hath founded it upon the seas.* It is God who lifts up the Earth from out of the sea, so that the dry land, which otherwise might in a moment be submerged, as in the days of Noah, is kept from the floods. The hungry jaws of ocean would devour the dry land if a constant fiat of Omnipotence did not protect it. *He hath established it upon the floods.* The world is Jehovah's, because from generation to generation he preserves and upholds it, having settled its foundations. Providence and Creation are the two legal seals upon the title deeds of the great Owner of all things. He who built the house and bears up its foundations has surely a first claim upon it.

Let it be noted, however, upon what insecure foundations all terrestrial things are founded. Founded on the seas! Established on the floods! Blessed be God the Christian has another world to look forward to, and rests his hopes upon a more stable foundation than this poor world affords. They who trust in worldly things build upon the sea; but we have laid our hopes, by God's grace, upon the Rock of Ages; we are resting upon the promise of an immutable God, we are depending upon the constancy of a faithful Redeemer. Oh! you worldlings, who have built your castles of confidence, your palaces of wealth, and your bowers of pleasure upon the seas, and established them upon the floods; how soon will your baseless fabrics melt, like foam upon the waters! Sand is treacherous enough, but what shall be said of the yet more unstable sea?

EXPOSITION:

Verses 3–6. Here we have the true Israel described. The men who shall stand as courtiers in the palace of the living God are not distinguished by race, but by character; they are not Jews only, nor Gentiles only, nor any one branch of mankind peculiarly, but a people purified and made meet to dwell in the holy hill of the Lord.

Psalm 24:3 *Who shall ascend into the hill of the LORD? or who shall stand in his holy place?*

EXPOSITION: **Verse 3.** *Who shall ascend into the hill of the Lord?* It is uphill work for the creature to reach the Creator. Where is the mighty climber who can scale the towering heights? Nor is it height alone; it is glory too. Whose eye shall see the King in His beauty and dwell in His palace? In Heaven He reigns most gloriously, who shall be permitted to enter into His royal presence? God has made all, but He will not save all; there is a chosen company who shall have the singular honor of dwelling with Him in His high abode. These choice spirits desire to commune with God and their wish shall be granted them. The solemn enquiry of the text is repeated in another form. *Who shall be able to stand or continue there?* He casts away the wicked, who then can abide in His house? Who is He that can gaze upon the Holy One, and can abide in the blaze of His glory? Certainly none may venture to commune with God upon the footing of the law, but grace can make us meet to behold the vision of the divine presence. The question before us is one which all should ask for themselves, and none should be at ease until they have received an answer of peace. With careful self-examination let us enquire, "Lord, is it I?"

Psalm 24:4 *He that hath clean hands, and a pure heart; who hath not lifted up his soul unto vanity, nor sworn deceitfully.*

EXPOSITION: **Verse 4.** *He that hath clean hands.* Outward, practical holiness is a very precious mark of grace. To wash in water with Pilate is nothing, but to wash in innocency is all-important. It is to be feared that many professors have perverted the doctrine of justification by faith in such a way as to treat good works with contempt; if so, they will receive everlasting contempt at the last great day. It is vain to prate of inward experience unless the daily life is free from impurity, dishonesty, violence, and oppression. Those who draw near to God must have clean hands. What monarch would have servants with filthy hands to wait at his table? They who were ceremonially unclean could not enter into the Lord's house which was made with hands; much less shall the morally defiled be allowed to enjoy spiritual fellowship with a holy God. If our hands are now unclean, let us wash them in Jesus' precious blood, and so let us pray unto God, lifting up pure hands.

But "clean hands" would not suffice, unless they were connected with *a pure heart.* True religion is heart work.

We may wash the outside of the cup and the platter as long as we please; but if the inward parts be filthy, we are filthy altogether in the sight of God, for our hearts are more truly ourselves than our hands are. We may lose our hands and yet live, but we could not lose our heart and still live; the very life of our being lies in the inner nature, and hence the imperative need of purity within. There must be a work of grace in the core of the heart as well as in the palm of the hand, or our religion is a delusion. May God grant that our inward powers may be cleansed by the sanctifying Spirit, so that we may love holiness and abhor all sin. The pure in heart shall see God, all others are but blind bats; stone blindness in the eyes arises from stone in the heart. Dirt in the heart throws dust in the eyes.

The soul must be delivered from delighting in the groveling toys of Earth; the man who is born for Heaven *has not lifted up his soul unto vanity*. All men have their joys, by which their souls are lifted up; the worldling lifts up his soul in carnal delights, which are mere empty vanities; but the saint loves more substantial things; like Jehoshaphat, he is lifted up in the ways of the Lord. He who is content with the husks will be reckoned with the swine. If we suck our consolation from the breasts of the world, we prove ourselves to be its home-born children. Does the world satisfy you? Then you have your reward and your portion in this life; make much of it, for you shall know no other joy.

Nor sworn deceitfully. The saints are men of honor still. The Christian man's word is his only oath; but that is as good as twenty oaths of other men. False speaking will shut any man out of Heaven, for a liar shall not enter into God's house, whatever may be his professions or doings. God will have nothing to do with liars, except to cast them into the lake of fire. Every liar is a child of the devil, and will be sent home to his father. A false declaration, a fraudulent statement, a cooked account, a slander, a lie—all these may suit the assembly of the ungodly, but are detested among true saints: how could they have fellowship with the God of truth, if they did not hate every false way?

Psalm 24:5 *He shall receive the blessing from the LORD, and righteousness from the God of his salvation.*

EXPOSITION: Verse 5. It must not be supposed that the persons who are thus described by their inward and outward holiness are saved by the merits of their works; but their works are the evidences by which they are known. The present verse shows that in the saints grace reigns and grace alone. Such men wear the holy livery of the Great King because he has of his own free love clothed them therewith. The true saint wears the wedding garment, but he knows that the Lord of the feast provided it for him, without money and without price.

He shall receive the blessing from the Lord, and righteousness from the God of his salvation. Because the saints need salvation; they receive righteousness, and the blessing is a boon from God their Savior. They do not ascend the hill of the Lord as givers but as receivers, and they do not wear their own merits, but a righteousness which they have received. Holy living ensures a blessing as its reward from the thrice Holy God, but it is itself a blessing of the New Covenant and a delightful fruit of the Spirit. God first gives us good works, and then rewards us for them. Grace is not obscured by God's demand for holiness, but is highly exalted as we see it decking the saint with jewels, and clothing him in fair white linen; all this sumptuous array being a free gift of mercy.

Psalm 24:6 *This is the generation of them that seek him, that seek thy face, O Jacob. Selah.*

EXPOSITION: Verse 6. *This is the generation of them that seek him, that seek thy face, O Jacob.* These are the regeneration, these are in the line of grace; these are the legitimate seed. Yet they are only seekers; hence learn that true seekers are very dear in God's esteem, and are entered upon His register. Even seeking has a sanctifying influence; what a consecrating power must lie in finding and enjoying the Lord's face and favor! To desire communion with God is a purifying thing. Oh to hunger and thirst more and more after a clear vision of the face of God; this will lead us to purge ourselves from all filthiness, and to walk with heavenly circumspection. He who longs to see his friend when he passes takes care to clear the mist from the window, lest by any means his friend should go by unobserved. Really awakened souls seek the Lord above everything, and as this is not the usual desire of mankind, they constitute a generation by themselves; a people despised of men but beloved of God.

The expression, *O Jacob*, is a very difficult one, unless it is indeed true that the God of Jacob here condescends to be called Jacob, and takes upon himself the name of His chosen people. The preceding verses correct the inordinate boastings of those Jews who vaunted themselves as the favorites of Heaven; they are told that their God is the God of all the Earth, and that He is holy, and will admit none but holy ones into His presence. Let the mere professor as he reads these verses listen to the voice which saith, *Without holiness no man shall see the Lord* [Hebrews 12:14]. Selah. Lift up the harp and voice, for a nobler song is coming; a song of our Well beloved.

328

Psalm 24:7 *Lift up your heads, O ye gates; and be ye lift up, ye everlasting doors; and the King of glory shall come in.*

EXPOSITION: Verse 7. These last verses reveal to us the great representative man, who answered to the full character laid down, and therefore by his own right ascended the holy hill of Zion. Our Lord Jesus Christ could ascend into the hill of the Lord because His hands were clean and His heart was pure, and if we by faith in Him are conformed to His image we shall enter too. We have here a picture of our Lord's glorious ascent. We see Him rising from amidst the little group upon Olivet, and as the cloud receives Him, angels reverently escort Him to the gates of Heaven. The ancient gates of the eternal temple are personified and addressed in song by the attending cohorts of rejoicing spirits.

> Lo His triumphal chariot waits,
> And angels chant the solemn lay.[96]
> "Lift up your heads, ye heavenly gates;
> Ye everlasting doors, give way."[97]

They are called upon "to lift up their heads," as though with all their glory they were not great enough for the All-glorious King. Let all things do their utmost to honor so great a Prince; let the highest Heaven put on unusual loftiness in honor of the King of Glory. He who, fresh from the Cross and the tomb, now rides through the gates of the New Jerusalem is higher than the heavens; great and everlasting as they are, those gates of pearl are all unworthy of Him before whom the heavens are not pure, and who charges His angels with folly. *Lift up your heads, O ye gates.*

---

96. A narrative in song or poem.
97. "Psalm 24," verse 7, from *Psalms and Hymns,* by Charles Wesley (1743).

Psalm 24:8 *Who is this King of glory? The LORD strong and mighty, the LORD mighty in battle.*

EXPOSITION: **Verse 8.** The watchers at the gate hearing the song look over the battlements and ask, *Who is this King of glory?* A question full of meaning and worthy of the meditations of eternity. Who is He in person, nature, character, office and work? What is His pedigree? What His rank and what His race? The answer given in a mighty wave of music is, *The Lord strong and mighty, the Lord mighty in battle.* We know the might of Jesus by the battles which He has fought, the victories which He has won over sin, and death, and hell, and we clap our hands as we see Him leading captivity captive in the majesty of His strength [See Ephesians 4:8.]. Oh for a heart to sing His praises! Mighty hero, be crowned forever King of kings and Lord of lords.

Psalm 24:9 *Lift up your heads, O ye gates; even lift them up, ye everlasting doors; and the King of glory shall come in.*

EXPOSITION: **Verse 9.** *Lift up your heads, O ye gates; even lift them up, ye everlasting doors; and the King of glory shall come in.* The words are repeated with a pleasing variation. There are times of deep earnest feeling when repetitions are not vain but full of force. Doors were often taken from their hinges when Easterners would show welcome to a guest, and some doors were drawn up and down like a portcullis, and may possibly have protruded from the top; thus literally lifting up their heads. The picture is highly poetical, and shows how wide Heaven's gate is set by the ascension of our Lord. Blessed be God, the gates have never been shut since. The opened gates of Heaven invite the weakest believer to enter.

Dear reader, it is possible that you are saying, "I shall never enter into the Heaven of God, for I have neither clean hands nor a pure heart." Look then to Christ, who has already climbed the holy hill. He has entered as the forerunner of those who trust him. Follow in His footsteps, and repose upon His merit. He rides triumphantly into Heaven, and you shall ride there too if you trust Him. "But how can I get the character described?" you ask. The Spirit of God will give you that. *He will create in you a new heart and a right spirit* [Ezekiel 36:26]. Faith in Jesus is the work of the Holy Spirit, and has all virtues wrapped up in it. Faith stands by the fountain filled with blood, and as she washes therein, clean hands and a pure heart, a holy soul and a truthful tongue are given to her.

Psalm 24:10 *Who is this King of glory? The* LORD *of hosts, he is the King of glory. Selah.*

EXPOSITION: **Verse 10.** The closing note is inexpressibly grand. Jehovah of hosts, Lord of men and angels, Lord of the universe, Lord of the worlds, is the King of glory. All true glory is concentrated upon the true God, for all other glory is but a passing pageant, the painted pomp of an hour. The ascended Savior is here declared to be the Head and Crown of the universe, the King of Glory. Our Immanuel is hymned in most sublime strains. Jesus of Nazareth is Jehovah Sabaoth.[98]

---

98. Lord of the Sabbath.

PSALM 25
PSALM 25:1–PSALM 25:22

Psalm 25:1 *Unto thee, O Lord, do I lift up my soul.*

EXPOSITION: **Verse 1.** *Unto thee, O Lord.* See how the holy soul flies to its God like a dove to its cote.[99] When the storm winds are out, the Lord's vessels put about[100] and make for their well-remembered harbor of refuge. What a mercy that the Lord will condescend to hear our cries in time of trouble, although we may have almost forgotten Him in our hours of fancied prosperity. *Unto thee, O Jehovah, do I lift up my soul.* It is but a mockery to uplift the hands and the eyes unless we also bring our souls into our devotions. True prayer may be described as the soul rising from Earth to have fellowship with Heaven; it is taking a journey upon Jacob's ladder, leaving our cares and fears at the foot, and meeting with a covenant God at the top. Very often the soul cannot rise, she has lost her wings, and is heavy and Earth-bound; more like a burrowing mole than a soaring eagle. At such dull seasons we must not cease our prayers, but must, by God's assistance, exert all our powers to lift up our hearts. Let faith be the lever and grace be the arm, and the dead lump will yet be stirred. But what a lift it has sometimes proved! With all our tugging and straining we have been utterly defeated, until the heavenly loadstone of our Savior's love has displayed its omnipotent attractions, and then our hearts have gone up to our Beloved like mounting flames of fire.

---

99. A coop for doves.
100. Change direction.

Psalm 25:2 *O my God, I trust in thee: let me not be ashamed, let not mine enemies triumph over me.*

EXPOSITION: **Verse 2.** *O my God.* This title is dearer than the name Jehovah, which is used in the first sentence. Already the sweet singer has drawn nearer to his heavenly helper, for he makes bold to grasp him with the hand of assured possession, calling him, my God. Oh the more than celestial music of that word—"My God!" It is to be observed that the psalmist does not deny expression to those gracious feelings with which God had favored him. He does not fall into loathsome mock modesty, but finding in his soul a desire to seek the Lord he avows it. Believing that he has a rightful interest in Jehovah he declares it, and knowing that he has confidence in his God he professes it; *O my God, I trust in thee.*

Faith is the cable which binds our boat to the shore, and by pulling at it we draw ourselves to the land; faith unites us to God, and then draws us near to Him. As long as the anchor of faith holds there is no fear in the worst tempest; if that should fail us there would be no hope left. We must see to it that our faith is sound and strong, for otherwise prayer cannot prevail with God. Woe to the warrior who throws away his shield; what defense can be found for him who finds no defense in his God? Let me not be ashamed. Let not my disappointed hopes make me feel ashamed of my former testimonies of your faithfulness. Many were on the watch for this. The best of men have their enemies, and should pray against them that they may not see their wicked desires accomplished.

Let not mine enemies triumph over me. Suffer no wicked mouth to make blasphemous mirth out of my distresses by asking, "Where is thy God?" There is a great jealousy in believers for the honor of God, and they cannot endure that unbelievers should taunt them with the failure of their expectations from the God of their salvation. All other trusts will end in disappointment and eternal shame, but our confidence shall never be confounded.

Psalm 25:3 *Yea, let none that wait on thee be ashamed: let them be ashamed which transgress without cause.*

EXPOSITION: Verse 3. *Yea, let none that wait on thee be ashamed.* Suffering enlarges the heart by creating the power to sympathize. If we pray eagerly for ourselves, we shall not long be able to forget our fellow sufferers. None pity the poor like those who have been or are still poor, none have such tenderness for the sick as those who have been long in ill-health themselves. We ought to be grateful for occasional griefs if they preserve us from chronic hardheartedness; for of all afflictions, an unkind heart is the worst, it is a plague to its possessor, and a torment to those around him. Prayer when it is of the Holy Ghost's teaching is never selfish; the believer does not sue for monopolies for himself, but would have all in like case to partake of divine mercy with him. The prayer may be viewed as a promise; our Heavenly Father will never let His trustful children find Him untrue or unkind. He will ever be mindful of His covenant.

Let them be ashamed which transgress without cause. David had given his enemies no provocation; their hatred was wanton. Sinners have no justifiable reason or valid excuse for transgressing; they benefit no one, not even themselves by their sins; the law against which they transgress is not harsh or unjust; God is not a tyrannical ruler, providence is not a bondage: men sin because they will sin, not because it is either profitable or reasonable to do so. Hence shame is their fitting reward. May they blush with penitential shame now, or else they will not be able to escape the everlasting contempt and the bitter shame which is the portion of fools in the world to come.

Psalm 25:4 *She me thy ways, O LORD; teach me thy paths.*

EXPOSITION: **Verse 4.** *Shew me thy ways, O Lord.* Unsanctified natures clamor for their own way, but gracious spirits cry, "Not my will, but thine be done." We cannot at all times discern the path of duty, and at such times it is our wisdom to apply to the Lord himself. Frequently the dealings of God with us are mysterious, and then also we may appeal to Him as His own interpreter, and in due time He will make all things plain. Moral, providential and mental forms of guidance are all precious gifts of a gracious God to a teachable people. The second petition, *teach me thy paths,* appears to mean more than the first, and may be illustrated by the case of a little child who would say to his father, "Father, first tell me which is the way, and then teach my little trembling feet to walk in it." What weak dependent creatures we are! How constantly should we cry to the Strong for strength!

Psalm 25:5 *Lead me in thy truth, and teach me: for thou art the God of my salvation; on thee do I wait all the day.*

EXPOSITION: **Verse 5.** *Lead me in thy truth, and teach me.* The same request as in the last verse. The little child, having just begun to walk, asks to be still led onward by its parent's helping hand, and to be further instructed in the alphabet of truth. Experimental teaching is the burden of this prayer. "Lead me according to thy truth," and prove yourself faithful; lead me into truth that I may know its preciousness, lead me by the way of truth that I may manifest its spirit. David knew much, but he felt his ignorance and desired to be still in the Lord's school; four times over in these two verses he applies for a scholarship in the college of grace. It would be good for many who profess to be Christians if instead of following their own devices, and cutting out new paths of thought for themselves would enquire for the good old ways of God's own truth, and beseech the Holy Ghost to give them sanctified understandings and teachable spirits.

For thou art the God of my salvation. The Three in One Jehovah is the Author and Perfecter of salvation to His people. Reader, is He the God of your salvation? Do you find in the Father's election, in the Son's atonement, and in the Spirit's quickening all the grounds of your eternal hopes? If so, you may use this as an argument for obtaining further blessings; if the Lord has ordained to save you, surely He will not refuse to instruct you in His ways. It is a happy thing when we can address the Lord with the confidence which David here manifests; it gives us great power in prayer, and comfort in trial.

On thee do I wait all the day. Patience is the fair handmaid and daughter of faith; we cheerfully wait when we are certain that we shall not wait in vain. It is our duty and our privilege to wait upon the Lord in service, in worship, in expectancy, in trust all the days of our life. Our faith will be tried faith, and if it is of the true kind, it will bear continued trial without yielding. We shall not grow weary of waiting upon God if we remember how long and how graciously He once waited for us.

Psalm 25:6 *Remember, O LORD, thy tender mercies and thy lovingkindnesses; for they have been ever of old.*

EXPOSITION: Verse 6. *Remember, O Lord, thy tender mercies and thy lovingkindnesses.* We are usually tempted in seasons of affliction to fear that our God has forgotten us, or forgotten His usual kindness towards us; hence the soul puts the Lord in remembrance, and beseeches Him to recollect those deeds of love which once He wrought towards it. There is a holy boldness which ventures thus to deal with the Most High, let us cultivate it; but there is also an unholy unbelief which suggests our fears, let us strive against it with all our might. What gems are those two expressions, *tender mercies and lovingkindnesses!* They are the virgin honey of language; for sweetness no words can excel them; but as for the gracious favors which are intended by them, language fails to describe them.

> When all thy mercies, O my God,
> My rising soul surveys,
> Transported with the view, I am lost
> In wonder, love and praise.[101]

If the Lord will only do unto us in the future as in the past, we shall be well content. We seek no change in the divine action, we only crave that the river of grace may never cease to flow. For they have been ever of old. A more correct translation would be "from eternity." David was a sound believer in the doctrine of God's eternal love. The Lord's loving kindnesses are no novelties. When we plead with Him to bestow them upon us, we can urge use and custom of the most ancient kind. In courts of law men make much of precedents, and we may plead them at the throne of grace. "Faith," said Dickson][102] "must make use of experiences and read them over unto God, out of the register of a sanctified

---

101. Hymn: "When All Thy Mercies, O My God," written by Joseph Addison in 1712.
102. Horace H. Dickson, English clergyman.

memory, as a recorder to Him who cannot forget." With an unchangeable God it is a most effectual argument to remind Him of His ancient mercies and His eternal love. By tracing all that we enjoy to the fountain head of everlasting love we shall greatly cheer our hearts, and those who try to dissuade us from meditating upon election and its kindred topics do us sorry service.

Psalm 25:7 *Remember not the sins of my youth, nor my transgressions: according to thy mercy remember thou me for thy goodness' sake, O LORD.*

EXPOSITION: **Verse 7.** *Remember not the sins of my youth.* Sin is the stumbling block. This is the thing to be removed. Lord, pass an act of oblivion for all my sins, and especially for the hot-blooded wanton follies of my younger years. Those offences which we remember with repentance God forgets, but if we forget them, justice will bring them forth to punishment. The world winks at the sins of younger men, and yet they are not so little after all; the bones of our youthful feastings at Satan's table will stick painfully in our throats when we are old men. He who reasons his youth for his unrepentant actions is poisoning his old age. How large a tear may wet this page as some of us reflect upon the past!

Nor my transgressions. Another word for the same evils. Sincere penitents cannot get through their confessions at a gallop; they are constrained to use many regrets, for their swarming sins smite them with innumerable griefs. A painful sense of any one sin provokes the believer to repentance for the whole mass of his iniquities. Nothing but the fullest and clearest pardon will satisfy a thoroughly awakened conscience. David wanted his sins not only forgiven, but forgotten. *According to thy mercy remember thou me for thy goodness' sake, O Lord.* David and the dying thief breathe the same prayer, and doubtless they grounded it upon the same plea, viz., the free grace and unmerited goodness of Jehovah. We dare not ask to have our portion measured from the balances of justice, but we pray to be dealt with by the hand of mercy.

───────────── **EXPOSITION:** ─────────────

Verses 8 – 10. These three verses are a meditation upon the attributes and acts of the Lord. He who toils in the harvest field of prayer should occasionally pause awhile and refresh himself with a meal of meditation.

Psalm 25:8 *Good and upright is the LORD: therefore will he teach sinners in the way.*

EXPOSITION: **Verse 8.** *Good and upright is the Lord: therefore will he teach sinners in the way.* Here the goodness and rectitude of the divine character are beheld in friendly union; he who would see them thus united in bonds of perfect amity must stand at the foot of the Cross and view them blended in the sacrifice of the Lord Jesus. It is no less true than wonderful that through the atonement the justice of God pleads as strongly as His grace for the salvation of the sinners whom Jesus died to save.

Moreover, as a good man naturally endeavors to make others like himself, so will the Lord our God in His compassion bring sinners into the way of holiness and conform them to His own image; thus the goodness of our God leads us to expect the reclaiming of sinful men. We may not conclude from God's goodness that He will save those sinners who continue to wander in their own ways, but we may be assured that He will renew transgressors' hearts and guide them into the way of holiness. Let those who desire to be delivered from sin take comfort from this. God himself will condescend to be the teacher of sinners. What a ragged school is this for God to teach in! God's teaching is practical; He teaches sinners not only the doctrine but the way.

Psalm 25:9 *The meek will he guide in judgment: and the meek will he teach his way.*

EXPOSITION: **Verse 9.** *The meek will he guide in judgment.* Meek spirits are in high favor with the Father of the meek and lowly Jesus, for He sees in them the image of His only begotten Son. They know their need of guidance, and are willing to submit their own understandings to the divine will, and therefore the Lord condescends to be their guide. Humble spirits are in this verse endowed with a rich inheritance; let them be of good cheer. Trouble puts gentle spirits to their wit's ends, and drives them to act without discretion, but grace comes to the rescue, enlightens their minds to follow that which is just, and helps them to discern the way in which the Lord would have them to go. Proud of their own wisdom fools will not learn, and therefore miss their road to Heaven, but lowly hearts sit at Jesus' feet, and find the gate of glory, *for the meek will he teach his way.* Blessed teacher! Favored scholar! Divine lesson! My soul, be familiar with the whole.

Psalm 25:10 *All the paths of the LORD are mercy and truth unto such as keep his covenant and his testimonies.*

EXPOSITION: **Verse 10.** This is a rule without exception. God is good to those that are good. Mercy and faithfulness shall abound towards those who through mercy are made faithful. Whatever outward appearances may threaten we should settle it steadfastly in our minds that while grace enables us to obey the Lord's will we need not fear that Providence will cause us any real loss. There shall be mercy in every unsavory morsel, and faithfulness in every bitter drop;

let not our hearts be troubled, but let us rest by faith in the immutable covenant of Jehovah, which is ordered in all things and sure. Yet this is not a general truth to be trampled upon by swine, it is a pearl for a child's neck. Gracious souls, by faith resting upon the finished work of the Lord Jesus, keep the covenant of the Lord, and, being sanctified by the Holy Spirit, they walk in His testimonies; these will find *all things working together for their good* [See Romans 8:28.] but to the sinner there is no such promise. Keepers of the covenant shall be kept by the covenant; those who follow the Lord's commandments shall find the Lord's mercy following them.

Psalm 25:11 *For thy name's sake, O LORD, pardon mine iniquity; for it is great.*

EXPOSITION: Verse 11. This sentence of prayer would seem out of place were it not that prayer is always in its place, whether in season or out of season. Meditation having refreshed the psalmist, he falls to his weighty work again, and wrestles with God for the remission of his sin. *For thy name's sake, O Lord.* Here is a blessed, never failing plea. Not for our sakes or our merit's sake, but to glorify your mercy, and to show forth the glory of your divine attributes. *Pardon mine iniquity.* It is confessed, it is abhorred, it is consuming my heart with grief; Lord forgive it; let your lips pronounce my absolution. For it is great. It weighs so heavily upon me that I pray you to remove it. Its greatness is no difficulty for you, for you are a great God, but the misery which it causes to me is my argument with you for speedy pardon. Lord, the patient is sorely sick, therefore heal him. To pardon a great sinner will bring you great glory; therefore for your name's sake pardon me. Observe how this verse illustrates the logic of faith, which is clean contrary to that of a legal spirit; faith looks not for merit in the creature, but has regard to the goodness of the Creator; and instead of being staggered by the demerits of sin it looks to the precious blood, and pleads all the more vigorously because of the urgency of the case.

Psalm 25:12 *What man is he that feareth the* LORD? *him shall he teach in the way that he shall choose.*

EXPOSITION: Verse 12. *What man is he that feareth the Lord?* Let the question provoke self-examination. Gospel privileges are not for every pretender. Are you of the royal seed or not? *Him shall he teach in the way that he shall choose.* Those whose hearts are right shall not err for want of heavenly direction. Where God sanctifies the heart He enlightens the head. We all wish to choose our way; but what a mercy is it when the Lord directs that choice, and makes free will to be goodwill! If we make our will God's will, God will let us have our will. God does not violate our will, but leaves much to our choice; nevertheless, He instructs our wills, and so we choose that which is well pleasing in His sight. The will should be subject to law; there is a way which we should choose, but we are so ignorant that we need to be taught, and so willful that none but God himself can teach us effectually.

Psalm 25:13 *His soul shall dwell at ease; and his seed shall inherit the earth.*

EXPOSITION: Verse 13. He who fears God has nothing else to fear. *His soul shall dwell at ease.* He shall lodge in the chamber of content. One may sleep as soundly in the little bed in the corner as in the Great Bed of Ware;[103]

---

103. A bed 3 meters (approximately 9 feet) wide built in 1590. It is on display in the Victoria and Albert Museum in London.

All-glorious it is not abundance but content that gives true ease. Even here, having learned by grace both to abound and be empty, the believer dwells at ease; but how profound will be the ease of his soul forever! There he will enjoy the *otium cum dignitate;*[104] ease and glory shall go together.

Like a warrior whose battles are over, or a husbandman whose barns are full, his soul shall take its ease, and be merry forever. His seed shall inherit the Earth. God remembers Isaac for the sake of Abraham, and Jacob for the sake of Isaac. Good men's sons have a goodly portion to begin the world with, but many of them, turn a father's blessing into a curse. The promise is not broken because in some instances men willfully refuse to receive it; moreover, it is in its spiritual meaning that it now holds good; our spiritual seed do inherit all that was meant by "the Earth," or Canaan; they receive the blessing of the New Covenant. May the Lord make us the joyful parents of many spiritual children, and we shall have no fears about their maintenance, for the Lord will make each one of them princes in all the Earth.

Psalm 25:14 *The secret of the LORD is with them that fear him; and he will shew them his covenant.*

EXPOSITION: **Verse 14.** *The secret of the Lord is with them that fear him.* Some read it "the friendship:" it signifies familiar conversation, confidential intimacy, and select fellowship. This is a great secret. Carnal minds cannot guess what is intended by it, and even believers cannot explain it in words, for it must be felt to be known. The higher spiritual life is necessarily a path which the eagle's eye has not known, and which the lion's whelp has not traveled; neither natural wisdom nor strength can force a door into this inner chamber. Saints have the key of Heaven's hieroglyphics; they can solve

---

104. Leisure with dignity.

celestial enigmas. They are initiated into the fellowship of the skies; they have heard words which it is not possible for them to repeat to their fellows.

And he will shew them his covenant. Its antiquity, security, righteousness, fullness, graciousness and excellence, shall be revealed to their hearts and understandings, and above all, their own part in it shall be sealed to their souls by the witness of the Holy Spirit. The designs of love which the Lord has to His people in the covenant of grace, He has been pleased to show to believers in the Book of Inspiration, and by His Spirit He leads us into the mystery, even the hidden mystery of redemption. He, who does not know the meaning of this verse, will never learn it from a commentary; let him look to the Cross, for the secret lies there.

Psalm 25:15 *Mine eyes are ever toward the Lord; for he shall pluck my feet out of the net.*

EXPOSITION: Verse 15. *Mine eyes are ever toward the Lord.* The writer claims to be fixed in his trust, and constant in his expectation; he looks in confidence, and waits in hope. We may add to this look of faith and hope the obedient look of service, the humble look of reverence, the admiring look of wonder, the studious look of meditation, and the tender look of affection. Happy are those whose eyes are never removed from their God. *The eye,* says Solomon, *is never satisfied with seeing* [See Proverbs 27:20.], but this sight is the most satisfying in the world. *For he shall pluck my feet out of the net.*

Observe the conflicting condition in which a gracious soul may be placed, his eyes are in Heaven and yet his feet are sometimes in a net; his nobler nature ceases not to behold the glories of God, while his baser parts are enduring the miseries of the world. A net is the common metaphor for temptation. The Lord often keeps His people from falling into it, and if they have fallen He rescues them. The word "pluck" is a rough word, and saints who have fallen into sin find that the means of their restoration are not always easy to the flesh; the Lord plucks at us sharply to let us feel that sin is an exceeding bitter thing. But what a mercy is here: Believer, be very grateful for it. The Lord will deliver us from the cunning devices of our cruel enemy, and even if through infirmity we have fallen into sin, He will not leave us to be utterly destroyed but will pluck us out of our dangerous state; though our feet are in the net, if our eyes are up unto God, mercy certainly will interpose.

Psalm 25:16 *Turn thee unto me, and have mercy upon me; for I am desolate and afflicted.*

EXPOSITION: Verse 16. His own eyes were fixed upon God, but he feared that the Lord had averted His face from him in anger. Oftentimes unbelief suggests that God has turned His back upon us. If we know that we turn to God we need not fear that He will turn from us, but may boldly cry, *Turn thee unto me.* The ground of quarrel is always in ourselves, and when that is removed there is nothing to prevent our full enjoyment of communion with God. *Have mercy upon me.* Saints still must stand upon the footing of mercy; notwithstanding all their experience they cannot get beyond the publican's prayer, *Have mercy upon me. For I am desolate and afflicted.* He was lonely and bowed down. Jesus was in the days of His flesh in just such a condition; none could enter into the secret depths of His sorrows, He trod the winepress alone, and hence He is able to comfort in the fullest sense those who tread the solitary path.

> Christ leads me through no darker rooms
> Than he went through before;

He that into God's kingdom comes,
Must enter by this door.[105]

Psalm 25:17 *The troubles of my heart are enlarged: O bring thou me out of my distresses.*

EXPOSITION: **Verse 17.** *The troubles of my heart are enlarged.* When trouble penetrates the heart it is trouble indeed. In the case before us, the heart was swollen with grief like a lake surcharged with water by enormous floods; this is used as an argument for deliverance and it is a potent one. When the darkest hour of the night arrives we may expect the dawn; when the sea is at its lowest ebb the tide must surely turn; and when our troubles are enlarged to the greatest degree, then we may hopefully pray, *O bring thou me out of my distresses.*

Psalm 25:18 *Look upon mine affliction and my pain; and forgive all my sins.*

EXPOSITION: **Verse 18.** *Look upon mine affliction and my pain.* Note the many trials of the saints; here we have no less than six words all descriptive of woe. "Desolate, and afflicted, troubles enlarged, distresses, affliction, and pain." But note even more the submissive and believing spirit of a true saint; all he asks for is, "Lord, look upon my evil plight;" he does not dictate, or even express a complaint; a look from God will content him, and that being granted he asks no more. Even more noteworthy is the way in which the believer under affliction discovers the true source of all the mischief, and lays the axe at the root of it.

---

105. Hymn, "Lord, It Belongs Not to my Care," words written in 1681 by Richard Baxter, nonconformist minister, put to music and titled in 1850 by Lowell Mason.

Forgive all my sins, is the cry of a soul that is sicker of sin than of pain, and would sooner be forgiven than healed. Blessed is the man to whom sin is more unbearable than disease, he shall not be long before the Lord, for He shall both forgive his iniquity and heal his diseases. Men are slow to see the intimate connection between sin and sorrow, a grace taught heart alone feels it.

Psalm 25:19 *Consider mine enemies; for they are many; and they hate me with cruel hatred.*

EXPOSITION: **Verse 19.** *Consider mine enemies.* Watch them, weigh them, check them, and defeat them. *For they are many.* They need the eyes of Argus to watch them, and the arms of Hercules to match them, but the Lord is more than sufficient to defeat them. The devils of hell and the evils of Earth are all vanquished when the Lord makes bare His arm. *They hate me with cruel hatred.* It is the breath of the serpent's seed to hate; their progenitor was a hater, and they themselves must imitate him. There is no hate as cruel as that which is unreasonable and unjust. A man can forgive one who had injured him, but one whom he has injured he hates implacably. *Behold, I send you forth as sheep in the midst of wolves,* is still our Master's word to us [Matthew 10:16].

Psalm 25:20 *O keep my soul, and deliver me: let me not be ashamed; for I put my trust in thee.*

EXPOSITION: **Verse 20.** *O keep my soul out of evil, and deliver me* when I fall into it. This is another version of the prayer, "Lead us not into temptation, but deliver us from evil." *Let me not be ashamed.* This is the one fear which like a ghost haunted the psalmist's mind. He trembled lest his faith should become the subject of ridicule through the extremity of his affliction. Noble hearts can brook anything but shame. David was of such a chivalrous spirit, that he could endure any torment rather than be put to dishonor. *For I put my trust in thee.* And therefore the name of God would be compromised if His servants were deserted; this the believing heart can by no means endure.

Psalm 25:21 *Let integrity and uprightness preserve me; for I wait on thee.*

EXPOSITION: **Verse 21.** *Let integrity and uprightness preserve me.* What better practical safeguards can a man require? If we do not prosper with these as our guides, it is better for us to suffer adversity. Even the ungodly world admits that "honesty is the best policy." The heir of Heaven makes assurance doubly sure, for apart from the rectitude of his public life, he enlists the guardian care of Heaven in secret prayer: *for I wait on thee.* To pretend to wait on God without holiness of life is religious hypocrisy, and to trust to our own integrity without calling upon God is presumptuous atheism. Perhaps the integrity and uprightness referred to are those righteous attributes of God, which faith rests upon as a guarantee that the Lord will not forfeit His Word.

Psalm 25:22 *Redeem Israel, O God, out of all his troubles.*

EXPOSITION: **Verse 22.** *Redeem Israel, O God, out of all his troubles.* This is a very comprehensive prayer, including all the faithful and all their trials. Sorrow had taught the psalmist sympathy, and given him communion with the tried people of God; he therefore remembers them in his prayers. Israel, the tried, the wrestling, the conquering hero, fit representative of all the saints. Israel in Egypt, in the wilderness, in wars with Canaanites, in captivity, fit type of the church militant on earth. Jesus is the Redeemer from trouble as well as sin, He is a complete Redeemer, and from every evil He will rescue every saint. Redemption by blood is finished: O God, send us redemption by power. Amen and Amen.

STUDY GUIDE

1.) Here you can review the themes of the first twenty-five psalms. Which one made strongest impact on you? (In other words which ones met a current need for you and helped you to have more faith in the Lord?) Why?

1. The contrast between the righteous and the wicked; wisdom

2. The foolishness of rebelling against God

3. Having confidence in the Lord in the face of one's enemies

4. The strong benefit of trusting God in midst of conflict

5. Crying out for help and wrath against evildoers

6. Expression of weariness with conflict, ending in confidence

7. Calling for God's help because of an adversary

8. God is great simply because He is the Creator

9. Psalm of praise for God's righteousness

10. A plea for help for orphans and others who are oppressed

11. Tempted to flee, the psalmist instead trusts in God's righteousness

12. Calling for God's help because of human faithlessness

13. Trusting despite unanswered prayer about enemies

14. A psalm of lament about human foolishness

15. Prerequisites for drawing near to God

16. Rejoicing in a good relationship with the Lord

17. A right relationship with God means one can ask Him for help

18. Praising God for help that came because of the psalmist's righteousness

19. Praising God for both His natural revelation and written revelation (the Law)

20. Exhortation to trust in the Lord instead of weapons of war

21. Praise for God's blessing on the king and victory over his enemies

22. Psalm of the suffering Messiah

23. Psalm of the Good Shepherd

24. Psalm of the Lord, the King of Glory

25. Humility, plea for help in time of trouble

2.) Psalm 1:1—What seven-letter word is used both at the beginning of the first psalm and at the beginning of the Sermon on the Mount in the fifth chapter of Matthew? _____ If you have a study Bible or a concordance, look up the expanded meaning of the word.

_____

3.) Psalm 1:3—When we keep the Word of God in our minds and hearts daily, what three benefits can we expect to see?

　　1. _____

　　2. _____

　　3. _____

4.) Look back at Spurgeon's commentary on Psalm 5:3, about fervent prayer. List five of the ten metaphors that he makes. (Look for key words such as "archer," "sacrifice/altar," "king/petition," "mill," "dead dog,"

"blind falcon," "well-kindled fire," "ostrich," "seed/
harvest," and "windows.") Are your own prayers
fervent enough? If not, what can the psalmist teach
you about prayer?

1. _____

2. _____

3. _____

4. _____

5. _____

5.) Psalm 9:7—*But the* LORD *shall endure for ever: he
hath prepared his throne for judgment.* About this
verse, Spurgeon comments "Term-time lasts all the
year round in the court of King's Bench above."
What does this mean? Explain in your own words.

_____

_____

_____

_____

_____

6.) Psalm 10:13—*Wherefore doth the wicked contemn God?
he hath said in his heart, Thou wilt not require it.* In
Spurgeon's commentary, he summed up the point of this
verse as follows: "If there were no hell for other men,
there ought to be one for those who question the justice
of it." Can you put this in your own words? Do you
know of any individuals to whom this pronouncement
might apply?

7.) Psalm 15:1–2—David asks the Lord: *Lord, who shall
abide in thy tabernacle? who shall dwell in thy holy hill?*
Fill in the blanks: The Lord answers: *He that walketh
u_____, and worketh r_____, and speaketh
the t_____ in his heart.*

8.) Psalm 19:14—*Let the words of my mouth, and the meditation of my heart, be acceptable in thy sight, O Lord, my strength, and my redeemer.* When we pray these words, just as when David prayed them, our goal is to become [choose one]:
— successful and prosperous
— obedient and pleasing to God
— skilled in preaching
(See also Matthew 7:21; Ephesians 6:6; 1 John 2:17.)

9.) Psalm 23—This familiar psalm is David's great statement of faith, in which he declares many reassuring *promises* of the Lord as his Shepherd (and ours). See if you can find at least seven of them:

1. _____

2. _____

3. _____

4. _____

5. _____

6. _____

7. _____

If you have never memorized the twenty-third psalm, consider doing it now.

10.) Psalm 16:11—*Thou wilt shew me the path of life: in thy presence is fulness of joy; at thy right hand there are pleasures for evermore.* When you seek Him, you will find Him. You will find Him in the psalms as well as in other parts of the Bible. Seek Him now, read a few verses, and relax in His presence and be filled with joy. Get alone with the Father, the Son, and the Holy Spirit. Listen. Respond. Worship.